TARGET

TARGET

CAUGHT IN THE CROSSHAIRS OF BILL AND HILLARY CLINTON

KATHLEEN WILLEY

World Ahead Publishing, Inc.

TARGET: Caught in the Crosshairs of Bill and Hillary Clinton
A World Ahead Book
Published by World Ahead Media
Los Angeles, CA

Cover Design by Linda Daly

World Ahead Books are distributed to the trade by:

Midpoint Trade Books
27 West 20th Street, Suite 1102
New York, NY 10011

World Ahead Books are available at special discounts for bulk purchases. World Ahead Publishing also publishes books in electronic formats. For more information call (310) 961-4170 or visit www.worldahead.com.

First Edition

ISBN 10-Digit 0974670162
ISBN 13-Digit 9780974670164
Library of Congress Control Number: 2007933737

Printed in the United States of America

10 9 8 7 6 5 4 3 2 1

To my Hero, thank you for your love, devotion, and encouragement, the gifts you gave me, the lessons you taught me, and the courage to face all of my tomorrows. I will forever hold you in my heart with abiding hope.

CONTENTS

PREFACE

I WAS A POLITICALLY ACTIVE and aware Democrat for most of my life, but politics is only a small part of who I am. An ordinary American woman, I was a housewife and a soccer mom. But ten years ago, as impeachment loomed for the president of the United States, I was suddenly involved in the biggest political crisis since Watergate. *This* frenzy intertwined both national politics and sexual behavior. What could be more scandalous?

Of course, I wanted nothing to do with it.

But what do you do?

Do you tell your girlfriends? Do you trust the authorities?

Or do you lie? Do you swear under oath that nothing happened, even though it did? Do you let good and innocent people be smeared, while the guilty walk away with impunity?

Do you cave in the face of fear?

I chose not to. I chose to tell my story: President Bill Clinton assaulted me in the Oval Office.

I went through intensive FBI interrogations, gave depositions, and testified before the grand jury. In the process, I hurt Clinton. His machine came after me and defamed me in the media. They coerced others to lie about me. They violated my right to privacy. I suffered a public ordeal of humiliation and frustration. That was the fight that the American public saw.

But there was another side of my ordeal. It was the private side—my private terror.

They threatened my children. They threatened my friend's children. They took one of my cats and killed another. They left a skull on my porch. They told me I was in danger. They followed me. They vandalized my car. They tried to retrieve my dogs from a kennel. They hid under my deck in the middle of the night.

They subjected me to a campaign of fear and intimidation, trying to silence me. It didn't work.

When Bill Clinton assaulted me, he betrayed my trust and our friendship. This was a personal betrayal. But that which followed was not. That which followed was a betrayal of the public trust, of political power, and of the Democratic ideology that the Clintons and I once held dear. Subjected to sexual abuse at the hands of Bill Clinton, I was then subjected to abuse of power at the hands of the Clinton administration. More than any other's, these were Hillary Clinton's hands.

When the White House released letters in which I asked President Clinton to help me find a government job, they broke the law and violated my right to privacy. That was Hillary's call. When my corroborating witness recanted her story, a very powerful Washington lawyer whom she could ill afford stepped in to represent her. That was Hillary's good friend. When a White House aide predicted my reputation would sink just days after my first public appearance, he told a friend he could go to jail for what he was doing. That was Hillary's aide. When White House lawyers hired private investigators, those thugs terrorized me. They were Hillary's investigators.

Did Hillary attack me because she was the heartbroken and destroyed wife of an adulterer? Did she do it out of revenge? Or did she do it out of lust for power? The answer is complicated. It calls to mind yet another question, the popular guessing game of our generation: Do Hillary and Bill have a "real" marriage?

Yes, I think they do have a real marriage—a real dysfunctional one.

Consider the legendary pairing of polar opposites that makes their political partnership so ideal. Like chocolate with merlot, they blend perfectly. She is calculating while he is childlike. She is rigid while he is spontaneous. She is cold while he is charming. She has the guts for a knock-down, drag-out fight. He just wants everyone to like him.

Such compatibility is equally obvious in at least one aspect of their marriage: He is a sexual addict and she is his compulsive enabler.

With more than thirty years of practice behind them, their behaviors are automatic, their patterns entrenched, their denials well rehearsed. And though they perfected the dynamic, their "private issue" became public because Bill's addiction was so advanced. For her part, Hillary is not a typical codependent housewife, but a woman with vast money, power, and people at her disposal. Further, their political milieu—which is no accident— allowed them to skirt self-destruction.

Now, however, we have a new and even graver concern. To Hillary's half of the professional partnership—the calculating, rigid, cold, and aggressive politician—add something deeper and darker to the mix: the psyche of a compulsive enabler in a person who wants to become president of the United States. That is a fearsome combination.

Ironically, theirs is a partnership that depends on the favor of women for its success. Just as a pedophile loiters around playgrounds, so the sex addict surrounds himself with willing (and unwilling!) women. And just as the convict loudly professes his innocence, so the sexual predator professes his feminism. And so does his wife.

But make no mistake: Bill Clinton is no feminist. He raped Juanita Broaddrick. He assaulted me. He promised young Monica Lewinsky a future with him. He objectifies women, treats them like trash, and calls them names *much* worse than "bimbo." He holds all women in contempt, all women except those who tell him what to do, who guide him and discipline him and *mother* him, as Hillary does.

Bill Clinton is no feminist, and neither is his wife.

Hillary enabled her husband to degrade, abuse, and assault women for more than thirty years. She *condoned* his behavior, *facilitated* it, and *swept up* after it. In doing so, Hillary stopped at nothing. While Bill victimized women, Hillary kicked us when we were down—smearing us in the media, digging into our backgrounds, humiliating and terrorizing us.

He stabbed us, and she twisted the knife.

This was my life, every day, for five years. I struggled to summon the personal strength to stand up to them. I tried to retain my dignity and it cost me. Though I am an outgoing person, I went into hiding, became self-conscious in public, and shied away from crowds. I've spent ten years lying low. I never was paranoid, but became overly sensitive to being in public.

People sometimes recognize me and it's still hard for me to believe that it was *me*. When Sean Hannity mentions my name on his television show, it still shocks me. When I'm sitting at a stoplight with Rush Limbaugh on the radio and he says, "And Kathleen Willey..." I get the funniest feeling, look at the people in the cars around me, and wonder if they are listening too.

I've kept a newspaper clipping for nearly ten years. I was working in a bookstore one Christmas, wrapping books for people who made a donation to our animal shelter. I met a woman, another shelter volunteer, who was also a reporter for *Style Weekly*, our Richmond alternative newspaper. She stopped by our book-wrapping table and later wrote that I was "a woman who can travel amongst us, volunteer for our local animal shelter, and shop amongst us like a normal person."[1] I have kept that clipping on my refrigerator ever since, but I think now is the time for it to come down.

A friend looked at me recently and said, "It's time for Kathleen Willey to come out of hiding. This is not you. You're an outgoing person. You need to come out of hiding." And she is right.

After ten years of living my private life, I need to come forward again, to remind America, especially American *women*, what Hillary and her husband will do. It is not a matter of what they are *capable* of doing, but what they *have done* in their lust for the presidency. They have wielded an ugly power over me and over many other women and witnesses. They will do it again and, worst of all, they will do it *in the name of feminism!*

America is ready to elect a woman president. The planets are perfectly aligned in Hillary's favor, and many women will likely vote for her just because she is a woman, because it *is* time for a woman to be our president. But Hillary Clinton is the *wrong* woman.

This is why I need to tell my story. I know it will open old wounds for me, subject me to more dirty tricks, and make me vulnerable to an onslaught of attacks. As an American and as a woman I have to share my story, because Hillary Clinton cannot claim to be an advocate for women if she victimizes us when no one is looking. She cannot claim to support our empowerment when she uses power to betray us. She cannot claim to be a feminist when she enables her husband as a sexual predator. Hillary claims one thing and does another. She is a lie.

INTRODUCTION

HE CAN TELL that something is wrong. I am on the verge of tears. My adrenaline has gotten the better of me and I am trembling. He greets me with a hug. I know—*he hugs everyone*. But at this moment, it is sincere and just what I need. A flurry wells up in my stomach, a mixed rush of fear and solace, all raw, all at the surface. He is my friend—the most powerful man I know, the most powerful man *anyone* knows. Surely he can help me, give me some hope, maybe a job, *anything* to help me out of this crisis. A hug is a good start. Then he looks into my face, into my eyes.

"What's going on?"

"I just really need to talk with you about something," I start to explain as we sit at his desk. "I've got some real problems." I have helped him for a long time, worked for him, supported him when other people didn't. I figure a relationship like that goes both ways, and I don't think twice about asking him for help. But I don't want to cry in front of him, and I try not to let go of the tears. "I don't know what will happen with Ed and me. He's gotten himself into real financial problems and we need help."

"I can see how upset you are," he said. "Would you like a cup of coffee?"

"Oh, yeah, okay."

"Well, come on," he says. "Let's go back to my kitchen."

He opens a side door that's discreetly integrated in the paneling of the office wall, and I follow him through it into a narrow hallway. There's a small bathroom on the right and just past it, a little galley kitchen. A steward starts to ask what we would like but he is quickly dismissed and we are alone.

"I will fix you a cup of coffee," he says. "Decaf?"

"No, high test."

We stand in the hallway for a minute or two. He pulls down a Starbucks cup and pours my coffee into it, mentioning that he only takes decaf.

"How do you like it?"

"Um, cream."

He hands me my cup. My hands are shaking and I worry about spilling, so I quickly taste the coffee.

"Come on back here to my study," he says, "where it's easier to talk."

I follow him through a narrow hallway into his private study. He rests on the back of a chair while I stand, leaning against the doorjamb. At six feet two, he is a big man, but half-sitting he no longer towers above me and we are at eye level with each other. It's subtle, yet I wonder if he knows that this makes me feel a little more at ease. Still, I tremble. Holding the full cup of coffee, my hands are shaking. I think, *Now just calm down!* I grip the warm mug to steady myself.

"I can tell you are really upset," he says, looking at his watch. "Are you okay? Tell me more about what's going on."

"I'm frightened," I said. "And worried about my family and where this is going to all end."

My voice trembles as I quickly tell him about my crisis, passing over the details. I have a serious problem. I don't know what's going to happen with my husband. I don't know if we're going to get divorced, and I don't know what's going to happen to us. I only know that Ed is in trouble, owes a lot of money, and I have to do something. I am scared to death. I've got to rise to the occasion. I have not had a paying job in twenty years, but my volunteer days are over.

I've got face time with a very powerful friend who only has a few moments for me, so I'm going to make the most of it. Tears well up in my eyes. I try to maintain my dignity. I don't want to lose it in his office. I just need him to point me in the right direction. That's basically how I look at it. I want him to know that times are bad and this is very serious. With all this desperation and nervous energy, I run my mouth for five or ten minutes. He looks at his watch again. His assistant said he would see me before a three o'clock meeting, and I came in at about two forty-five, so I should finish talking and get out of his way. "I hope you can give me assistance because I desperately need a job. Please, send me anywhere."

"We'll see what we can do."

But my coworkers wanted me to tell him about some office problems, so I tag them on as an aside. "And you really need to know this too," I add. Still on the verge of tears, I think talking about work will help me to level out the conversation and distract me from my panic. "The office is just chaos. It's a mess. There's no protocol, no rhyme or reason, no organization. There's no language code, and it's very inappropriate." Finally, I conclude, "You really need to do something about that." I know it's nervy of me to tell him what to do. But that's just who I am!

Again he looks at his watch. I'm not paying much attention to the time but I know it's close to three o'clock and time to leave. We move back into the small hallway. I set my coffee cup on a shelf to steady myself again.

He promises to help.

There is a loud knock beyond the door from the outer office, and an assistant calls out, "It's time for your meeting!"

He ignores this. He doesn't say anything, not one word. I'm thinking, *How can he ignore this?* But he does not answer at all. He doesn't even say "Give me a minute," or "Hold on." *Why don't they just come in? What must they think if he doesn't answer?*

Again he looks at his watch. Obviously, he's trying to show me he needs to get to that meeting, so I should go.

"Well," I say, "I'll be going."

"No, you don't have to rush."

"But you have an important meeting here, and I know you have a lot to do that's more important."

"No, it's all right."

But again he looks at the watch. I think that contradicts his words and my time is up. "Okay, well, I'm open to any possible job, and I could go anywhere," I conclude. "I've taken enough of your time, so I should leave."

The assistant beyond the door resumes knocking. "You're late!"

Somebody's got to move to the door here, and obviously it's not going to be him. You'd *think* it would be him—or that somebody would come through the door and say, "Okay, it is time to move along." Yet there's no such person. Instead, he looks at the watch. It crosses my mind: *Why does he keep looking at that watch if he's not going to usher me out?*

The assistant bangs on the door again. I decide to ease myself out of there.

"Well, thank you for listening. I'd better go, and if you could help me, I'd really appreciate it." I retrieve my coffee cup. I have no idea why, just that I was so full of distracted, nervous energy. I move to the door and head back toward his office. He follows me and moves closer. I turn around and he is right next to me, but it's a narrow hallway, so I don't really feel like he's crowding me. I finish the conversation, "So, you know, whatever you can do for me..."

"I'm so sorry this is happening to you."

He reaches around to hug me but I'm holding my coffee cup at my waist, with both hands. He presses into the cup between us.

"I'm going to spill my coffee."

He takes the cup and puts it on a shelf, then gives me a big hug. But this hug lasts a little longer than a hug should. I pull back. All of a sudden, his hands are in my hair and around the back of my neck. *What the hell?* And then he kisses me on my mouth. Somehow, before I know it, I'm backed up in the corner by the little bathroom, against the wall behind his office. I am trying to maintain my space but he's all over me, just all *over* me. And all I can think is, *What the hell is he doing?*

I try to twist away. He is a foot taller than I am and nearly double my weight. I can barely think. *What do I do?* He is my friend, my boss. He is a very powerful man. And I am trying to be a *lady*.

"What are you *doing*?" I finally manage.

"I've wanted to do this since the first time I laid eyes on you."

I am totally unprepared for this. I have been off on this other plane—terrified for my husband, for my family, for our future—and he says, "I've wanted to do this..."

What?

He takes my hand and places it on his genitals, on his erection—perhaps to show me how much he's "always wanted to do this." *What is he doing?* I am shocked! I yank my hand away but he is forceful. He is all hands—just *all* hands. His hand goes up my skirt, he touches me everywhere, pressing up against me and kissing me. His face is red, literally beet red. It is as though this bizarre scene gives him a different kind of rush.

My mind is racing. *I should slap him. That would shake it out of him. Can I slap him? I don't know if I can slap him!* I'm pinned in the corner against the bathroom door and the wall, and his hands are all over me, up my skirt, over my blouse. I think he is trying to unhook me...

"Aren't you afraid that somebody's going to walk in here?" This should give him pause.

He doesn't miss a step. "No. No, I'm not."

"What if your wife or daughter walks in here?"

"I know where they are," he says, "all the time."

The aide outside the office is frantic, banging on the door and yelling from the other side, "You're late for your three o'clock meeting." But the assistant doesn't come in. *Why doesn't he come in? Where is everybody? Where is that steward? What about security? Why doesn't someone come in?*

I realize why they don't come in. They've been told to stay out. *Oh, God! I've got to get out of here! I just have to get to that door. I have got to get out!*

CHAPTER ONE

A SOCCER MOM MEETS A GOVERNOR

ON ELECTION DAY, November 8, 1960, I was fourteen years old, a Catholic schoolgirl in a small, sheltered community. The world beyond my little life was brimming with political fervor, which I was only starting to notice. Though political news was just coming on to my radar, it was compelling. I started to pay attention to everything that was happening out there. And what was happening was fantastic. America was electing a new president. And—incredibly—he was a Catholic.

I *loved* John Kennedy. In my little Catholic community, we all loved him. I was young and unaware of the cultural importance of his victory, but both my mind and my world were infused with passion and joy for the political process. It was not about ideology, but was a lesson in the joy of empowerment. It was a liberation. Of all that happened, one thing was obvious above all others: The nuns at St. Gertrude's were ecstatic. And *that* was something!

My life as a child centered around St. Bridget's, our parish, our whole community. Isolated in this enclave, it never occurred to me that people would discriminate against Catholics. Other than my dad's friends from work, all of my parents' friends were from the parish. My brother went to Benedictine, the boys' military school down the street, and we had a little strip of neighbors and a few children on the street who weren't Catholic. But I didn't know any other public school kids. All of my friends were Catholic and went to Catholic school, as my sister and brother later did. That was our life.

My dad, who sold cash registers for NCR, went to work every day to support the family. A Russian Ukrainian, Mike Matzuk was a dreamer and a quiet man. My shanty-Irish mom more than made up for his serenity. My parents were from Philadelphia, where I was born, before they moved and settled in Richmond, Virginia. All of our relatives were still in Philadelphia and vacationed on the Jersey Shore every summer, so we'd sometimes take vacations there to see them.

We were a typical middle-class family. Mom, of course, stayed home to raise us. We lived in the west end of Richmond in a new suburban tract home, which was a standard three-bedroom house. When we moved out there, it was nothing but woods— maples and dogwoods under tall pine trees.

The families in our neighborhood started one of the first neighborhood club pools. They put a pool in the ground and built up everything around it. In time, every family had their own little plot of grass at the pool club. The pool became a great place for me to socialize. I had an independent streak and *loved* meeting the public school kids at the pool. By ninth grade, I wanted to move beyond my small social circles. While my siblings and friends were content in the parochial schools, I'd had enough nuns in my life! I desperately wanted to go to the new public high school.

"*Please* let me go to public school," I begged my parents. "I can't stand nuns. I don't want nuns anymore. Please let me go to that school."

They finally relented and off I went to the beautiful, brand-new Douglas Freeman High School. Life was good until my senior year. When I graduated from high school in 1964, I was eighteen years old and three months pregnant. Imagine my mother's anger and shame. The Irish-Catholic attitude toward unwed mothers at the time was severe, to say the least, and my mother rushed me out of town. As soon as I graduated from high school, she sent me to a home for unwed mothers—run by nuns—in Columbus, Ohio. It was awful. *Awful*. We were sinners, all of us.

My son, Sean, was born on January 23, 1965. I could only look at him through the glass. Within minutes, he was gone. I was forced to give him up for adoption. I was devastated. Six months later, I went by myself to Catholic Charities in Richmond to sign the final papers. I came home and never talked about it, wasn't allowed to talk about it. I couldn't tell a soul what I was going through.

Not only was I utterly powerless, I was also heartbroken. Sadly, I was right on the cusp of a cultural revolution. Only a few years later the world changed and women could walk around pregnant and unmarried with their lovers. But what happened to me happened to young women all the time. It was a real shame, and it was wrong. I missed Sean and mourned this loss for many, many years.

Most of my friends married after high school. Some went to college and earned their degrees, but about half of them dropped out after a couple years to get married. They'd go to work so their husbands could get their degrees. That's the way it was back then. In the end, ninety-nine percent of my peers from Richmond became secretaries, nurses, or teachers. I was part of the remaining one percent. I didn't think the way most young women at that time did.

Maybe it's the Irish blood in my veins, but I always thought slightly outside the box. I was strong for a young woman of my time. I had my own ideas about my life, thank God! I would have liked to go to college, study pre-med, and become a doctor. But first, there was something I really wanted to do: I moved to New York, went to flight school, and became a flight attendant for TWA.

I flew from 1967 to 1969. At that time, it was all about the "flyer." Flying was a privilege, and women would dress up in special outfits to take a flight. What a different culture that was! Those were the days when airlines would do weight checks, insist that a flight attendant's hair didn't touch her collar, and frown upon married flight attendants. They had a long list of sexist rules we had to follow. But there were few careers that provided women such liberating experiences.

On two different flights, Jack Lemmon was one of my passengers. The first one was a red-eye flight. He was traveling from Los Angeles to Philadelphia for a funeral. We were on an old 707 that had a lounge in front, and I sat and talked to him all night. It was fascinating. On another flight, I saw him with his wife and he remembered me. Famous people were always on the flights out of California, and I met different movie directors and even Lucille Ball once.

The pilots I flew with were also interesting, good guys who had just gotten back from fighting in Vietnam. They'd been jet or helicopter pilots in the war and had seen everything. The airlines hired them right and left.

We often flew out to places like Dallas or Los Angeles or San Francisco, but I never saw parties like people sometimes talk about. I swear that is an undeserved stereotype. We'd go out for dinner and we'd all go back to our rooms and that was it for the night. There might have been a couple of times when flight attendants drank a little too much and the next morning had to deal with it. But every pilot I ever met was *always* extremely careful about the alcohol deadline before flying. Of course there was always a little fooling around, just like anywhere in life. But the whole time I was flying, I saw little evidence of the loose partying that people associate with flight attendants.

There's a mind-set that a woman who is a flight attendant is a party girl who "gets around." This chauvinism continues to revisit me. Though I was a flight attendant for only two years in the 1960s, I have been called a "former flight attendant" *ever since*! Of course, people never say, "So-and-so is a former nurse" or "She's a former teacher"! But once a flight attendant, always a flight attendant. Yes, it's funny. And it's wrong.

Working as a flight attendant in my early twenties was a valuable life experience. It allowed me to get out in the world and expand my horizons. In the end, I think it helped me think more globally than most of my female peers. As the women's movement got moving, I was flying right along with it, because my experience as a flight attendant gave me an awareness of sexism before we even had a word for it.

Though I flew out of New York, I had moved back to Richmond and was commuting from there to New York. In the '60s, this meant I had to take a puddle jumper, which was a real hassle. Finally I quit. But looking back, I wish I'd flown much longer.

Ed Willey Jr.

I lived in an apartment complex in Richmond. A friend there had pointed out a divorced man, a lawyer who was the son of a famous Virginia senator. In fact, his dad had been the senator pro tem of the state senate for years and years. Father and son had the same name: Ed Willey.

I was at the swimming pool one day and he was there, sitting on the side of the pool with two young children in the water. Let's just say I noticed him. He was a *very* handsome man and I wanted to strike up a conversation with him. Though he was at least ten years older than I was, he had dark hair, sophisticated good looks, and an overt, Kennedy-like charm.

I swam up to him. "So, what kind of lawyer are you?"

"A damn good one."

Okay, well, that answers that.

It went from there. This "damn good" lawyer had recently divorced and he cared for his two kids every other weekend. The rest of the time the children lived in Roanoke with their mom. On top of this, Ed was also getting out of a relationship that he'd been in after his divorce. None of this stopped me!

Our courtship was quick. Before long, Ed took me to meet his parents, and I found myself living a scene right out of the movie *Love Story*. Ryan O'Neal played Oliver Barrett IV and Ali McGraw played his girlfriend, Jennifer Cavalleri. Carefree and in love, they drove his little MG with its top down from Harvard out to the suburbs, and pulled up to the Barrett mansion. Oliver introduced Jennifer to his parents, but his father disapproved of the common college girl and cut off Oliver's inheritance.

We pulled into the drive and went around to the back door, the way most people enter homes in the South. Just inside the kitchen, Ed came up close behind me, leaned in, and whispered into my ear.

"Don't tell them you're Catholic."

"*What?*"

He repeated, "Don't mention that you're Catholic."

I was aghast. I turned around and blurted, "Don't tell them I'm *Catholic?*"

"Shh!"

I was taken aback. *Why wouldn't I tell them?* For the first time in my life, I felt discriminated against. Until that moment, I had no idea that anyone in the world thought being Catholic was anything but good. Besides, I was utterly intimidated about meeting Ed's mother and the great senator Ed Willey Sr. I was stunned and hurt and angry. I was also twenty-four years old and scared to death, so I decided to shush.

We sat in the parlor, where a life-size picture of *The Senator* hung over the fireplace. Our conversation was polite and formal.

"And what does your father do?" Ed's mother asked me.

"Uh, he sells cash registers…"

Irish

Our relationship survived all of it. We married three months after we met and within two years I had two babies, Shannon and Patrick.

Though people called me "Kathy" when I was a girl and I started going by "Kathleen" when I grew up, Ed always called me "Irish." I like to think it was my red hair and green eyes, but it might have been my temperament. Though I had come of age before the women's movement, I was strong-willed as a girl, and as a woman I still am. As much as Ed wanted me to be a shrinking violet, he also liked my fire—and he got plenty of it! I had a temper and he had one too, so we butted heads a lot. And although I was not a submissive wife, he always won because he was the strong one, the husband, the father. He was a man, a Southern gentleman who commanded a situation and did things his way. He built his law practice, made the decisions, and paid the bills. That's the way it was. I was still me, but whatever else we were, we were both Virginians, *Southerners*, and we had a very Southern marriage.

Ed grew up in North Side, the old beautiful part of Richmond where his dad—who was not a lawyer but a pharmacist—had a pharmacy. We bought a house on that side of town, a little tri-level. Ed started his own law office and I worked there a couple of days a week off and on for years, helping when people were sick or filling in during their vacations.

One day in 1975, we visited friends on the south side of the river in Midlothian, a suburb. They lived on a pretty street with old oak trees that towered above the houses and sheltered open lawns adorned with dogwoods. Three doors down from our friends' home, a house was being built. Already under roof, it was a simple house, a typical New England saltbox. Even without landscaping, the lot was nice. It was wooded, with a gentle, curving slope up to the house. We bought it and it became the home in which our children grew up. We had a good life there.

I was the wife and mom, and I stayed home to take care of the house and Ed, Shannon, and Patrick. I joined the PTA and got involved with my children's sports teams. I liked it. I volunteered at school, coached soccer, and I worked to make our home nice. I grew flowers in the garden, set a pretty table, and made macaroni and cheese from scratch. I loved doing all kinds of canning and giving people Christmas gifts of peach jam, hot pepper jelly, and corn relish. Looking back, I wonder where I found the time to do all those projects while I was driving my kids across town from school to soccer and everywhere else, but I did it and I enjoyed it.

Our neighborhood had a country club with a golf course, but we didn't live a country-club lifestyle. We didn't travel in "social circles" and I didn't join the junior league or women's clubs or anything like that. We weren't that kind of family. I wasn't that kind of woman.

In the summertime, our children went off to summer camp for six weeks. I didn't really know the meaning of "summer camp" because the only camp I'd ever experienced was a week with the Girl Scouts. But Ed had gone to summer camp. That's the way *he* grew up, so when our children were young, they went away for most of the summer. Other than those periods, my life as a "housewife" was busy, filled with school functions, T-ball games, soccer practices, and outings with the children.

Though I was a Martha Stewart–type homemaker, I was also an activist mom. At my children's high school, I started the first alcohol-free after-prom party. Other schools were starting to throw parties to keep teens from drinking and driving, so I talked to MADD and introduced the idea to our school. I invited parents to an information night to promote it and discuss what this all-night party would be like. Surprisingly, plenty of parents vociferously opposed it. "Who are *you* to tell us how to raise our children?" they challenged me, adding, "As parents, we need to teach our children how to drink!" But in the end, I won. The school has held this all-nighter every year since.

Bullseye

I started hearing stories about the drunken high school "Beach Weeks," when high school students went to the beach, drank a lot, and got into some serious trouble. So when my children were in middle school, after school let out for summer vacation, I started taking them and their friends to the beach, and continued until they graduated. At first, I only wanted to start my children on a healthier version of "Beach Week." Ed usually came for part of the week. When the children were older, I would take them with fifteen or twenty of their friends. Shannon had good friends, and I'd take her whole gang and Patrick's friends too, since Shannon and Patrick were just two years apart. We would rent a large house on the beach, usually down at Cape Hatteras. I'm sure some of them snuck out and bought beer, but for the most part it was volleyball in the sand or a fire pit on the beach. Since then, a few of these young adults have come up to me and said, "Mrs. Willey, I have the best memories of junior and senior Beach Week!"

One year, when the children were about fourteen and twelve, they each brought just one friend to Beach Week. We stayed at my sister's little condo down on the Chesapeake Bay side of Virginia Beach. There was a narrow point where the beach comes in to some culvert pipes that drain a little trickle into the bay. When we went out to the beach each day, a young cat began to greet us. He was about six months old, apparently living in one of those pipes, and he'd come out and play with Shannon and Patrick. Damn if that cat didn't follow the children right into the water! I mean cats don't *do* that! He especially latched on to Patrick and as the week wore on, he and the other children started in on me. Patrick never let up. After all, the cat *was* pretty amazing. And he was a stray. So what was the harm?

"Mom," Patrick pleaded. "Can we *please* take him home?"

The harm was that Ed was not a cat lover. We had an Irish setter and a rescue dog, Murphy and little Meg. But we did not have any cats. And Ed did not intend to have any cats. But *this* cat? This cat was pretty cool.

"What are we going to do about the cat, Mom?"

"Well, we're going to have to make up some bizarre story about him," I said. "We're going to have to stick together on this one, so don't blow it for me, okay?"

"This is what we'll do…" I rehearsed the scenario. "We'll tell Dad that we were leaving, driving down the road to the highway, and this cat ran across the road and the car kind of bopped him, just knocked him out. And there he was in the gutter and, you know, we couldn't leave him there, poor cat! Of course we couldn't leave him…"

"Yeah, yeah!" Shannon and Patrick agreed. "That's good. That'll work."

"Okay, so we'll stick to this?" Yes, they promised.

When we walked into the house with this cat, Ed zeroed in on him instantly. Then he looked at me.

"What is this, Irish?"

"Oh, wait till you hear this!"

The children were no help at all, as they were barely stifling their giggles.

"…So we couldn't leave him in the gutter. We didn't know where any vets are down there, and we needed to come home, so we *had* to bring him with us."

He didn't like it. "All right," he grumbled. "Okay. But *you* take care of him. He is *your* cat."

"Well, actually," I looked at my giggling children, "Shannon and Patrick felt real bad too…" After all, there's enough Catholic guilt to go around.

He was a pretty cat, a light yellow tabby with a bull's-eye pattern on his sides, so Shannon's friend Beth named him "Bullseye."

About a week later, Ed and Shannon were washing the cars. Water was spraying everywhere and Bullseye was right there with them. The cat was acting like he was in a spring shower, lounging around under the spray, totally in his element, tipping his head back to face the fountain of water with his eyes closed. He was the picture of springtime bliss, just loving it.

"That is the damnedest cat I've ever seen!" Ed said to Shannon. "I've never seen a cat that liked the water like that."

"Oh, man, that's *nothing*!" Shannon blurted. "You should have seen him chasing us in the waves and following us into the water at the beach!"

We were toast.

But by then, even Ed had to admit that Bullseye was a cool cat. He was Patrick's cat because they had made a real connection from the start. After all, what boy wouldn't love a cat as nuts as Bullseye? Those two would be on the hardwood floor and Patrick would grab him by the tail and twirl him around on the floor—and Bullseye loved it.

Ed was more of a dog man. We had an Irish setter, Murphy, a great dog who was at Ed's feet every night, so when it came to the cat, Ed insisted on playing the role of the outraged, duped father. And he played it up! He wasn't at all serious, but he got as much mileage out of that as he could. He'd needle the children, calling the cat "Target" instead of "Bullseye."

The children protested, especially Patrick. "Dad! It's *Bullseye*!"

"Nah, it's Target," Ed would say. "I think Target's better."

But eventually Ed took a liking to him. He had to, because Bullseye was a love bug. In the winter, I'd build a fire in the fireplace and sit reading or knitting or watching TV, and Bullseye always climbed up in my lap and cuddled.

The Streakers

As a mom, I spent many years, week in and week out, on the sidelines watching my children play soccer. Some of us moms learned to referee or coach the teams and finally we thought, *Hey, we know this game…We should play!* So we started a women's soccer league.

There was a cross section of women—some had children, some didn't, some even had grandchildren. The moms with children were like me. The most I ever did sportswise was shake the pom-poms in high school. Girls didn't have many other options before 1972, when Title IX was enacted. Before that, when I was in school, we didn't have any girls' teams, so women my age had never engaged in competitive sports before. Some of the women who played with us, though, were young, athletic college PE majors who didn't have children.

In 1983, we pulled together a wonderful bunch of women, formed teams and a league, and created a special bond in the process. College girls to grandmothers and every age in between, we came from all walks of life and went through everything together, supporting each other through our childrens' births, illnesses, teenage strife, and family deaths. These are the kinds of friends who open their homes to one another, for whom a guest is just part of the family, so our sisterhood was the beauty of this group of women. We called our team the Streakers, and every Sunday we played soccer against other women's teams. We played together for a long time, and our husbands and children came out to cheer *us* on for a change!

Ed and the Dixiecrats

"He's such a dreamer," Ed's parents used to say about him. "We couldn't keep his attention, could never get him to focus." Unfortunately, until the mid-1980s, attention deficit disorder (ADD) was not on anyone's radar—certainly not ours. But it was our life! Ed was *always* blowing in late to soccer games, baseball games, and meetings. "I'll get there," he'd say. "I'll be there late and I have to leave early, but I'll get there." Ed would charge in a few minutes late in a big flurry, shaking the change in his pocket and going on about how he had locked his keys in his car so he needed to call his secretary to come and get him.

There were many times when I literally could not get his attention. I always followed up after him and took care of the details. I was simply accustomed to living my life like this. I was oblivious to its implications, and it took me a long time to realize that Ed likely had ADD. Adults with ADD didn't receive treatment until the early 1990s, and it never occurred to me—to either of us—that he might have a problem. I often wonder if it would have helped Ed if he'd been diagnosed, but it was too late for him. He struggled a lot and had many problems in his life. As the son who couldn't live up to his great father, he suffered many demons. I often think that if he had sought treatment or counseling he might still be alive today.

When it came to our children, Ed had a soft touch and I was the disciplinarian. He grew up in a fairly middle-class family and wanted the children and me to have all the things he didn't have when he was growing up, so he enjoyed providing for us. While I encouraged our children to get summer jobs, do their chores, and live on an allowance, Ed indulged all of us in the lifestyle he wanted to give us. I was oblivious to the financial resources, or lack of them. Whenever I asked about the money, Ed would say, "Well, uh, Jane-Lee..."

Jane-Lee was Ed's right-hand girl, the one who cleaned up the rest of his life: his law office. Ed was terrible about returning phone calls to clients, and Jane-Lee and the other women in the office would cover for him, especially at the end when he was really in trouble. They were very loyal to him because he was a good and caring boss. But he was very female-dependent. It was as though the females in his life were a means to an end.

Every April hundreds of politicians—including my husband—attended a bizarre gathering in the Virginia woods to celebrate politics and fish, of all things. Shad is a bony fish that doesn't taste good at all. They took the shad and nailed it to planks of wood, then propped the planks into the sides of a fire pit dug into the ground. They'd cook the fish and talk politics, but I think the "Shad-Planking" was an excuse for a bunch of guys to get drunk. The state troopers in attendance would look the other way when all the drunk drivers got in their cars, but they'd make sure they all made it home. The Shad-Planking has been around as long as I have and it is vital to Virginia's political process. Back in Ed's day, everybody who was anybody went to it: our state legislators, former governors, senators, Washington congressmen and senators, and absolutely anyone else who was politically connected. Of course, I *desperately* wanted to go. There was only one problem—it was all men.

"What do you mean, *all men*?"

"Don't start, Irish," Ed pleaded.

"Well it's time for women to go! What's wrong with having a woman along?"

"Irish, this is not the place for you to burn your bra."

"Oh, come on!" I begged. "I won't look when they're peeing in the woods!"

This is the way our marriage was, the way we were. But I still could not go to the Shad-Planking.

Having evolved from southern Dixiecrats, Ed's father and his cohorts were "Democrats," but they were *not* McGovern Democrats. Far from it. They held tightly to their socially conservative ideology. Still, they were Democrats on paper. At least we had that in common.

A Virginia senator from 1952 until his death in 1986, my father-in-law was an extremely powerful legislator. As chairman of the state finance committee, he controlled the budget, which gave him authority over the state's purse strings. Everybody bowed, scraped, and groveled at Senator Willey's feet, and he was very good at being bowed to. He loved it.

His clout, which exceeded that of the governors, is evident today in the Willey Bridge, which spans the upper James River. Of course, the son of such a man would always be involved in politics. My husband ran his father's campaigns. Ever since I was a young girl and John Kennedy was elected, I have been interested in politics. In the 1960s, I was politically aware and I was pretty liberal. Though I never went to marches or protests, I supported equality for women and believed in the civil rights movement. As a political "child" of JFK, I held on to the idealism for which he stood.

When Shannon was about sixteen years old and Patrick was fourteen, I realized I could do political work during the school day, so I started volunteering. The timing was good. Ed's law practice was successful. At the time, he worked on land-use, condemnation, and zoning cases. Our family life allowed me to dig in to politics and I was enthusiastic about doing so.

I met a Democrat named Mary Sue Terry. In 1985, Doug Wilder ran for lieutenant governor and Mary Sue ran for attorney general. I joined her campaign, doing anything that needed to be done. We didn't do many mass mailings back then. It was more footwork. We didn't have fax machines, and copy machines were just starting to be common. The lucky campaign offices had copiers, but we had to borrow somebody's copier or run down to a copy office. We did a lot of that kind of legwork.

Where I helped most was fundraising. More than anything, that meant using the phone, but I was also good at organizing fundraisers. All those years as a housewife paid off when it came to planning events to raise support and money. We won, and Mary Sue Terry became the first female attorney general in the state of Virginia and in the country. Wilder, who eventually became Virginia's first black governor, was elected lieutenant governor. After that, I went to work for him as "unpaid staff," mostly handling constituents' problems and helping anyone who contacted the office for help on any issue.

The Rock Star

Four years later, Doug Wilder was ready for a promotion. He ran for governor in the fall of 1989. John and Patricia Kluge were honorary chairs of Wilder's campaign, and I volunteered, planning events and raising money. The Kluges held a grand fundraiser for him at their expansive estate in Charlottesville, Virginia. Their mansion was like nothing I had ever seen in my life. With Roman pillars and every extravagance, it was beyond grandiose.

We were excited about the event because we knew the campaign was going to bring in substantial donations that night. Coinciding with the fundraiser, President George H. W. Bush had gathered the nation's governors in Charlottesville for a summit on education. In addition to all the people who had come just for the fundraiser, many of America's Democratic governors also came to support Wilder.

Among the governors at the Kluge fundraiser was a rising star, the governor of Arkansas, Bill Clinton. He was *very* up and coming. Word was that Pamela Harriman doted on Clinton. She had a Washington "salon" where all the Democratic thinkers would sit and jawbone. He was one of her favorites. Besides, Bill Clinton is Bill Clinton. He was a rock star!

Clinton offered to support Doug's race for the governorship and I told him that we would be delighted. I was constantly fundraising and suggested that we could use his help. "We'd love to have you come to a fundraiser in Richmond," I said, "whenever you're in Washington." He was always in Washington. I gave him the phone number of Doug's campaign office.

"Yeah," he said. "Sure."

Ed and I were impressed by Bill Clinton. He was our age. He was attractive, charming, and personable. When Ed introduced himself and mentioned that he was a lawyer, Clinton said his wife was a lawyer too. That was all I knew of Hillary at the time, but Bill seemed down to earth and had so much charisma that Ed and I thought he had a lot to offer.

In the evening, the event moved from the Kluges' estate to a historical home for dinner and dancing. Ed and I found seats at a dinner table and just as our table was filling up, Governor Clinton quickly tried to sit next to me. Somebody else had already claimed the seat, so he moved to the next table. Still, he zeroed in on us and continued to make eye contact with me throughout dinner. He was being flirty and assertive, and I felt uncomfortable, for myself and also for my husband.

About a week later, I was at campaign headquarters and a young intern working at the campaign during the summer stopped me. "Oh, I forgot to tell you," he said. "Governor Clinton called you."

"What?" I said. "When?"

"Well, it was the day after that fundraiser at the Kluges'," he said.

"Did he say what he wanted?"

"He just wanted to talk to you."

"Well," I said, "did he leave a number or anything?"

"I don't think so…"

"Well, do you want to go back and look? See if you can find something?" I wanted Clinton to come to Richmond to do a fundraiser for Doug. *For goodness sake, kid, find the damned message.* He couldn't find it.

Though I didn't know it at the time, meeting Bill Clinton that night was only the beginning of a long and difficult period of my life. At the end of it, my pleasant life as a homemaker would be in shambles and my loyalty to the Democratic Party—the party of my childhood hero JFK—would be in serious jeopardy.

But at the beginning it was sheer excitement. After all, I was about to become involved in a heady, victorious presidential campaign for the man who would eventually become America's forty-second president. I was determined to make the most of the opportunity.

CHAPTER TWO

THE FIRST CAMPAIGN

WHEN BILL CLINTON announced his bid for the presidency in October 1991, I met with Richmond's Main Street businessmen and other politically active people to discuss his campaign. I met with Bob Burrus, a lawyer who was a big Democrat, and Alan Wurtzel, the president of Circuit City. Together, we formed the state campaign, "Virginians for Clinton," and set up campaign headquarters in Ed's office suite.

Ed's practice had continued to grow and he had another lawyer, a secretary, and his paralegal, Jane-Lee, working for him. His offices took up part of the first floor of a nice building, with floor-to-ceiling windows overlooking the lake. For its headquarters, the campaign occupied one of the offices.

The national campaign sent Doug Bonner down from Washington to manage the state campaign part time. But everyone knew that Virginia wasn't really in play. Clinton would not win the state, so it wasn't much of a priority to his national campaign and Bonner's job there was very low-level. He manned the fort but wasn't all that engaged. We gave him space while we went about the business of raising as much money as we could. I planned several fundraisers in Virginia and met often with national campaign coordinators in Washington.

The following January, just before the New Hampshire primary, a tabloid proclaimed that Clinton had engaged in a long-term affair with a woman named Gennifer Flowers. More news started trickling in about Gennifer and the revelations almost derailed his campaign. I was so angry I ripped the bumper sticker off my car. But Clinton denied the story. Since my husband and I supported him, we talked

at length about it and decided that there are women out to get powerful men. That happens all the time. We were loyal Democrats and
we thought, "Who is this troublemaker?" Besides, we thought Clinton would make a very good president. In the end, Ed believed in
him and I believed in him—and I didn't believe *them*. So we continued to support him. It should have been my first warning and I
should have known better, but like most Democrats, I believed him,
and the self-proclaimed "Comeback Kid" prevailed.

We had planned a fundraiser for February 10, which was
right on the heels of the Gennifer Flowers scandal. Clinton was
planning to attend but he canceled at the last minute, promising
to make it up to us.

Into the summer, I worked on his campaign nearly full time.
Since Ed and I had started "Virginians for Clinton," people in Virginia came to us at the campaign headquarters if they wanted to go
to an event.

Whenever Clinton was scheduled to attend an event, the Secret Service arrived in advance. They'd get to know who was involved in the planning and organizing, because we needed to be
able to move around freely at the event and they needed to feel
comfortable talking to us, asking questions, or requesting help.
As a security mechanism, the Secret Service gave us a little button
that signified that they had checked us out. I got a button at all
the events I worked at, and Ed would just *die* for one! He kept
saying, "Get me one of those." I finally gave him one of my old
ones and he wore it around town.

In addition to my work organizing fundraisers, Ed and I attended several events for Clinton. One time, we drove up to Washington to attend a seated dinner. We brought another couple, Ed's
colleague Michael Morchower and his wife, Beth. Clinton was going to attend the fundraiser but, at the last minute, he couldn't get
there and Hillary filled in for him, delivering a speech and working the room. She didn't strike me as anyone interesting at all, and
we were disappointed that Governor Clinton hadn't come.

Ed and I attended another splendid fundraiser in the spring
of 1992 in Annapolis, Maryland, at Tom and Debbie Siebert's
home. Tom Siebert had gone to law school at Georgetown with

Bill and Hillary, so they had a history. Enormously wealthy, he gave a lot of personal money to Clinton's campaign. Clinton later appointed him ambassador to Sweden and Tom's wife, Debbie, later volunteered in the White House Social Office, where I really got to know her. A seated dinner for at least a hundred people, the fundraiser was on the grounds of their home overlooking the Severin River. Clinton, of course, was an hour and a half late, but at least he showed up.

After dinner, the party moved onto an elegant wooden boat modeled after the *Sequoia*, the old presidential yacht. The boat accommodated about fifty people, so only about a third of the guests could board the yacht at one time. With all the fundraising I had done, I had learned how to keep an eye on the Secret Service, so we stayed close to them and the candidate, moving along with them just ahead of the crowd, down the big steps to the dock and onto the boat.

Though it was crowded, the cruise down the river was delightful. Ed and I were in the salon when Clinton came in. Don Henley music played in the background and Clinton told us that Henley was one of his favorite singers. We exchanged small talk but I was thinking about the fundraiser, when he canceled at the last minute, and I wanted him to make up for it. I knew that with him we had the opportunity to put on a high-dollar fundraiser.

I finally said, "Remember—you owe us another fundraiser."

"Sure," he said. "I'll do it."

He promised again to come to Richmond. We talked about the Democratic Convention coming up in July in New York, and he asked if we would be there. I went to the convention at Madison Square Garden with a bunch of Virginia politicos, and Clinton was nominated. It was thrilling! We attended many of the events, including a big dinner where we again spoke with Clinton. Like a broken record, he again promised to come to Richmond for a fundraiser.

In the late summer, we attended an event at Pamela Harriman's estate in Middleburg, Virginia. The epitome of Southern gentility and elegance, Pamela opened her lovely home where her political memorabilia was on display. Her huge, well-manicured estate offered views of the peaceful countryside and the pastures and forest beyond her lawn, on which she had a tent set up for the party.

In October, Governor Clinton *did* come to Richmond—for the third presidential debate with Ross Perot and President George H. W. Bush. And I finally got my fundraiser!

Virginia's lieutenant governor's office called and invited me to go to the airport to welcome Clinton because I worked with them. I was part of a delegation that included Lieutenant Governor Don Beyer and some of his staff members. About six of us carpooled to Richmond's airport and waited on the tarmac in the clear and breezy morning. Finally, more than an hour late, Clinton's jet arrived and he emerged with his entourage.

The national press corps had front-row access, while envious local reporters struggled to get clear footage of the popular candidate. Off to the side on the grass, a few fans with campaign signs tried to catch a glimpse. We had a little ceremony for him and Clinton made quick rounds, shaking hands and talking with Don Beyer. Clinton spoke as little as possible. He'd lost his voice and the debate was the next day.

After about five minutes, Clinton and his cortege moved toward their motorcade. He moved close to one of his assistants, a stunning, polished-looking woman with long blonde hair, and he spoke discreetly in her ear. Then he pulled her by the arm, closer to his body, and turned her away from him. He put his face down next to hers, lined up their view, and pointed at me.

In a minute, she approached me, encumbered by several briefcases and bags hanging from her shoulders. "Excuse me," she said. "The governor would like yours and your husband's phone number."

"Oh, okay," I said. "But, uh, who are you?"

"I travel with the governor as his personal aide," she said. "And he would like your phone number."

I gave it to her.

Clinton and his party boarded limousines and the motorcade pulled away, off to Williamsburg where Clinton was to prepare for the debate. Our carpool gathered and everyone was abuzz as we got in the car. They had heard the conversation I had with the aide and were thrilled. We wanted tickets to the debate, which was going to be at the University of Richmond. All the tickets went to students and alumni of the university, so extra tickets were not to be had. I don't care who you were—*nobody* could get them. But now that Clinton had noticed me, we thought maybe I could get a few tickets.

I got home and no sooner did I put down my purse than the phone rang. It was Governor Clinton.

"Hi, Kathleen," he scratched, really hoarse. "How're you?"

"Well, I'm fine." Actually, I was in shock.

"It was so nice seeing you there at the airport." Though he had no voice, his Arkansas twang came through. "Where am I?"

It occurred to me that candidates are flying all over the place and understandably have to be told where they are.

"You're in Williamsburg, just down the road." I added, more urgently, "How are you going to do the debate tomorrow night when you've got no voice?"

"I've got doctors coming. They're gonna help me out with this."

"Can they help you talk? I mean, how are you going to get your voice back to get ready for the debate?"

"Ah, I'll be all right. They know what they're doing."

"But what are you going to do about your voice?" This debate was the biggest political event Richmond had ever seen. We all wanted him to do well, but his laryngitis seemed like a disaster.

"It sounds like you need some chicken soup," I suggested casually.

"Would you bring me some?"

That took me off guard. "Well, I guess I could," I said automatically. Really, I *could*. It's *possible*. I didn't happen to have any chicken soup on the stove at that moment, but I could whip some up. I was good at that sort of thing. After all, I'm a Martha Stewart kind of woman. I probably had some homemade stock in the freezer.

"How far are you from me?"

"Well, I'm about an hour away, but..." I started thinking, *Okay, what's this all about? Is this what I think it is?* I didn't know what to say. *Maybe these rumors about him are true.* But the man is *good.* He knew exactly what he was doing, exactly the position that he was putting me in. I was thinking, *Did he just say that? You think he meant that? Or did he mean this?* It was like, "It depends on what the definition of 'is' is." *Exactly!* That's how good he was. In the end, something told me he wasn't interested in chicken soup.

"Well, I'm surrounded by Secret Service and I think Hillary's going to come in tonight, but maybe not until tomorrow," he said. "I have got to find out where Hillary is going to be tonight, so let me just check into a few things. I'll see what I can do here and I'll call you back at about six."

So I thought, *All right, now he wants to know where Hillary is and to get rid of the Secret Service.* Though there was a lot of speculation at the time about his womanizing, I still thought it was all just speculation. I would not allow myself to believe the stories were true.

I hung up and called Ed. "You're not going to *believe* this!"

"Did you get tickets?"

That was all we were thinking about. We wanted tickets to the debate. I was more involved in the Clinton campaign than Ed was, though Ed very much liked the political limelight. Bill Clinton knew me, but he'd also met Ed.

"I haven't asked yet," I said. "He's going to call me back and I'll ask him then."

I told Ed about the chicken soup.

"He wants you to take him chicken soup?" Ed was always a gentleman. He was a man, but he was also a Southern gentleman, always tight and guarded. "What does that mean?" Ed asked me.

"Well, you're a man," I said. "You tell me. What do you think I should do?"

"I don't know."

"I don't think I should go," I told him.

"Well, er, I think that's a good idea."

Sure enough, at about six o'clock, Clinton called back. He told me that he had "cleared the decks," found out where Hillary was going to be, and said it would be fine to leave anytime and bring him that chicken soup.

I told him, "I don't think I'd better do that."

"I think it would really help me."

"Well, you know, you're there at the Williamsburg Inn," I suggested. "I'll bet they make really good chicken soup, and you could probably just call room service." *You know, open a can of Campbell's or something.*

"Ah, I kind of cleared the decks here," he said, "and I just... ah...okay..."

Well, now's the time, I thought. "Before you go, you know, we'd really appreciate just two tickets to the debate."

"Oh, I don't know if I can get any."

"Well, if you can't, who can?" I mean really, he couldn't find two tickets? Obviously, he got a certain number of tickets, and probably as many as he wanted.

"I'll have to ask around," he said. "I'll see what I can do, but I don't know if I can get my hands on any. So, uh, I'll...I'll see."

He had obviously lost interest. So we didn't go to the debate.

Later, I think the FBI tried to make something of the issue that Clinton wouldn't get me the tickets because I didn't perform. That never went anywhere.

We watched the debate with a crowd at the Omni Hotel in Richmond. Bush kept looking at his watch as if to say, "Get me out of here," and Clinton found his voice and did very well. Richmond was electrified! We never saw this sort of thing in our city. That night, after the debate, everyone was buzzing. The planets were perfectly aligned for our high-dollar fundraiser and it was a *huge* success.

The room was jammed with about a hundred and fifty people. John Kerry, who had helped Clinton with debate preparation, was there, and somebody had invited Pierce Brosnan, who was making a movie in Richmond at the time. Clinton arrived and gave me a hug, and then I took him around the room and introduced him to everyone by name. Everyone was eager to shake his hand and spend a minute with him—and support his candidacy. The money poured in.

An account in the press years later quoted somebody as saying that Ed was going around the room that night saying things like, "Did you see the big kiss Bill Clinton just gave my wife on the mouth?" Ed "reportedly bragged about it for weeks."[1] That really galled me, because it wasn't true. What's more, that is not something that would come out of Ed Willey's mouth. I knew him well enough to know that just was *not* Ed.

After the fundraiser, late that night, Clinton spoke at a huge public rally that continued until one o'clock in the morning. It was mayhem. Richmond had never seen anything like it!

Early the next morning, they had another rally at Capitol Square, the largest gathering ever on the grounds of the Capitol! Clinton was already a rock star, but he did so well in the debate that he had turned sedate, conservative Richmond, Virginia, into a city full of fervor. Thousands of people came, from college students to older Democrats. The rally was huge.

I went with my mother and a good friend who attended all of these events with me. When Governor Clinton gave his big talk, we were right behind the stands where all the politicians were—Hillary Clinton, Governor Chuck Robb and his wife Linda, senators—all the Democratic big wigs.

As Clinton's speech ended, Secret Service agents paved the way for Bill and Hillary to shake hands along the rope line. The agents went all along the line, checking people out and saying, "Don't engage either one of these people in conversation. They've got a lot to do, so don't stop them for any kind of conversation. They don't have time for it. Let them keep moving," they instructed. "Shake his hand, smile at him, that's all. Don't do any more than that."

Hillary started at one end and Bill the other, and they headed toward each other. Hillary came along first, and we shook hands. I had seen her before, when she stood in for him at the dinner in Washington, but I hadn't really met her. She had already made the comment that, "I suppose I could've stayed home and baked cookies and had teas,"[2] which I thought was awful. I was one of those quintessential "soccer moms," staying home and baking cookies myself, so I felt personally insulted and thought it was a terrible thing for her to say.

Down the way, she and her husband crossed paths as they worked the rope line, and soon he came to us. Clinton came first to my mother, then me, and then my girlfriend. He stopped. Regardless of what the Secret Service had said, *he* was certainly going to be engaged!

"I'd like you to meet my mother," I said. And boy was he all over her! When Bill Clinton is talking to you, you are the only person in the universe, and my mother was dazzled by him.

"Well, aren't you pretty?" he said to her. "Aren't you just pretty?" He had his hand behind my head, touching the back of my hair—in public, while he was talking to my mother! "Well, I can sure tell that Kathleen takes after her mother. She looks just like you." My mother could not get words out of her mouth. She was just blubbering. And still, he had his hand in my hair while he was saying, "It's obvious that she really does look like you."

I was embarrassed and hoped no one else noticed. Here he was, flirting unabashedly with me while his *wife* was right down the rope line!

"She's done so much to help me in my campaign," he added, "and we just love her."

My mother couldn't get words out of her mouth. Literally, she was like, "Mblaaagh." People later told me that when she returned to work, my mother was giddy, bouncing off the walls. This is how people reacted to Bill Clinton. He had just won the big debate, and he was the star.

Then he turned to me, giving me both hands. "Thank you for everything you did last night."

Then he greeted my friend, who was also hardly able to speak. An African-American, she said, "I just want you to know, I got all the folk out for you." She beat herself up over that for about a month. "What in the hell was I thinking?" I told her there was nothing wrong with that.

Clinton spent a couple of minutes with us. Standing behind him, the Secret Service agents talked into their earpieces as if to say, "Ahem," until Clinton finally started moving down the rope line. As he did, he kept his eyes on me. He moved down the rope line, shaking hands, watching me the whole time. It was blatant! He shook hand after hand but didn't look at any of those people. He looked at me all along.

"Do you see that?" my girlfriend said. "Do you see the way he is looking at you?"

"Uh, yeah, I do," I said.

"I don't think I have ever seen a look like that before," she said.

"It's pretty intense," I said.

"Jesus, God!" she said.

It made me nervous and uncomfortable, just as it had at the Kluges' fundraiser. As he shook hands and walked farther and farther away, he kept looking back, maintaining eye contact the whole way down the line.

Hillary was working the other end of the rope line. I think she knew, but didn't want to see it. That's what I believe, because she's *not* clueless.

Bill Clinton is tall, but when he got to the end of the rope line he stood on his tiptoes, still looking. And as they all got ready to leave and get in the limo, he stood up on something and pointed at me. Nobody else would have known he was pointing at *me*, as it seemed like he was pointing at anybody. But he added a huge wave good-bye.

My friend was incredulous. "Do you see what he's doing?"

I thought, *Well, he's pretty friendly but this is a little over the top.* She and I talked about it later and wondered whether the rumors about him were true. But we talked ourselves out of it. We wanted this man to become the next president of the United States—and it was going to happen! As people say, he's a very charismatic man. So I left with a little doubt that started to seep in. It was there, but I didn't give it much attention, just filed it away.

On election night, Ed and I drove Patrick and a friend to meet Shannon at Washington National Airport in D.C., where we boarded a chartered plane filled to the brim with giddy "FOBs"— Friends of Bill. Supporters like Ed and me, and people from the campaign in Washington, were flown to Little Rock. We went to the invitation-only celebration at the infamous Excelsior Hotel. It was an electric night. The numbers were looking good and our candidate was going to win! It was intense, the most exciting time. The Fleetwood Mac song, "Don't Stop Thinkin' About Tomorrow" echoed in our minds. We were victorious. Our man won and it was thrilling!

Clinton arrived at the hotel very late and gave a short speech. Hillary left to go to bed but he stuck around, reluctant to leave. He worked the room and finally came our way.

Across the room, Shannon panicked. "Mom! Mom, wait!" My sophisticated, well-mannered daughter jumped tables to get back to us. "*Get me over there!*"

She made it. Clinton talked with her at length, asking about her studies at Harvard, talking about the election and campaign—especially in Virginia—and thanking her for her help.

Shannon was dazzled. *All* of us were dazzled. Even Patrick. As a teenager, he hung out with Woody Harrelson the whole time.

A few days later I was vacuuming Shannon's bedroom when the phone rang.

"Hello."

"This is Bill Clinton."

What? I thought. *Surely not!* I mean, I'm in my sweats, vacuuming! At first I thought it was a joke from a disappointed Republican friend or something like that, but I quickly recognized his voice.

"I just want to thank you for all that you did for us," he said. "I'm going to be up at Pamela's for a big dinner..." He was going to go to Washington right after Christmas, when all the major inaugural events would be gearing up. "Are you going to be up at any of those things?" he asked me.

I had call waiting and a call beeped in. "Could you hold on just a second?"

Ed was calling me. "Oh my God," I exclaimed. "You're not going to *believe* who's on the other line!"

"What?" Ed said. "*Who?*"

"I'm on the phone with Bill Clinton," I explained, "and he's talking about inviting us to the inaugural stuff!"

"And you put him *on hold*? Oh my God, Irish!" Ed said. "What in the hell are you doing, asking him to hold? Don't you think you ought to get back to him?"

Yes, I put the president-elect on hold. We laughed about that for years. But it was a weird phone call. I didn't know what it was about. It was as if he just called to chat, as if he didn't have enough to do with choosing cabinet members, hiring staff, and planning the inaugural events.

But during the conversation Clinton asked if I "might possibly" be able to meet him over dinner in D.C. to discuss my role in the inaugural. I later realized that this should have been another red flag. In my gut, I just didn't feel right about it, although I couldn't see at the time exactly why I hesitated. I gracefully demurred.

When I got off the phone, I called Ed right back. "You're not going to believe this…" I told him about Clinton's dinner idea.

I also called a friend who had worked on the campaign with us. Very politically savvy, he had traveled in a lot of political circles.

"Now, first of all," I said, "I just got off the phone with Bill Clinton."

"What?"

"Yeah," I said. "I'm in my sweats vacuuming and he just called here and thanked me."

"Really!"

"Yeah," I said. "He's going up to Washington for all the pre-inaugural stuff, and Pamela Harriman's giving him a big party and all that."

"That sounds cool."

"And he asked me to meet him for dinner."

"Oh, really?"

"Yeah," I said. "Now, how would that work?"

"Well, obviously, it would be someplace very private," he said.

"Like where?"

"You know, let's say if he was up in Washington doing something, it would probably be in his suite."

"Well," I stammered. "Uh…"

He kind of read my mind.

"It'd be very private," he added. "The Secret Service would know about it, but it would be really private. The Secret Service would know, and that's about all."

I didn't go. But I did volunteer to work with the Inaugural Committee. Mary Mel French and Rahm Emmanuel were inauguration co-chairs. Mel was a lovely, refined woman from Little Rock, but Rahm was an arrogant jerk. I commuted by train from Richmond to Washington as much as I could, and helped plan the inaugural events. It was chaotic. The only thing we knew for certain was that the inauguration would happen whether we were ready or not, because it happened every four years.

When it did happen, we *were* ready. Clinton was inaugurated on January 20, 1993. Ed and I attended all of the festivities, including a formal gala where we saw Barbra Streisand and sat behind the Kennedy clan, including John Kennedy Jr. and Daryl Hannah. It was incredibly exciting to be a part of all of it.

Looking back, I should not have been surprised when the scandals arose about the Clintons and money—the sale of the Lincoln Bedroom, for example. One could attend any and all festivities at the Clinton inaugural, for a price.

But the glitz and glamour of the inaugural were only the beginning. For the next few years, I would work in a White House that knew how to put on a very good show on the outside while it was corrupt on the inside. The only thing more offensive than the lack of decorum within the walls of the White House was the lack of concern among those who should have been most interested in preserving the dignity of the office of the president—namely, the president and his wife.

CHAPTER THREE

THE FIRST TERM

WITHIN A MONTH, the new Clinton White House was overwhelmed by mail. They sent out a massive request for volunteers, calling all the campaign offices around the D.C. area. One such call came in to the Virginia State Democratic headquarters, asking if any of us would be interested. I talked with Ed and thought, *Maybe this would be a really nice opportunity.* Our children were in college, Ed had his law practice, and the time seemed right. So I answered the call. Along with many volunteers who lived around the Washington and Bethesda areas, I volunteered to work in the White House Correspondence Office.

Linda Tripp was one of the first people I met. She kind of came out of nowhere and befriended me, and I enjoyed her. She was friendly, nice, helpful, and she had a funny side. Yet she constantly put herself down, especially about her appearance. She would sometimes come in with her long, beautiful hair straightened and she looked really pretty. But she never thought so. She was hard on herself. Her hair was naturally very curly, so she would go to a salon in Washington and have her hair straightened professionally. Washington women thought nothing of paying $250 for a cut and color, which was a shock to me because I paid twenty-two dollars for a haircut in Richmond. But Linda's self-esteem seemed to need that.

Linda was an insider, one of the very few holdovers from the Bush administration who stayed on in Clinton's White House. I thought it was dangerous to have someone like that there, but they needed people like her. After the inauguration and the parties, everyone moved into their offices but nobody knew what they were doing. They needed people with experience and Linda was one who provided it. I don't know whether she was actually good at her job or just good at promoting herself—probably some of both—but her background was definitely a commodity that helped her keep her job when Bush left. She worked as something of a floater, moving wherever they needed her day to day in the West Wing.

President Clinton

I started working at the White House in March. In April, I volunteered at Clinton's first White House Easter Egg Roll. It was great fun. The president was out in the crowd and came over to speak to me, greeting me warmly.

"Good to see ya."

"Good morning, Mr. President."

He asked in which office I was working.

"I'm in the Correspondence Office," I said, "in the Old Executive Office Building."

"Oh, you don't need to be there," he said. "You should be in a better place. I'll have Nancy call you."

I'd heard of Nancy Hernreich. She was the president's assistant, the director of the Oval Office and the keeper of the gate. When I got home that afternoon, she had already left a message on my answering machine! "The president asked me to call you and talk to you about maybe a different position in another place," her message said. She asked that I meet with her the next time I came to the White House.

I thought, *Wow, this is great!* I was only a volunteer, but I'd raised lots of money for President Clinton and I figured that was how it worked.

The next time I went to work at the White House, I called Nancy and made an appointment to see her. Walking from the Correspondence Office in the Old Executive Office Building, I embarked on my first trek over to the "real" White House. I walked down through the basement and up to the main floor. Mack McLarty walked by and George Stephanopoulos was there. I took in the majesty of the White House and eyed the people about whom I'd read and heard so much.

I found Nancy's office and was instantly shocked. She was the woman who had asked me for my phone number at the Richmond Airport before the debate. I had never put the name with the face. I sat across from her and she told me there was a slot open in the Visitors Office and one in the Social Office. And, she said, "We think you'd be better suited to that."

I was thinking, *This is an awful lot of interest they're taking in an unimportant volunteer who's riding up on the train from Richmond, Virginia. But I'll take it!*

"Just a second," Nancy said. "I need to take this file in to the president." When she came back, President Clinton strolled into Nancy's office with her. I thought, *Okay, well…Here's the president of the United States!*

He gave me a big kiss and a hug like he's famous for. "Come on in," he said. "I'll take you on a tour of the Oval Office."

Years later, press reports, pundits, and the public wondered at the access I had to the president. One article, for example, said I was "a questionable character of dubious qualifications, gaining access to the president only through the corrupting power of campaign contributions."[1] That was silly. Our own financial contributions were *nothing* compared to the work we did starting the Virginia campaign and raising support and money in our state. I never expected or assumed that those efforts would give me access to the president or the Oval Office. In fact, I was surprised and delighted that President Clinton welcomed me the way he did.

When he took me by the hand and led me in, I didn't think much of it. *He's famous for hugging people*, I thought. *He takes a lot of people by the hand.* At that time, Nancy's office was on the other side of the Oval Office and, to get there, he led me into the private dining room, past the galley kitchen and the private study, and into the Oval Office through a side door.

It was the first time I'd ever been there. I was overwhelmed, just dazzled by it, as President Clinton pointed out the Remington statue and the desk, which had been John Kennedy's desk. That was really something for me because Kennedy was a hero to me. I looked at that desk and thought about Caroline and John playing underneath it. Pictures of them ran through my mind. I was awestruck. I thought, *John Kennedy walked right on this spot where I'm standing. He sat at this desk, right here!* I walked around, nodding, thinking to myself, *Try to remember everything!* I didn't want to walk out and forget any of it. I asked for some autographed pictures for Ed and my children, and President Clinton gave them to me. He escorted me into his private study and showed me his extensive collection of old campaign buttons. I saw one of the stewards, a really sweet Filipino man, but he quickly went away.

As we talked, the president suggested that I could be better utilized in the White House Visitors Office or the Social Office, and I should call Melinda Bates at Visitors or Ann Stock in Social.

Then, all of a sudden, he seemed distracted, like he wasn't quite all there. He looked around a lot, and even though he was showing me the button collection and other artifacts in the study, I thought to myself, *I can't seem to get his attention.* It was as though he was going through the motions but not able to pay attention, as though there was something else—something big—going on in his mind.

I later realized that he was sizing up the situation, looking around, thinking, *Is there time for something here? Is anybody around? Where's Hillary?* Much later, I also realized the significance of the little lair to which he'd taken me. That little hideaway behind the Oval Office across from the galley kitchen—and beyond the view of the White House security cameras—would one day become famous.

After about fifteen minutes alone with the president, he gave me a hug. I started to feel a little bit uncomfortable. It was so subtle. The hug was a little long and we were in a private room. My feminine intuition recoiled. It was one of those things, a feeling I had as a woman, but he was the president of the United States! I didn't think of it as being alone with him, but as being shown the Oval Office by the president. This is where he's good. That was, of course, his whole MO. But I didn't realize that yet.

I raced back to my office to pick up the phone and call Ed—and everyone I've ever met in my entire life! I'd gone from soccer mom to working at the White House *and* getting a tour of the Oval Office by the president of the United States. That is the pinnacle! I loved it. I was thrilled.

Neither Ed nor I ever questioned—at all—whether it was inappropriate. We simply thought we were great fundraisers and our guy won the election, and this is what you get.

That was April 15, 1993, one of the best days of my life. When I returned to my desk in the Old Executive Office Building, I received the phone call for which I had been hoping for twenty-eight years. I had hired a search group to find Sean, the son I had given up for adoption, and they found him in Pittsburgh, Pennsylvania! A few months later, I finally met Sean while traveling through Pittsburgh. It was great. The spitting image of his father, he was in a huge crowd and I spotted him right away. About three months later, he came to Richmond to meet Ed and his new sister and brother.

Days after I met with President Clinton, I called Melinda Bates in the Visitors Office and told her that I was calling at Clinton's personal suggestion. Surprisingly, she was cold and unwelcoming. I found Ann Stock in the Social Office to be much friendlier. She said there was room for me, so I went to work in the East Wing.

Ann Stock

A lot of the volunteers in the Social Office were Democratic faithful who didn't have a relationship with either the president or the first lady. Still, whenever a new volunteer started working in the office everyone would ask, "So, are you a friend of *his* or *hers*?"

"Well, I know him better than her," was my standard answer. I was careful about that, because many people would say they were friends with the Clintons when they really weren't. I didn't like it when anyone bragged about a relationship with the Clintons, so I made a point of downplaying mine. But if I was walking with someone and we saw the president, he'd always stop and say, "Hi, Kathleen."

"Oh, you really *do* know him?" my coworkers would say. "So you really *are* close to him?"

"Well, yeah," I'd say. "Ed and I worked on his Virginia campaign," I would explain, "and we were at that fundraiser after the debate." I certainly didn't go around advertising it, but the longer I was there the more people saw it, and people generally knew that I had a history with Clinton.

Later, when the Clintonistas started to smear me, reporters gathered comments from my Social Office coworkers who supposedly said, "Kathleen was always throwing Bill's name around," and "She was always talking about how close they were." These were cheap shots. Each comment was anonymous. Nobody would stick her neck out for such lies.

Part of that was political, of course. But it was also the nature of the beast. There was a lot of appalling behavior in the Social Office, and it started at the top—with the president and his wife.

In *Living History*, Hillary claimed that she and Social Secretary Ann Stock "tried different combinations of linens and place settings before settling on the...china acquired by Mrs. Reagan. We worked on seating arrangements" and "consulted with the White House florist...as she arranged the tulips I had selected for each table."[2] Actually, Hillary hardly gave any input at all. We worked with the florist on her arrangements and prepared mock-up place settings with the china and crystal and silverware for Hillary's approval, but she never seemed to care. "Hillary would respond, 'I don't have time. I don't want to do this,'" wrote Carl Bernstein in his 2007 biography of Hillary, *A Woman in Charge*.[3] I think I saw Hillary in the Social Office maybe two times. Everything—all the planning that was done for the events and Christmas parties and state dinners—was left up to the staff. She didn't know anything about entertaining and never showed any interest in such things. Bernstein even noted, "There was little evidence throughout 1993 of Hillary as the hostess to the nation."[4]

To her credit, Ann Stock told Bernstein that, had the first lady "skillfully entertained," it might have helped her politically, laying a groundwork from which she and the president could promote their legislative agenda—starting with Hillary's health care plan. But Hillary would not get involved in such tasks. "The first lady's social secretary was flabbergasted by Hillary's initial unwillingness to engage in the usual protocols of White House entertaining," Bernstein wrote. "For better or worse, effecting change in the capitol, and thus changing the country, was an intricate process that involved a certain amount of bowing and scraping, and the first lady was no exception from the requirement ... [but] Hillary refused."[5] Obviously, bowing and scraping were not a part of Hillary's agenda as first lady.

Hillary hired Stock, who had graduated from Purdue University where she majored in elementary education. When Hillary gave her the White House job, Ann was vice president of public relations for Bloomingdale's in New York.[6] As the story goes, the first lady hired Ann Stock in fifteen minutes, such was her concern about the Social Office.

Stock was an outsider and many of the women in the office were more connected. Ann McCoy was one. A lovely woman, she was a very proper Southern lady who knew the right way to do things. A loyal Clinton supporter and "Friend of Bill," she had come to the White House from Little Rock because she loved Clinton, just *loved* him. But Ann Stock treated Ann McCoy like dirt.

Ann Stock had no sense of decorum or good taste, which was typical of the Clinton White House. She cussed like a sailor, dropping the "f-bomb" every other minute. That set the tone for the office. With no language code—never mind a dress code—the scene inside the White House was completely inappropriate. I often thought about Jackie Kennedy or Nancy Reagan and wondered what they would think.

The White House was populated with interns, some of whom were placed in sensitive positions. In the Social Office, we often had calls from high-dollar donors and very influential, important people from all over the world, inquiring about an invitation to an event or a visit to the White House. The fact is some people need careful and respectful handling. But these interns were college kids who didn't know anything about anybody. They had no manners, and treated these people with no particular respect. Time and again, people would call and the interns didn't even act like they recognized their names—because they didn't!

One woman in the Social Office who was a breath of fresh air was Vernon Jordan's wife, Ann Jordan. She really knew the ways of Washington and was a rare voice of reason in the office. I was so grateful that she was there because she knew how things were supposed to be.

But her kind of reason and civility were not requirements in the Clinton White House or in its Social Office, and they certainly weren't common. While most of the volunteers had a sense of dignity about working in the White House, not a lot of the regular staff seemed to have the same regard. Many of the volunteers, like Debbie Siebert and Harolyn Cardozo, would often tell me, "You need to tell the president what's going on around here!" *Yeah*, I thought, *I'll just go tell the president what to do!*

Harolyn Cardozo and I became good friends. I liked her a lot. But she was caught up in the ugly drama of the Social Office, the gossip and backstabbing. I really went to bat for her, but in the end Harolyn left. And Harolyn Cardozo is *not* the kind of person that you let walk out and quit. She came from a very rich family and knew how to run a party. She also had a lot of influence and knew her way around Washington. But she quit.

Despite all the drama, I enjoyed working in the Social Office and I was good at it. My experience as a housewife and fund-raiser had taught me how to organize beautiful dinners and events. Ruthie Eisen was another volunteer in the office, very adept at entertaining and a dear friend of mine. Almost immediately, Ruthie and I were put in charge of the White House Jazz Festival in July. At the same time, we were unpacking and evaluating crafts and ornaments for the Christmas tree and holiday decorations for the White House. We had the theme—a handmade country motif—and invited vendors from all over the United States to contribute ornaments to match our theme. One of our jobs, long before we worried about bombs or anthrax, was to screen the boxes of ornaments and decorations that came in. Essentially, we looked at all of them to make sure they were tasteful and appropriate, even if nothing else in the White House was. One guy made his ornaments out of roadkill and actually sent one in. The minute I saw it I was horrified!

Some of the volunteers in the Social Office were the least likely types you'd ever expect to be working anywhere in the White House, much less volunteering in the Social Office. These were fine older men, one of whom was a retired CIA agent. I later learned he had been one of our most notorious CIA spies. He told us that his daughter had been born under an assumed name in a foreign country. He wanted to tell more about his experiences, but many of those things are never to be known. He was a nice man—the last person you'd ever think would have been a deep-cover CIA agent—and here he was, working in the Social Office. I mean, there must have been something else he could do, rather than stuffing envelopes in the Social Office.

Just behind the Social Office was a military office. Every detail of every trip had to be planned with military logistics, and the office that coordinated them was just behind the Social Office. A really nice man who was left over from the Bush administration ran it. He hated the Clintons. And he wasn't alone.

The First Lady

Linda Tripp was another holdover who hated the Clintons. She knew that I was a staunch Democrat and that I was there because I was a Clinton person, but I quickly saw that she was extremely displeased with the Clintons. She had been a Bush person and obviously didn't support the Clintons' ideology. But the new administration's lack of decorum and its disrespect for the White House and the presidency antagonized her more than anything. Clinton had no dress code for the Oval Office, much less for the White House. And there was no language code, no protocol, nothing. There was no schedule. Nobody followed the rules. Everything was loosey-goosey, just sloppy. And Linda hated that.

One day, she told me with disgust, President Clinton had a hankering for a Big Mac, so they sent her out to McDonald's to get him one. I thought, *Surely the Secret Service isn't going to let somebody go out and bring the president a Big Mac?* I know they don't have food tasters, but they have to be a *little* careful, don't they? But the way the White House was run, it could have been true. That was the dichotomy of the Clinton White House: America had a bull in its china shop.

The Social Office problems were just symptomatic of the problems in the whole White House. A managerial anarchy trickled down through the ranks, starting at the top with the president and first lady. The White House didn't seem to follow any rules. The work had no rhyme or reason. It was chaos. And to top it off there was no sense of propriety.

The casualness of the Clinton crowd did not fit in the White House. It doesn't matter how casual the president is, nor does it matter that he came from Arkansas or that he's as popular as a rock star. It should not have been that way. It was inappropriate and wrong. It diminished the integrity of the White House from the top down.

According to Linda, during the Reagan administration, men were required to a wear a suit and tie to enter the Oval Office. George H. W. Bush did Reagan one better. In Bush's White House, women weren't even allowed to wear pants—dresses only! That's very sexist, but at least he upheld a sense of decorum. Believing in the dignity of the presidency, these leaders afforded due respect to the White House and to the office. Not so with the Clintons.

On three-day weekends and days when most of the workers were gone, President Clinton was known to walk around the White House wearing jeans, and James Carville and his cast of characters would also come in jeans, with their shirts out. I even heard they would sprawl on the sofa, eating pizza in the Oval Office and resting their feet on the desk—Jack Kennedy's desk. I thought to myself, *This is just is not right!*

Ann Stock confirmed this to Bernstein. The Clintons' gang "treated the White House as if it were a campaign venue," Stock told him. "They didn't really understand the significance of the president's house."[7]

The first lady was someone else who didn't seem to understand the significance of the White House, the people's house. People often described how rude and impatient Hillary was and how filthy her language was. She sometimes walked around the White House looking like she had just rolled out of bed. Her hair was dirty and hardly brushed and she didn't wear a stitch of makeup, not even foundation or something to improve her ruddy, uneven skin. She paid no attention to her clothes. When I saw her around the White House looking like that, I thought, *Doesn't anybody around here understand where they are?*

In the beginning, clothing designers and vendors begged her to wear their lines, so they sent racks of clothes to the White House. I like nice clothes. I always have. When I worked at the

White House, I was polished and appropriately dressed every day. When racks of Oscar de la Renta and Carolina Herrera fashions showed up, I just drooled! And everyone buzzed, "What's Hillary going to wear?"

Her wardrobe was so bad that people would say to me, "Kathleen, can't you tell her what to wear? Can't you make a suggestion?" Obviously, I wasn't about to tell the first lady of the United States that she wasn't dressed appropriately.

Visitors

Following the Clintons' example, their friends behaved just as inappropriately in the White House. An Arkansas couple, Harry Thomason and his wife, Linda Bloodworth-Thomason, was a famous example. He was a sleaze. All he did was walk around with his badge and his hands in his pockets, with his big gut hanging out over his belt. He walked around, with free rein of the place. He made me so uncomfortable. His wife was in California, but when she did come to the White House they couldn't wait to get to the Lincoln Bedroom so they could jump up and down on the bed. Some of the Clintons' friends notoriously had sex in the Lincoln Bedroom—even when they were *not* overnight guests!

Bernstein confirms that Harry Thomason lived part time in the White House in early 1993, and that he was"given a White House pass, an office in the East Wing, and a vague charter, known as the 'White House Project,' to continue shaping the public images of the president and first lady."[8]

Harry and his wife weren't the only ones. The White House was full of visitors with passes and some of them were the most flamboyant and bizarre people I have ever seen in my life. Sometimes it felt as though I were walking around a Hollywood movie studio. They moseyed around from the Old Executive Office Building over to the West Wing or wherever, and had free rein of the whole White House. Some looked like Elton John wannabes. And there were many *very* extravagant-looking women.

I would be working at my desk, with Secret Service agents around, and we'd see these clowns walk by and we all looked at each other like, "What is *this*?" We had no idea where these characters came from or what they were doing there. It was just crazy.

Vince Foster

The craziness turned serious when Vince Foster died. Among the thousands of unanswered questions about Vince was the issue of his relationship with Hillary. Everyone knew they were incredibly close. As Bernstein put it, "The relationship would confound Foster's wife (but not Bill Clinton)."[9]

Linda Tripp noticed it too. "I believe at one time they were very close," Linda observed. "She was dependent on him, which, over time, caused a strain." Vince was increasingly on the spot for Travelgate and, while Hillary claimed it had nothing to do with her, Linda said she had evidence that Hillary "masterminded the entire Travelgate massacre."[10]

Curiously, when Vince moved to Washington, he insisted on leaving his family in Little Rock until their youngest child graduated high school. His wife didn't like it. Bernstein recounts a telling story. "She and their children came to Washington for the inauguration, but Vince had no time for them." In fact, he ditched them when the ceremony was over, leaving them on the Capitol grounds, from which they had to find their way back to their host's house. Naturally, she was furious. "I was just angry at him for ignoring us and leaving us behind, and making me have to deal with everything, all the decisions, and he was getting all the so-called glory."[11]

According to Bernstein, Vince told Web Hubbell that he felt that, as deputy counsel to the president, he and Hillary "were the team he had always imagined they would be." That's an intriguing view, considering it was Hillary and *Bill* who were the infamous team. Sadly, as Bernstein adds, "The glow didn't last long."[12]

The fair-haired boy, Vince graduated magna cum laude from law school and became head of the *Law Review*. He did everything right. He and Bill Clinton had been buddies since kindergarten. Though Vince was tall, thin, handsome, and came from the right side of the street, he didn't have the tough skin that the Clintons have. Vince took a lot of political hits and the press really beat up on him. On July 20, 1993, he went to a park outside of Washington D.C., put a gun in his mouth, and shot himself.

Linda Tripp had worked with Vince. "His very being commanded respect—dignified, decent, kind, smart, immensely loyal," Linda said of him. "Vince Foster was a good man."[13] She was the last person known to have spoken with him. When she appeared on *Larry King Live* in 1999, Larry asked Linda if she knew he was troubled.

"I don't know that I knew he was troubled."

"Were you shocked when he killed himself?"

"I was shocked that he was dead, yes."

"Are you saying," Larry pressed, "you are not sure he killed himself?

"You know, I don't know," Linda said. "To this day, I don't know... It was the aftermath of that suicide that started to make me...question things."[14]

Hillary was not in Washington that night, and phone calls flew between Maggie Williams and Hillary. But Linda was there and saw that they were taking files out of Vince's office. It was suddenly a mad rush. Linda said Maggie Williams hauled all kinds of stuff out of there. It was "chaos, people milling around," Linda later said. "Finally, I closed the doors because there were no guards, no nothing. Security in the Clinton White House was lax at best. When you have a high-ranking administration official dead by other than natural means, there obviously should be an investigation," she added.[15]

Linda thought that the Capitol Police or other officials with some legal authority should supervise the file transfer, but they didn't. Linda knew what should and shouldn't be going on, and she wanted to ensure it was proper and legitimate. Linda said there was a lot of hush-hush activity. "Initially," she said, "there was shock and grief. But then doors shut, covert weirdness began." She knew the files in Foster's office were "sensitive" materials that would cause problems for Hillary, and she watched them being removed from his office to the Clintons' residence.[16]

Years later, chief investigative counsel for the House Judiciary Committee David Schippers said, "I think he was murdered. Absolutely. We were going to investigate that. All my investigators said, 'Let's investigate the Vince Foster thing.'" But once the Republicans lost the midterm election, they were called off of everything. "We were called off the Ron Brown thing. We wanted to get into that. We wanted to get into Chinagate," Schippers said. "But they called it all off. We were all told we had to stop dead."[17]

"Formers"

Our offices were always full of women from Arkansas, some of whom were Southern ladies, flawless and elegant. I became good friends with one such woman, Mel French, who had headed up the inaugural before becoming chief of protocol at the State Department. But when Arkansas women came to town it often was a different story. It usually raised Linda's antennae. She seemed to know whenever an Arkansas woman set foot in the White House.

"Who is *she*?" Linda would quiz us. "Is she a *former*?" I still didn't believe that the president *had* any former flings, but according to Linda there were many. She seemed to revel in the drama and intrigue, and she perpetuated it, frequently pointing out women in the White House, saying, "Now *she* is *definitely* a former!" or "There's a former," and "So-and-so is a former." I'm not convinced that it wasn't all just in her mind.

Linda

Linda was a promoter, and during 1993 I noticed that she was particularly promoting scandal. Until she had something real to go on, she would try to make something out of nothing. For a while, that "nothing" was me.

Linda and I would often take a break and walk outside together so she could have a cigarette. On our way, we would sometimes see President Clinton in the Rose Garden as he went from the Oval Office to the residence. Other times, we encountered him in the White House corridors. Whenever we saw him, he was familiar and friendly with me. He would stop and give me a hug, say hello, and talk for a moment. As soon as we went on our way, Linda would say, "Did you see that? Did you see the way he looked at you?" I thought she was being ridiculous. I mean, the president didn't save those kinds of greetings for me. Men and women alike, that's just what he did. That was Clinton's way, I thought.

As a Social Office volunteer, I frequently helped at receptions and parties. If the president was expected to attend an event, Linda would be in my ear a few days beforehand. "What are you going to wear?" she'd ask me, as if I weren't a married woman. It did occur to me that Linda seemed to be trying to get the president in trouble. It was pretty clear she was out to get him, and she seemed to think I might be the way.

Not surprisingly, Linda would repeat the tactics that she used with me on a more susceptible woman—Monica Lewinsky. Linda used to say something to me that echoed back a few years later. While working in the office, I heard my own voice on an answering machine. I thought, *God, I sound so nasal—and I can still hear my parents' Philadelphia accents*. Linda and I were casually talking about this, and I mentioned that, like most people, I hated the sound of my own voice. "Oh no, Kathleen," Linda told me, "you have such a sexy voice." Linda said the same thing to Monica Lewinsky! Years later, in one of the infamous recorded conversations between Linda and Monica, Linda said to her, "You've just got the most seductive voice. No wonder he calls you for phone sex, that voice of yours." When I heard and read the transcripts of Linda's conversations with Monica, I recognized that many of her comments to the young woman echoed things she had said to me a few years before. It was as if she used the same playbook, trying to finesse information out of Monica, while steering her in a particular direction. Unlike me, though, Monica obviously followed that path.

The Clinton White House was full of interesting characters, some of whom were respectable while others were not. The work we did was chaotic, and the atmosphere was often less edifying and dignified than what was appropriate in that situation. But the undisciplined, loose environment was simply a symptom of a deeper, far-reaching problem—a problem, as I would unfortunately soon discover, that started with the man who sat behind John Kennedy's desk.

CHAPTER FOUR

ASSAULT IN THE OVAL OFFICE

E D LOVED being connected, loved that I worked in the Social
Office. There were times when he helped me write notes to
the president or had me bring him gifts. Once Ed asked me to
give President Clinton a Jeffrey Archer book. Another time, Ed
bought a Nicole Miller tie for the president. She named her ties,
and this one was called "Presidential Shoes." It had pictures of
presidents' shoes back to Abe Lincoln. Ed asked me to leave it for
the president, so I dropped it off with Nancy, who was always
very gracious. Next thing I knew, I had a letter from President
Clinton sitting on my desk. Ed got a kick out of that and loved
saying, "My wife works at the White House."

It was a small pleasure, no doubt. For Ed, there couldn't have
been many pleasures that year. I didn't know it yet, but he was in
serious trouble.

Throughout our married life, Ed would do things that I
thought were ill advised, even reckless. For example, he would
move his law practice relatively frequently. He had about five offices in his career. One of them was ten minutes from our home,
but Ed fought with the landlord of the office building and stopped
paying the rent. Finally, the owner of the building locked the door
on him. I found out and called Jane-Lee. As usual, she and all the
women at the office covered for him.

Finally, I talked to Ed. I was in a panic. "Where are you going
to go? What are you going to do?"

"Oh, don't worry," Ed said. "I have it all figured out."

And he did. He always had it figured out. He always had an ace in the hole, always landed on his feet. Always. Until he didn't.

At the top of the list of Ed's recklessnesses was his approach to taxes. He wasn't big on paying them. Worse, he didn't seem to have a problem with that. This bothered me to no end, but he always lived on the edge and liked it there. Still, it scared me. They were *our* taxes. There wasn't much I could do, because Ed kept financial details from me. But he had been playing fast and loose with the Internal Revenue Service and was getting behind on the taxes. I didn't know that things were getting dicey for him. In the end, Ed had an accountant file my taxes separately so I wouldn't fall into the hole. Instead, I inherited it.

Ed had won a land-condemnation case for some clients and their money went into escrow. But it was too tempting, and Ed made a terrible mistake. He borrowed from Peter to pay Paul, using his clients' money to pay the IRS and other bills. The clients figured out what Ed had done. They wanted their money, and they called him constantly to demand it. Ed dodged them. Jane-Lee and the other secretaries covered for him. But the clients kept calling for the money, and finally they caught up with him.

Ed owed the money to a man named Tony Lanasa who was represented by Bubba Marshall, another country good ol' boy. Ed slipped out early one morning and met with Bubba and Lanasa at the Chesterfield courthouse parking lot at six thirty in the morning. They told him they knew what he had done. They gave him two weeks to repay the money in full or they would turn him in. They gave him a promissory note to sign and demanded that I cosign the note. It had to be in Bubba's office by noon.

I went to the dentist that morning and was on my way to deliver Meals on Wheels, as I did about once a month. It was eleven fifteen and I had to be there at eleven thirty, so I was in a rush, running a little late. We didn't have cell phones back then, but big car phones, and Ed called me in my car.

"I have something I need to talk to you about," he said.

"Yeah," I answered. "What's up?"

"No, I have to see you at the house."

This is weird, I thought. He'd never done this before. I was just a few minutes from his office.

Why did I have to go all the way back home? Something must be wrong.

"I have to talk to you at the house," he said. "*Now*."

We stood in our kitchen, separated by the island counter. Ed had his hands in his pockets, jiggling his change. He was nervous, anxious, wired. Finally, he sat down.

"I have gotten myself in some trouble," he blurted out. "I need you to cosign a note."

"For what?"

"I won a condemnation case for these clients and I put the check in escrow and I borrowed the money."

"Why?"

"We needed it. I spent it."

"On *what*?" I was starting to get panicky.

"Office expenses and tuition and…"

"How *much*?"

"Two-hundred and seventy-four thousand dollars."

"You have got to be kidding me!" I started to raise my voice.

"And Irish," he said, "these aren't nice people."

Ed explained that he had "illegally borrowed" the money and the clients found out about it and demanded that I cosign this note, which was to be in their hands by noon that day. He said they had threatened us.

The note would come due on Monday, November 29. My husband had two weeks to come up with more than a quarter of a million dollars.

I was in shock and upset with him, but he was my husband and he was in trouble. He needed my help and I wanted to help him. I signed the note and Ed promised that it would be "taken care of."

He took the note to Lanasa and Bubba, and they agreed to let bygones be bygones if they had their money in two weeks. They shook on it, the kind of "gentlemen's agreement" that usually means something in the South.

I went into high gear. I was going to fix it, to keep our lives from falling apart. I scrambled for alternatives. We had a condo in Colorado, but it was in Shannon and Patrick's names, and we'd had a thirty-year note on our house since 1975.

"We have to do something," I said to Ed. "Maybe we can sell the house?"

Ed couldn't live with that. He liked our nice home and lovely neighborhood. But more than that, losing the house meant losing his reputation. He did a lot of work at the county and was well liked, and he had a name to live up to. Losing the house was too much. He wouldn't agree to sell it. He kept saying I shouldn't worry and he would not discuss it with me. When I brought it up, he dismissed me and said that it was "handled."

By then, it didn't really matter. The die was cast.

We didn't know it, but that morning, despite signing promissory note, shaking on it, and saying, "Bygones will be bygones," Bubba and Lanasa had marched into the courthouse and told the commonwealth's attorney what Ed had done. Ed had helped him with his campaign and they were very good friends. "There's the door," he told the two good ol' boys. "Get out!"

Instead, Bubba and Lanasa reported Ed to the state bar. The bar sent letters and called Ed. He would probably be disbarred and go to jail. And Ed Willey Jr., the Southern gentleman, son of the great senator of the Commonwealth of Virginia, would certainly be humiliated.

Ed kept all this to himself. Of course, I worried about the unknown—jail, disbarment, humiliation. I knew it would ruin him, both of us. Adrenaline, the fight-or-flight reflex, kicked in, and I was all about *fight*. I had to try to fix it, to grasp at whatever might help my family survive.

Days went by. The deadline loomed. I kept asking Ed what he was going to do, what *we* were going to do. He stalled me. "Don't worry," he said. "I've got it taken care of. Don't worry."

Of course I worried. Where could he possibly come up with that kind of money?

Thanksgiving was almost always at our home, but that year we went to my brother's house for a change. It was strained. Shannon and Patrick came home from college, and everyone vaguely knew something was going on. We were tense, but we managed to have a lovely day and Ed even regaled us with funny stories during dinner. It was our last Thanksgiving together.

The clock was ticking. I kept nagging Ed, telling him that we had to talk to our children about the crisis. Things had to change, and they needed to understand what was going on. They needed to seek grants and loans and jobs. And, I kept telling Ed, if we have to sell the house to get out of this, we're just going to have to do it.

On Saturday, the four of us finally sat down at the kitchen table for our family discussion. Ed hemmed and hawed. He couldn't tell them. He couldn't even say, "I stole money." The only way he could get it out was to say, "I illegally borrowed," with a few sketchy details of what he had done.

We're in trouble, and I need to fix it, I thought, going into takeover mode. I explained that times were going to change and we all had to help. We would have to tighten our belts, we may have to sell the house, and I was going to get a job for the first time in twenty years. I told them I was going to go to Washington to see the president on Monday to ask for a paying job. And they needed to help, too.

The "discussion" didn't go well. With my adrenaline in charge, I lost control of my fear. "I'm scared to death, Ed! I mean, my God, what are we going to do?" I lashed out at him. *"Why did you do this?"*

The kids also became really upset. Shannon, about to enter medical school, panicked about whether she'd be able to attend. Patrick, defending his father, was incensed at my accusation. "I don't like what you're calling my dad!" he stood up and said. "You're calling my dad a thief!"

Ed remained quiet through it all. He just sat there, subdued, watching us argue. He didn't say a word as the three of us blew up at each other. It turned into an ugly brouhaha. We yelled and hurled insults, and it ended badly. My guilt over that scene plagued me for years. I was burdened with regret. I could have handled it all so differently. But we have no idea what tomorrow is going to bring.

After the awful family scene, we went our separate ways. Shannon decided she couldn't stay for the rest of the weekend, so later Saturday she drove back to Baltimore. Patrick and his friend went back to school the next morning. On Sunday, I felt badly about how the conversation had gone and was still upset with Ed. He went upstairs, packed a small bag, and went to bunk with a friend. I thought it was a good idea, because we all needed space. But that wasn't why Ed left. He had a plan, and unless he was graced by an eleventh-hour miracle, he knew what he was going to do. If only he would have done something else.

The President of the United States

I woke up on Monday morning at about five thirty. I usually wore a blouse and skirt with heels when I worked in the White House, but that morning I was on autopilot. My mind was elsewhere. I cannot for the life of me remember what I wore that day.

I left my empty house, drove to the train station, and caught the eight o'clock train. Three or four days a week, I took that two-hour train ride, usually reading the *Richmond Times-Dispatch* and the *Washington Post* on my way to the White House. But on this day, the news did not concern me. Though I tried to read, my mind was racing. I had to get my name on the list to see the president. Then I would call Ed.

I arrived at the White House at about ten-fifteen and the minute I got to my desk, I called Nancy Hernreich. "I've got a real problem," I said, "and I need just a few minutes with the president at some point today."

"Just sit by the phone," Nancy said. "You won't have much notice but I'll call you."

I called Ed's car phone but he didn't answer. I called Jane-Lee. "Is he there?"

"No, he's not here," she said. "I have tried to reach him many times."

"Well, did he have a court case?" I asked her. "Where do you think he is?"

"I'm trying to find him," she said. "He's out there somewhere."

I tried to work, but I was upset and getting more and more worried about Ed. *Where is he?* I repeatedly called his car phone but he never answered. *Why doesn't he answer his phone?* I left message after message. "Ed, where are you? Please call me back. I'm worried about you."

I kept calling Jane-Lee, "Have you heard from him?"

"He'll show up," she told me. "Don't worry, Kathy."

But I was beyond worry. I started to panic, pleading with his voice mail. "Ed, please just call me and let me know you're okay! Just call. Please leave a message." And I said I was going to see the president and would hopefully have some news for us.

At about two o'clock, Nancy Hernreich called. "Come on over," she said. "We'll fit you in, but it's going to be tight. Be prepared to wait." I was amazed that she was able to get me any time with the president.

I walked into her office at about a quarter after two and Nancy could see that something was wrong. I sat outside her private office, in a chair across from Betty Currie's desk, and waited to see the president. All of a sudden Al Gore came flying in. Everywhere he went, Al Gore ran. Anyone who wanted to keep up with him had to run too. So he came flying in, ran right up to the little peephole and peeked into the Oval Office.

"Is he in there? What's he doin'?" Gore asked. "Is he in there? Is he with somebody?"

"Yes, he's in there and he is with somebody," Nancy said, always perfectly poised. "And Kathleen's next."

My jaw fell open.

"Oh, okay," said the vice president of the United States. "See ya!" And—*whoosh*—out he went, a storm of dust behind him!

I sat there and thought, *This is too screwed up. This just should not be this way.* But it *was* that way. And much, much worse.

In about fifteen minutes, Nancy showed me into the Oval Office. As he walked from his desk to give me a hug, President Clinton could also see how upset I was.

I had been in a prolonged state of panic. But greeting the president, I felt a flash of hope. I knew he could help me. Of course, *anything*—any guidance or a suggestion from the most powerful man in the world—could help turn me from raw distress to action. We talked briefly in the Oval Office before he offered to get me a cup of coffee from his kitchen. Then he suggested we go to his private study, where we could talk more comfortably. The president asked a few questions while I prattled on about our family crisis for five minutes or more, and I told him I needed a paying job.

While I talked, President Clinton looked at his watch a couple of times. Nancy had told me that he had an important meeting with cabinet members at three o'clock, so I knew I should finish talking and leave. I added a comment about the Social Office and some of the problems there, and again he looked at his watch. Time to leave. We moved back into the hallway toward the door to the Oval Office.

Suddenly, there was a loud knock at the Oval Office door. "Mr. President," Andrew Friendly called out. "It's time for your meeting!"

The president ignored him. I said I should leave and moved toward the door, but the president told me not to rush, said he had time. He looked at his watch again. I mentioned his important meeting and he again encouraged me to stay. But then Andrew Friendly began banging on the door and calling more loudly, "You're late!"

I turned and went through the small hallway toward the Oval Office and President Clinton followed closely behind me. When I turned around at the end of the small hallway, he was right next to me. He expressed his regret for my situation and gave me a big hug, but his hug lasted a little too long. I pulled back. All of a sudden, he was running his hands in my hair and around the back of my neck.

What the hell?

He kissed me on my mouth and, before I knew it, I was backed up into the corner, against the closed bathroom door and the wall behind the Oval Office. The president's hands were all over me, just all *over* me. And all I could think was, *What the hell is he doing? Just what is he doing?*

I tried to twist away. He was too powerful. President Clinton is almost a foot taller than I am and nearly double my weight. I couldn't get away and could barely think. I didn't know what I was supposed to do. He was my friend. And he was the president of the United States.

I finally managed to say, "What are you doing?"

"I've wanted to do this," he said, "since the first time I laid eyes on you."

What?

I was terrified for my husband, for my family, for our future, and the president says he's wanted to do this since he laid eyes on me? I was totally unprepared for that.

Then he took my hand. I didn't understand what he was doing. The president put my hand on his genitals, on his erect penis. I was shocked! I yanked my hand away but he was forceful. He ran his hands all over me, touching me everywhere, up my skirt, over my blouse, my breasts. He pressed up against me and kissed me. I didn't know what to do. I could slap him or yell for help. My mind raced. And the only thing I noticed was that his face had turned red, literally beet red.

I reminded him that Hillary or Chelsea could come into the room. I thought that would give him pause, but he said he always knew where they were and he wasn't concerned about them just then.

Andrew Friendly banged on the door and yelled. But he didn't walk in. I didn't understand why he didn't come in. If the president of the United States doesn't answer, wouldn't the Secret Service come and check on him? Someone should have come in. Finally, I realized why no one came: The president had told them to stay out!

In a different setting, with a different man, I probably would have yelled for help. Were it not for Andrew Friendly banging on the door and Bentsen and Panetta pacing outside, I would have felt more vulnerable. Indeed, I would have *been* more vulnerable. Had he the opportunity—the time and the privacy—I believe Clinton would have raped me that day, just as, I believe, he raped Juanita Broaddrick.

As it was, he violated me. He exploited me and betrayed my trust, but he did not injure me. More than all that, I thought, *My God, this is the president of the United States, and this is the way he acts in the Oval Office?* It conveys my heritage and upbringing that the main thing on my mind was that what he had done to me was *just not proper*. The man disgraced himself. He was humiliated in my eyes. I was truly embarrassed for him.

I made a dive for the door, yanked it open, and burst into the Oval Office. He followed me. As I scurried across that stately room, brushing my hair with my fingertips and checking that my blouse was tucked in, Clinton walked directly to his chair. His lechery aborted, the president of the United States concealed the remains of his arousal behind John Kennedy's desk in the Oval Office.

As I reached the door to the reception area, I turned to President Clinton and said, "Thank you for taking the time to see me, Mr. President." Apparently, part of me still respected the presidency, if not the president, and propriety if not the person. Stunned, I was polite to the last and, to my horror, those words tumbled out of my mouth. *Thank you for taking the time to see me? Thank you for taking the time to assault me when I came to you in despair!*

My heart was pounding. Thoughts raced through my head about what he'd done. The stories and rumors I'd heard came flooding in. I'd never believed those stories before, but now I had to process all of it over again, rethink it all. *This is really the truth here. This is what he does.* I was messed up. I thought about my makeup. *Get yourself together!* Whoever was outside that door, I didn't want them to think something was going on.

Sure enough, I opened the door and looked straight into the eyes of Treasury Secretary Lloyd Bentsen. Leon Panetta, chairman of the OMB, stood behind him, and there was Laura Tyson, chairperson of the Council of Economic Advisors. I was mortified. *What would they think of me?* I came out the door and they were all there. Andrew Friendly had been banging on the door and yelling, and everyone had to have heard that. Given the fact that the president was late, given his reputation, and given that I emerged from the Oval Office, I *knew* what they thought! Then I had to walk past Nancy's office and Betty Currie at her desk. And though I had done nothing wrong, it felt like I was walking the walk of shame. They all looked at me. I felt embarrassed and started to get really angry. I couldn't get out of there fast enough.

On any other day, being assaulted by President Clinton would have measured pretty high on my Richter scale. But on November 29, 1993, it was a mere blip on my radar. Not only did he not help me that day, but the twenty-four hours that followed would bring me such agony that all my recent despair and panic and even Clinton's assault would pale by comparison. And it would be many years, in fact, before the president's behavior became important in my life at all.

Linda

Discrepancies arose later about whether I looked unkempt or not. I have a general sense that I went straight from the Oval Office to a restroom. I normally would have done so to make sure that I looked okay, because I wouldn't let myself walk around the White House looking disheveled. But my memory is vague. After all, I was in a state of shock. It was as if my brain had reached its limit and I couldn't think anymore. I was going through the motions. I wanted to talk to somebody, as if dumping it out of my brain, talking about it, would make it go away.

I went to see Linda Tripp, who was working in Bernie Nussbaum's office. She glanced at me and said, "Where's your lipstick?" In an interview with George Magazine, Linda described me as "flustered: hair messy, red face, no lipstick, an overall disheveled wreck," and that I was highly agitated. She added, "It's possible I misread her excitement for joy."1

"I need to talk to you," I said.

A smoker, Linda suggested we go outside. We walked out a side entrance to a VIP parking lot where people went to smoke.

I said, "You're just not going to believe this!" And I told her.

Linda went into high gear. "All right," she said, her mind working double time. "This is going to lead to an affair and, now, this is how it's done. They're going to be finding a safe house for the two of you, and you'll be going to Camp David, and..." I sat there, staring at her. I felt indignant. I wasn't interested in him that way and besides, Linda knew that this scene with the president came in addition to my panic about Ed. I had told her that my life was falling apart, that my family was in trouble, that I couldn't find him, and instead of supporting me and listening to me, she started describing a *novel*. It was as though she'd expected it and been waiting for it. She had it all figured out. She assumed I was the player she wanted me to be. And because it fit her agenda, Linda *assumed* that I welcomed the president's abuse.

A few years later, in the *George Magazine* interview, Linda said her "instant reaction was, 'It happened,'" meaning "some sort of romantic thing." But she finally acknowledged that I described it as "rough and violent," even though she says I attributed this and his red face to passion.[2] Still, going with her assumptions, she started in on me.

"This is how it's going to be…" she went on.

I thought she was nuts.

I went back to my desk and tried to call Ed about every thirty minutes. I called his office, home, his car, but I couldn't find him and he never called me back. I was desperate to hear his voice, to know that he was okay. And I wanted to talk to him, to tell him what had happened, to find out what we were going to do about the deadline.

Ed

I took a cab to Union Station and caught the five o'clock train. Two hours later, back in Richmond, I got in my car and drove as fast as I could to Ed's office. When I pulled up, my heart sank. The office was dark. It was seven thirty and the secretaries were gone. Everyone was gone. Where could he be? I drove past our house to see if he was there, but he wasn't. I became frantic and drove around the village looking for him. I called Jane-Lee at home. I stopped at my friend Julie's house. I checked for him at bars. I thought, *God, maybe he's drunk. I hope he's somewhere just drunk.* But he wasn't. He wasn't anywhere.

God, Ed, would you just appear!

It was late when I finally gave up. I was thinking *I'm going to go home and his car's going to be in the driveway.* I went home, exhausted. He was not there.

Alone and scared out of my mind, I didn't sleep much. The phone woke me at seven in the morning. It *had* to be Ed.

"Your husband there?" a man barked at me.

"No he's not," I said. "Who's this?"

"This is Bubba Marshall."

"You know, it's seven o'clock in the morning," I said, annoyed. "I'm trying to find my husband. I don't know where he is, frankly. So what is it that you want?"

"You people owe me some money!" He was irate, yelling. We had missed the deadline on the note the day before. "Somebody better be showing up today with my money!"

"I don't have any money for you," I said. "I can't help you."

He said he was going to find me that day and *get* the money.

"I don't have any answers for you. I don't have *anything* for you!" I hung up.

I didn't know that they had turned on Ed and reported him. But Ed knew. He'd already received letters from the state bar.

I kept trying to call Ed.

At nine, the phone rang again and I jumped at it. It was the sheriff of King and Queen County—a remote area about sixty miles away. He wanted to speak to Shannon Willey. He had found her car on the side of the road with a flat tire.

"Where are you?" I asked the sheriff.

"I'm in King and Queen County."

"Where is that?"

I started to worry. Shannon had gone home to Baltimore on Saturday night. How did she get from there to King and Queen County on *Tuesday* morning? And why? It didn't make sense. I needed to find Shannon. A scary thought popped into my head. "Irish, these are not nice people," Ed had said.

Oh my God, maybe they abducted Shannon! Maybe they were holding her until they got their money? Shannon was always at her desk at Johns Hopkins, so I called there. She didn't answer. *Why didn't she answer? Where was she?* My worry turned to raw terror. *Had they hurt her? Have they murdered her?* I was beside myself. I sat on my bed and felt like all the blood had drained out of my body. My legs shook so badly I couldn't walk, and my whole body tingled. I thought, *My God, my daughter is dead. I can't find my husband and my daughter is dead. What in the hell am I supposed to do here? I don't know where King and Queen County is. Should I go there? Do I need to call somebody? I don't know what to do!*

I was desperate to hear her voice, to hear *somebody's* voice. I called my brother and Jane-Lee, but nobody could answer my questions. The adrenaline and panic continued for an hour. I needed Ed. I needed to find him.

"Where can we look?" I asked Jane-Lee. "Who else can we call? Should I call the police?"

The phone rang again. It was the sheriff. This time, he asked for Ed.

The cars were mixed up. When Ed had received the stickers that coordinated with the car registrations, he had just put them on whatever license plate for whatever car. So the tag registered to Ed's blue Isuzu Trooper was on Shannon's aqua Mitsubishi.

While I was on the phone with the sheriff, Shannon beeped in. The second I heard her voice, I knew she was okay. But I didn't want her to panic either, so I tried to act casual.

"Oh, I'm just calling to see how you're doing," I said. "Are you feeling better?"

"Have you talked to Dad?" she asked me.

"Well, no," I said. "But he's upset and I'm upset."

"Well, is he okay?"

"Oh, yeah," I tried to assure her—and myself. "He'll be all right."

Back on the phone with the sheriff, we finally figured out it was Ed's car, not Shannon's. Now it all made sense. Ed had gone down there for some court case that he hadn't told me about, I reasoned, and he had gotten a flat tire, so he called one of his friends to pick him up. That's why he hadn't answered the car phone. He was at somebody's house. I had the whole thing solved. And I knew that, wherever Ed was, I would find him and then we would manage to repair our life together. It would all turn out fine.

My brother called. "I'm on my way over," he said.

"Well that's nice," I said. I felt I already had the answer to all my confusion by then, so I was relieved.

He walked into my house. "It looks like something *has* happened."

"What are you talking about?" I said. "What do you mean something has happened?"

"They found a body."

"Well, so, whose body?" I asked him. I knew it wouldn't have anything to do with me.

"They think it's Ed," he said. "But Buford is on the way down to see."

"Well, that just that can't be," I stated flatly. And then I did something very bizarre. I walked outside with bare feet at the end of November and filled up all my bird feeders.

The county sheriff had called the state police, and they called Jane-Lee. She asked Ed's best friend, Judge Buford Parsons, to go and check it out. And she called my brother to come and be with me. Before long, Buford pulled into my driveway and when I saw his face, I knew. A big, burly man, Buford was sobbing, just *sobbing*. He had identified Ed's body at the scene.

On Monday, Ed had pulled off to the side of a dirt road onto a hunter's path. His car was blocking the road, so some hunters had slashed the tires. Ed never knew. He had walked into the woods, over a little berm to a small marsh. It was cold and the forest was darkening on that late November afternoon when Ed sat down on an old tree stump beside the dreary swamp, put a gun in his mouth, and pulled the trigger.

At just about the same time that Clinton assaulted me on Monday afternoon, a gunshot cracked through the forest in King and Queen County. From a distance, someone heard the shot. My husband was dead.

Some time later, when conspiracy theories started to emerge about Vince Foster's death, people accumulated names of former Clinton associates who had died abruptly—and conveniently for the Clintons. The list includes a plane crash here, a car accident there, a suicide here... My husband, "Clinton fundraiser, Ed Willey Jr." is on that list. And it has not escaped my notice that, less than five months after the left-handed Vince Foster drove to a wooded area in Virginia and used both hands to put a .38 caliber pistol into his mouth, so did my husband.

People ask me whether I believe Ed's death was a suicide. It is a wrenching question, and I doubt I will ever completely resolve it in my mind.

For one thing, I could never answer one question: *Why* would someone kill Ed?

After his death, my friend Carole told me something I hadn't known. Ed and I spent Christmas 1992 in Colorado with Carole and her husband. One evening during that trip, Ed confided to Dann that he'd taken briefcases full of cash to Little Rock during the campaign. When Carole told me this, I was shocked.

"Well, think about it," she said. "Is there any way he could have done that without your knowing?"

"Well, yeah, sure," I said. I was home all day and I assumed Ed was either at his office or out looking at property. "He had land-use and zoning meetings out in neighborhoods all the time," I said. "I guess he could have flown to Little Rock in the morning and come home the same day, especially if private planes were involved." But *if* he had done that, I was oblivious. I never saw any hint of it. Still, it makes me wonder. Ed may have been more involved in the Clinton campaign than I was.

I recently saw something on a blog, *The Cocaine Candidacy*, that explored early, illegal fund-raising activities by the Clintons. In its list of campaign "officials" who died, the site includes this curious notation: "Ed Willey, the manager of the Clinton 1992 presidential campaign finance committee, and notable for handling large briefcases full of cash, reportedly avoided airplanes. He died of a gunshot wound which was declared to be a suicide (not unlike Vincent Foster)."[3] Unless the writer of this blog talked to my friend Carole and her husband, I have no idea how anyone other than the Clintons would know that Ed might have carried cash in briefcases. So *why* would he be killed? Because he was carrying illegal money? That's probably not enough reason. But what if, in his desperation, Ed had "illegally borrowed" from the campaign?

After Ed died, I asked the police where he'd gotten the gun, a Smith and Wesson .38 Special. They told me it was unregistered, though they later tracked it to a woman in North Carolina. I still don't know who she was. To this day, I think there's a lot the state police didn't tell me, to protect me.

I watch criminal dramas on television, so I asked Dan, my lawyer, if there were powder burns on Ed's hand. Yes, he assured me, the evidence is solid. Ed had powder burns on his right hand. I shivered. Ed was left-handed.

Writing this book opened old wounds as I began to question Ed's death again. I requested a copy of his autopsy report and spoke to a medical examiner, who told me the powder burns were consistent with suicide. When I asked if the burns were indicative of a *left*-handed person committing suicide, she said no. The room started to spin, and I went into the bathroom and threw up. By the time she sent me the full report, though, she'd reconsidered, saying it *could* be consistent with a left-handed person. She suggested that he held the gun with both hands but pulled the trigger with his right. That's exactly how Vince Foster is said to have killed himself.

The report raised other questions, too. For one, it said that there was blood spatter, not on his palm, but on the *back* of Ed's left hand. If he pulled the trigger with his right hand, why would his left hand have been facing away from his face?

I noticed something else.

After death, the blood in the body pools to the lowest parts of the body due to gravity. In several hours, the blood "fixes" in this position, no longer shifting when the body is moved, so medical examiners look for "livor" or "livor mortis" to indicate the position of the body in the hours after death. When the sheriff found Ed, he was lying face down with the gun underneath him. He had been in that position overnight, so livor should have been fixed on the front of his body. But, according to the autopsy report, livor was complete, it's distribution posterior, on the *back* of his body. His body might have been moved.

Also, according to the autopsy, the bullet was not recovered.

I have not seen the police report, so I do not know if they searched the woods for the bullet. I do not know if they examined the area for blood spatter or other evidence that Ed did, indeed, die beside that swamp. I do not know why Ed would have gone to King and Queen County, to that particularly ugly place. I do not know where in the world Ed would have obtained a .38 Special, or whether he had personally purchased the box of bullets that the police recovered in his car. There's a lot I don't know.

I had been told that Jane-Lee found Ed's suicide notes were in his office, but the medical examiner's report noted, "Exam at site revealed five notes." There was one for each of us—me, Shannon, Patrick, and a couple of others. Ed wrote his good-byes, said he'd done a bad thing, and wished us well. He told me he was a fool and out of control. He told Shannon that she was going to be a great doctor. He told my son to look after Shannon and me. And he asked us to forgive him. How anyone could sit and write such letters is beyond me. But then, I could never understand how he could leave us, either. And while the letters are in *his* writing, I also know that anyone would write anything at gunpoint.

I know, this is the point where people say, "Ah, she's nuts."

Despite the unanswered questions, I reconciled in my mind, long ago, that Ed killed himself. In my heart, I don't want to think so and I still wonder, *How could he possibly do that?* I go back and forth. And, as I do, the possibility lingers, logical or not, that Ed was murdered.

Family and Friends

The worst part was that I had to call my daughter and son and tell them over the telephone that their father had killed himself. How do you possibly do that?

Ed's death was shocking to many people. He had helped a lot of people and had endeared himself to them. He was a well-known lawyer. And he was a *Willey*, so it was big news in Richmond. Immediately, the phone started to ring and the house filled with people. The newspaper called. Barbara McGonagha, another volunteer in the Social Office, informed everyone at the White House. When she heard, Nancy Hernreich called me and I sobbed. Nancy later reported that I had asked her to have the president call me, but I only remember that we talked and she said that the president would want to speak to me. I told her he could call me anytime.

I don't remember much of that week. I don't remember going to bed at night or getting up in the morning. People gathered around the table, talking about Ed, trying to figure out what had happened. Buford brought Ed's letters over. Shannon came home and my family arrived—my brother, sister, and my mother, who walked in the house shaking and asking for a Kleenex. I was worried sick waiting for Patrick. He refused to fly so he drove home, but I couldn't rest until he arrived late that night.

The Streakers, my women friends from the soccer team, stayed in touch and brought food. They were wonderful. On Wednesday, there were more visitors in the house. A friend answered the phone and told me, "The president is on the phone." It was noisy so I went upstairs to take the call. I have only a vague memory of that phone call. I cried uncontrollably and I recall Clinton saying, "You didn't see this coming, did you, kiddo?" He said something about attending the funeral and encouraged me to return to the White House soon.

Thinking about it later, it crossed my mind that Clinton might have assumed that I came home that Monday and told Ed what Clinton did to me in the Oval Office. When he heard about Ed's death, Clinton was probably worried. He didn't know anything about the circumstances yet, so it certainly might have occurred to him that his own behavior could have had something to do with Ed's suicide. With Clinton's MO, I'm sure he felt *entitled* to abuse me, but the master egotist had to be concerned about whether Ed's death involved *him*.

After all, Clinton had a pattern of risky behavior. I think he got off on that. I think it was part of the thrill for him. The risk seemed to make it more exciting, more arousing. Flirting with danger is part of his dysfunction, part of his sexual game. His recklessness was a common denominator in his affair with Gennifer Flowers, in his rape of Juanita Broaddrick, in his abuse of Paula Jones, in his assault on me, and in his seduction of Monica Lewinsky in the Oval Office.

But if the sexual danger in that little hallway behind the Oval Office stimulated Clinton, Ed's death certainly raised the stakes. It likely scared the hell out of him. I think that's the reason why Clinton called me that day. I think he needed to know what was going on. Did I tell Ed? And did Ed kill himself because of Bill Clinton?

I have just a vague recollection of sitting with the minister in the funeral home and planning the services. I had picked out Ed's suit and tie, though I don't remember what suit or what tie. I don't remember much, but we had an open casket in a side parlor. It was too hard for my children and my sister and brother to see him, but my mother and a best friend and a few other friends came with me. That night, the funeral home was like Grand Central Station and the line of people was down the block. There were hundreds of people at the visitation, but I can only remember talking to about three people. I was in shock.

I have a foggy recollection of seeing Ed in the casket. My young niece had always loved Ed. She knew that Ed had loved to fish, so my sister gave me a little fishing trinket that her daughter had found for him. I didn't have any experience with people dying and I certainly had never touched a body, but I needed to put this little thing in Ed's hands and I remember trying to pry his fingers open. "I'm so sorry," I sobbed to his body. "Why did you do this?"

Ed's funeral was on Friday, December 3. I remember very little of it. Patrick and I both spoke. I read a beautiful poem but, other than that, I don't know what I said or how I got through it. It just became part of the blur. A lot of my women friends from the White House drove down from Washington to attend the funeral. They were good to me, a big part of my support system at that time. Linda was as well, but she didn't come to the funeral. She knew I had been looking for Ed, saw my panic and held my hand through the day he died, so it seemed weird to me when she didn't show up. But the rest of the women were there and they encouraged me to come back to work soon. "It'll be good for you," they said.

Of course, returning to the White House was now more awkward than ever. In addition to dealing with the death of my husband, I had to consider how I would navigate my relationship with Bill Clinton, but I was facing a financial crisis, and the president of the United States is a very good friend to have when in need. It was a dilemma that I could not avoid.

CHAPTER FIVE

PROMISES, PROMISES

THE DAY after the funeral, reality pounded at me. Piling on top of my shock and grief, I was still in a financial crisis. Ed had isolated me from our financial life through twenty-three years of marriage. Now, thrust into the middle of it, I didn't know how to resolve those issues that Ed had always handled. And worse, I was alone. My husband, my best friend, my closest companion and confidant, was gone. It was too much for me. And then, there was more.

Dan Gecker

A process server showed up and served Shannon, Patrick, and me with papers demanding $500,000. A friend of Ed's brought an attorney, Dan Gecker, to my house and we started piecing together the details about why Ed killed himself. Though Bubba and Lanasa had promised they wouldn't do it, they had reported Ed to the state bar. My gregarious, generous, well-liked husband faced certain disbarment—and public humiliation.

I blamed Bubba and Lanasa for Ed's death and took my grief out on them. I didn't threaten them but, brokenhearted and overwrought, I apparently started harassing them on the phone. I called Lanasa at work the day Ed's body was found. I called them both, but mostly Bubba. I called them at two and three in the morning. I don't remember doing any of it, but they were furious at me for it. They started taping the calls.

A few days after the funeral, Bubba and Lanasa requested a warrant for my arrest. But the magistrate at Henrico Court was the son of a man who served in the senate with Ed's father. He looked at Bubba. "Good *God*, man! What are you thinking?" he exploded. "I'm not going to serve her with this! I'm just not going to do it. *You* figure it out." So Bubba hired a process server to serve me with a warrant for making "threatening" phone calls during the week. Rather than being arrested, I turned myself in on Monday. Dan came with me. I remember walking in, but not much else.

That week, I tried to find some kind of normalcy in my life, but it was too much for me. I took painkillers for my back and Valium and other sedatives—you name it. I was still hysterical and, though I wasn't threatening to do anything, I didn't want to feel anything. I was taking all those pills inappropriately. Everyone was worried about me. My friend Julie Steele helped me a lot. One week after the funeral, she drove me to the hospital and I checked myself in. They sedated me, watched me, and helped me get over the trauma. I was there for three days.

I was still grief-stricken several weeks later when I had to face the trial for those phone calls, but it was just a misdemeanor. God knows what I looked like when I showed up in court. I don't remember getting up, brushing my teeth, or getting dressed. I was still a mess.

Dan and I thought the whole thing was all going to be dismissed, but then Bubba walked in with a tape recorder. I looked at Dan, frantic. *What's going on here?*

I started to freak out. "Whatever you do, I don't want to hear that. I don't want to hear *me*," I pleaded with Dan. "I don't want to hear *me*! I just can't hear me in that state. Please, don't! Please…"

The judge was not very sympathetic and took the case under advisement. I didn't know what he was doing, and my worst fear was that it would be in the paper, that my family would be mortified and ashamed of me yet again. But as we expected in the first place, the judge dismissed it.

Dan helped me survive this first of many legal hurdles. The following March, I told him about the president's assault on me in the Oval Office. For many years to come, Dan would help me build a new life out of the chaos.

The Streakers

My women friends also helped me find life after Ed and taught me that I would eventually be okay on my own.

A few weeks after I buried Ed, I got a call from one of the Streakers.

"Did I ever tell you what was going on with the girls at the funeral home that night?" she asked. I had no idea what she was talking about. I didn't remember much about that night.

The soccer women all knew Ed and wanted to come to the funeral home to support me, but a lot of them were young and had never been to a funeral home before. They didn't know what to expect, what to do, how to act. "What do we say to her?" they asked each other. "We don't know what to say."

One of the older women gathered her "little ducklings" and brought them down to the funeral home. A few of them, especially my buddy Beth, got it in their heads that the only way they could handle it was with a beer—or two. They loaded up a big cooler of beer and piled in the car. By the time they got to the funeral home, they were all a little more comfortable and made it through the formalities at the funeral home without anyone making fools of themselves.

After the service, a lot of people were still there and the Streakers stayed around a while too. Then they hit on an idea. "Ed Willey deserves an Irish wake!" they decided. "We're going to give him one!" So they piled into the car out in the funeral home parking lot and had their wake for Ed. They drank beer and told war stories about Ed, how he had always come to our soccer games, all prim and proper, the dutiful husband on the sidelines.

Naturally, this bunch of women made a big dent in that cooler of beer and they all had to go to the bathroom. A couple of them made a bathroom run, scurrying through the funeral parlor lobby and into the ladies' room. Then they hustled back out, through the cold December night to the warm car, then another cluster of girls darted into the funeral home and found the restroom, only to be followed by another group of girls. The car's windows were steamed up and everybody was lit, coming and going and laughing and reminiscing.

But they weren't the only people lingering there. Some other guests were still visiting at the funeral parlor, including a state senator who had been a peer of Ed's father. He was there with his wife and they had driven in from the west end in their luxury car.

On one of these bathroom runs, the senator's wife encountered two of the women coming out of the bathroom. At this point, they were feeling no pain, laughing and talking and telling stories about Ed.

The senator's wife stopped them and said, "What's going on here?"

"Oh, hell," my friend Beth answered loosely. "We're having an Irish wake for Ed Willey over there in the car."

"Well," the lady said, "I've got my martini in the car. I'll be right over!"

So the senator's wife joined the Streakers. She was probably drinking on the way down to the service too—just like a lot of people.

Ed would have loved that story. And he would have been glad to know, as I continued to learn, how we women take care of each other, how girlfriends support each other through the tough times. I have been blessed with great women in my life. I don't know what I would do without them.

Clinton

Christmas was always big at our house, and I'd already begun making plans and decorating for the holiday season, but of course all that stopped. Shannon was staying in Baltimore to have Christmas with her future husband and his family. Patrick was home from school and had no schedule, so all of a sudden we were around each other all the time, which we weren't used to. And neither of us was handling our grief well. We were trying to help each other but we didn't know how. One minute we smothered each other, crying our eyes out, and the next we tried to be normal and make a joke.

Christmas, I knew, was going to be hell. I was basically not going to have Christmas that year and the depression and worry were weighing on me. I had to get out from under it, had to get my life going again. I needed to get out of the house, find something normal. I needed Christmas.

Since summer, I had been working on Christmas events and decorations for the White House and all my friends in the Social Office encouraged me to come back. I thought, *All right, I helped these people plan Christmas and if I'm going to have Christmas at all, it's going to be at the White House.* I decided to go back a couple of days a week. Ann McCoy in the Social Office said, "Come right up here and find me and we'll keep you busy." I don't know how I did it, but I went back to work a few weeks after the funeral.

The Social Office volunteers helped at the White House Christmas parties by greeting guests and playing hostess. So I dressed up and went to work. During the holidays, the White House had parties constantly, entertaining members of the press, congressional families, military VIPs, underprivileged children, diplomats' families, you name it. These parties were held on the State Floor, but guests were invited downstairs to the beautifully lit hallway with the arched ceiling, where they could have their pictures taken with the Clintons in front of a Christmas tree.

It was good to get out of the house, but I still had a mountain of debt and no income. My legal and financial situation was dire. Some dear friends sent me a check that sustained me for two months, but the fact remained: I needed a job. In December I started writing letters to the president. My attorney, Dan, whom I later told about the incident in the Oval Office, reviewed every letter. Each one was conversational. Each one mentioned my need for a paid position. And each one sent the message that our relationship was as I had always assumed it to be: friendly, respectful, and professional. In other words, as far as I was concerned, the incident was over—and it would not happen again. On December 20, 1993, I wrote:

Dear Mr. President –

I just wanted to wish you a wonderful Christmas. I can only imagine how you must be looking forward to your first Christmas here – Thank you for the opportunity to work in this great house –

After this bittersweet year, my first resolution for 1994 will be the pursuit of a meaningful job. I hope it will be here –

Merry Christmas,
Kathleen

The president had asked me to see him upon my return, so I went to the Oval Office and spoke to him alone. I told him that what had happened shouldn't have happened and that day was history. I would not bring it up again. He didn't acknowledge one word I said, but looked right through me. So I reiterated my need for a paying job. Halfheartedly, he told me to stay in close touch with Nancy.

I saw him again soon after that. I was wearing a black dress and pearls because I was working at an evening reception for members of the press and high-dollar donors. We were downstairs. Bill and Hillary were in a reception room having their pictures taken with guests in front of the Christmas tree. I was standing at the front of the line, escorting people to the tree and giving them the kid-glove treatment.

Clinton looked up and spotted me. He kind of nodded and I kind of nodded. I turned away. When I looked back in his direction, he was still looking at me. And he kept looking. Then he was interrupted. Tony Lake came in because he needed Clinton to sign some papers. The whole time, Clinton still looked at me. He was talking to Lake, flipping through the papers and supposedly signing them, but the whole while he was staring at me. It was just like the scene at the Richmond airport. It was unnerving.

Clinton had a way of doing that. People have said that when he talked to them one on one, he made them feel like they were the only person in the room. He had a way of locking in on you, like it's just the two of you. I think that's probably the first thing that got Monica. Linda Tripp validated that Clinton takes advantage of this particular talent. "He was so charismatic and mesmerizing," Linda told Larry King about Bill Clinton. "You can't be in his presence and not feel a sense of awe. He has a mesmerizing ability to draw you in."[1]

This time it seemed a little flirtatious, but also voyeuristic and domineering, like he was trying to read my mind. I looked away to pay attention to the next guest in line and, when I looked back, he was still watching me, as if to ask, "What are you thinking? Have you told anybody? Does anybody know?" His gaze said all of that. It was intense and intimidating. It made me uneasy.

Jerome Levin, Ph.D., is an addictions expert and author of *The Clinton Syndrome*, in which he describes Clinton's ability to zero in on a woman. "He can make every person he encounters in that crowd feel that they are the center of the world and the sole object of his attention. However," Levin adds, "the quid pro quo—the unspoken but understood contract—is that the feeling of being special will be returned, that the person in the crowd that Clinton singles out will feel adulation for him."[2]

But in my case, Clinton did not get any return.

Nathan Landow

In the spring, my friends in the Social Office encouraged me to start dating again. I didn't feel ready to date, but I was open to getting out and having a life. My girlfriend Ruthie was always trying to fix me up with somebody and Harolyn suggested that I meet her father. After prodding me for a few months, she invited me to spend Memorial Day weekend with her and her family at her father's place in Easton, Maryland. Harolyn set it up. Then I found out that Harolyn's father was Nathan Landow. Nate was a close friend of Al Gore's and big Gore supporter, a very influential Democrat and a powerful man. He was a huge fundraiser who had started his own political action committee and had been the national finance chair for Gore's 1988 presidential bid.

Ruthie was excited. "Wow, Nate Landow!" she gushed. "That would be perfect! He's really *rich*. *Really* rich! Let me find out for you." Ruthie found him listed in *Washingtonian Magazine* and called me. "Okay, are you sitting down?" She said, "One hundred million dollars!" I just sat there and didn't react.

Sheepishly, Ruthie asked, "Is that enough?"

Well, yes, a hundred million dollars is a lot of money. But it's not the most important thing.

I went with Harolyn to her father's home on Maryland's Eastern Shore. It was a big estate. In fact, everything Nate did was big. He had big cars—a big Range Rover and the most expensive Mercedes. And his house looked like a place that would have been created for J.R. Ewing on the television show *Dallas*! Everywhere I looked, I saw his initials "N.L.," which reminded me of *Laverne & Shirley*. Nate's house had a Western flair, an oversized Wyoming style with big overstuffed leather chairs and bear heads shipped in to decorate the walls, so it didn't exactly fit the beautiful beach property overlooking the Chesapeake Bay. Nonetheless, Nate was the perfect host and we had a great weekend.

A couple of weeks later, we had our first date. Nate invited me to go to New York with him and said I should take a cab and meet him at the executive airline terminal at National Airport in D.C. He was there waiting for me. The next thing I knew, we got into a limousine and drove out on the tarmac. We boarded his private jet and flew to New York, sipping champagne. I had never experienced anything like that.

His limo met us on the tarmac in New York and drove us to the Plaza Athenee, one of the nicest hotels in New York. Nate was obviously a regular there and we had adjoining suites. We had dinner at a beautiful restaurant. At some point, Nate showed me a diamond ring, the biggest I had ever laid eyes on. It was a *huge* diamond. "If you're a good girl," he said, "this might be yours." I knew what that meant.

I stayed in my own suite and Nate was a perfect gentleman.

The next morning, we left in his limo to make several stops. In his sixties, he had just had a facelift and needed to see his doctor for a follow-up visit. We dropped him off and Nate directed his driver to take me anywhere I wanted to go, then reached into his pocket, pulled out his American Express platinum card, and told me to "Go play." Instead, I went to Henri Bendel's with my Visa card and its $1,500 limit. When we picked up Nate, his next errand was to go to the Diamond District to see a jeweler friend. Everywhere we went people knew him, and he flashed the giant ring around. He was going to sell it. While we were driving, he opened the box and said, "That's what you could have had if you had *behaved* last night."

With that comment, I realized that there would never be anything between us.

So I never had an affair with him.

I saw him a few more times that summer. He flew me back and forth between Easton and Washington and I would see him at his estate. Sometimes he would charter a plane for me, not a jet, but a little a puddle jumper, or some of the time, I just enjoyed the drive up there.

Everything with Nate was cloak-and-dagger. When he took money out of his pocket, he hid it as if it were a poker hand. There were always little mysteries, things going on that I didn't understand. He had hushed conversations all the time. One day when I was with him in Easton, he had a hushed conversation with a woman on the board of supervisors about a zoning issue. It was always like that. Nate was new money. He got rich in real estate development and was always on the fringe.

Though my girlfriends in Washington thought he was a real catch, I was not willing to pretend I was attracted to him—or any man—no matter how much money he had. This was on the heels of the excesses of the '80s, when numerous New York trophy wives married old geezers who were rolling in money. But I looked at these young women with these older guys and I thought, *I don't care how much money the guy has, you still have to wake up with him in the morning.*

It would have been convenient if I *had* been physically attracted to him, but I wasn't. Not at all. With silver gray hair, he was a distinguished and nice-looking man and he always wore wonderful clothes. But his looks belied him. He was a bully—very gruff, profane, and rude. He had atrocious table manners. Relaxing out in Easton, for example, he would sit and eat his ice cream with the bowl resting on his stomach. I just thought, *I don't think so.* He had no class, was not my idea of a Rhett Butler, just not a Southern gentleman. Since there wasn't anything there on my part, the relationship didn't last long. I didn't want to hurt Harolyn's feelings, so I gracefully faded out of the scene by summer's end.

The White House Counsel

I still volunteered in the Social Office when Linda Tripp helped me get a volunteer position in the Counsel's Office as well. That was in the West Wing and I saw Clinton a lot when I was there. He was casual and dropped into our office a couple of times. About once a month, I'd run into him in the hall or see him going from the Oval Office to the residence. My good friend, Social Office volunteer Ruthie Eisen, was diagnosed with a brain tumor and I arranged a surprise luncheon and visit with the president for her. Whenever I saw Clinton, I was friendly but cautious.

In March 1994, White House counsel Bernie Nussbaum was the first to resign under a black cloud. We had a little going away party for him at the office and Clinton came up and surprised Bernie. After he left, Linda started in on me. "Did you see the way he looked at you?" she asked me. "He looked at you with such lust in his eyes! Oh my..." Then, the other women in the office and I went to Bernie's going-away party at his apartment in the Watergate. Janet Reno was there that evening, as well as Supreme Court justice Ruth Bader Ginsberg.

Lloyd Cutler came in as the new counsel and I got my part-time *paid* position as "staff support" in the Counsel's Office. I worked three eight-hour days a week for twenty thousand a year, plus the best health-care package known to man—which explains why our congressional representatives don't care about our health-care system. It is *unbelievable!*

A lot of people came through the Counsel's Office. One person whom I respected a lot was George Tenet. He was a gentleman. He was nice, pleasant, and always respectful. He was a professional. Louis Freeh was also nice, though he battled with Clinton and didn't like him at all.

One thing I learned when I went to work in the Counsel's Office was that there was no more discipline or sense of decorum in the West Wing than there had been in the East Wing. FBI background checks still hadn't been done for months, so people who hadn't been cleared continued to walk around the White House. At the same time, papers and confidential reports were left lying around. I walked into the office one day and Justice Stephen

Breyer's confidential FBI background check had been tossed on my desk and was lying there, half open. That's mildly problematic, to put it nicely. That's just not right.

Despite the grandeur of the White House, it is not as spacious as people think. Work areas are small and everybody fights for real estate. Outside of the White House Counsel's Office, we had our office area with four desks crammed together. We were on top of each other, squeezed in behind our chairs and desks. My chair even touched Linda's. Working so closely, I was aware of her activities. One thing I knew about Linda was that she had a relationship—of some sort—with Wolf Blitzer at CNN. They seemed to have a close tie and she was often whispering on the telephone with him.

Hillary

Right outside our door, the rickety elevator took people from the basement to the top floor. We saw everyone who got out of that old elevator—and we'd hear them. Some people we heard more than others.

When Hillary got off the elevator on the way to her office, which was next to ours, we all knew what kind of day it was going to be on our floor. She would emerge with her entourage, cursing up a storm. And all day long, we heard her raised voice through the wall. Hillary always seemed to be miserable, unhappy, and angry. Christopher Andersen, who wrote *American Evita*, said in an interview, "The staff was not afraid of Bill Clinton, the staff was afraid of Hillary Clinton—they were terrified of her. She had a tremendous temper.'"[3]

She didn't reserve her tirades for staff. She made the president plenty miserable, too. David Gergen wrote, "A chipper president would arrive at the office in the morning, almost whistling as he whipped through papers. A phone would ring. It was a call from upstairs at the residence…his mood would darken, his attention wander, and hot words would spew out…"[4] FBI agent Gary Aldrich wrote that he heard Hillary cuss at Bill about a newspaper article. "Come back here, you asshole!" she yelled at him. "Where the fuck do you think you're going?"[5]

That's the Hillary I saw. I've walked behind her when she was cursing an aide with a *very* foul mouth. Then she would see somebody who mattered and instantly pour it on, all sweetness and light. A doey-eyed expression on her face, she'd act so sincere. The minute they were gone, she'd turn around and explode again, cussing a blue streak. Lt. Col. Robert "Buzz" Patterson wrote in *Dereliction of Duty*, "While I got used to Hillary's wrath, her ability to turn it off and on amazed me."[6] She was one of the phoniest people I have ever seen.

Hillary treated her Secret Service agents like dirt. These were really good people—disciplined men and women with military backgrounds—who had a solid sense of how things should be done. But the Clintons hate the military. Hillary especially made it clear. Many of those guys were former Marines and some had gone to Vietnam. She saw this as reason enough to be horrible to them.

She spoke to her Secret Service agents just as she had to the state trooper bodyguards in Arkansas. Once, when one of her bodyguards greeted her with, "Good morning," Hillary replied, "Fuck off! It's enough that I have to see you shit-kickers every day. I'm not going to talk to you, too. Just do your goddamn job and keep your mouth shut."[7] As first lady, she maintained this attitude. On another occasion, she reportedly ordered a Secret Service agent to carry her bags, though he was reluctant to do so because "he wanted to keep his hands free in case of an incident."[8] Hillary's response to the diligent agent was, "If you want to remain on this detail, get your fucking ass over here and grab those bags."[9] In yet another incident, the first lady said to the Secret Service detail in charge of protecting her life, "Stay the fuck back, stay the fuck away from me! Don't come within ten yards of me, or else! … Just fucking do as I say, okay?"[10] *That* was our first lady! With obviously more class than she had, those men endured her with integrity. But I felt badly for them.

Linda

When the slow, old elevator was busy or not working, most people used the back stairs, a much faster way to get around. One day I was walking down those stairs and a girl, an intern, was walking up. I don't think she had on any underwear from top to bottom. I continued down, looked at her and thought, *No!* Obviously, her supervisor in the intern's office didn't look at her that day or couldn't be bothered to say, "No, I don't think so." So I turned around and went back upstairs and got in her face. "You know, I think you need to go home and change your clothes," I said. "I think you need to go home and put some clothes *on*." She looked at me like I had horns. "Do you understand where you *are* here? Do you understand what kind of people walked on these steps that you're walking on? Does that have *any* meaning to you? What you are wearing is really not appropriate. You need to go home and put on some more appropriate clothes."

Linda was fed up with all of it. The ridiculous style, the defiance of protocol, the degradation of the White House—it all really outdid Linda. Plus, it seemed impossible to get work done at all, much less properly. Work was done only because the administration had regular employees, people like Linda, who had been there a while and who sat at their desks and actually accomplished something. They were the only ones who knew how to *do* anything, how to get any work done.

Linda knew who everyone was so she always filled me in. She was also very conniving, a master at playing one person up against another, and she often pitted us against each other. And she told the women in my office lies about me, claiming that I had been having an affair with the president. She told them our rendezvous point was the private study behind the Oval Office— where Clinton would later have his secret meetings with Monica.

From day one, Linda hated one woman in our office. This woman went all the way back to Watergate with Hillary and Bernie Nussbaum and she was really tight with them. That was all the reason Linda needed. She was out to get her. Linda started in, trying to get rid of her. Linda secretly told me that the woman reeked of alcohol and came to work drunk every morning. I liked this woman a lot and I never ever saw any evidence of that, so I let Linda talk and reserved judgment. But Linda knew I wasn't going to confront my friend and say, "Hey, are you coming into work drunk?" She planted her ugly gossip and let it fester. In that way, she got away with it. She did that kind of thing to a lot of people, all the time.

Linda impressed me as an insider, and at some point she probably was. But there weren't many holdovers, and I don't know how Linda escaped the change in administrations. One problem was that she always compared the Clinton administration to that of the elder President Bush and First Lady Barbara Bush. She loved him, loved Barbara, and loved the way they ran the White House. And not only did she disagree with the Clintons ideologically, she *despised* the way they treated the "people's house."

Somebody finally labeled Linda the Forrest Gump of the White House: She was always where the action was. She was there with me, she was there the night that Vince died, and she was there with Monica. When the Clintons' biggest scandals happened, Linda was there every time. I don't think it was a coincidence. Linda had good antennae, a keen sense about what was going on with people, and a great knack for steering them in the direction she had in mind.

In time, Linda's whole agenda became hatred of the Clintons, and she *always* looked for trouble. Her animosity seemed to grow and she didn't hide it. I often thought how dangerous that was to the Clinton administration.

Finally, when Bernie had to resign and Lloyd Cutler came, they fired Linda. They said it was a cutback, but she was the only one. I think they could have kept her but got rid of her because of her attitude.

Linda thought I took her job, which was preposterous. She was making over fifty thousand dollars a year and I made a mere twenty grand as a part-timer. She wouldn't listen to reason and dismissed my argument about the salary discrepancy. All hell broke loose and threats flew. Linda later said that the real reason she was asked to leave was because Hillary had noticed that the president had been eyeing her.

Unfortunately, she didn't leave for two weeks, during which she spent a lot of time deleting files from her computer. She'd come and go, and we never knew when to expect her. A tall woman, Linda was actually rather thin at that time but, when she showed up, she looked like a battle-axe stomping in there. She was so irate that we would panic. "Oh, God, she's here!" we whispered to each other. "Oh, my God! What's she going to do? Is she going to hurt one of us?" We were afraid of her. Somebody in the office said Linda was so angry, she might bring a gun into the White House and do away with all of us and we'd have one of those shootouts in the West Wing. She scared us to death.

One afternoon, she told me that she knew "what's going on around here." She accused me of being the president's girlfriend and said that was why I replaced her. I think she really believed it. I think she had fostered this fantasy since Clinton assaulted me the day Ed died.

On her last day, as she walked out, she turned to me.

"I'm going to get you for this," she pronounced emphatically in front of everyone in the office, "before this is all over!"

The Network

In September of 1994, Clinton appointed another counsel, Judge Abe Mikva, who brought in his whole staff. There was no slot for me, so I lost my job. On my last day at the White House, I saw Clinton and thanked him for my previous employment, reiterating that I still had a pressing need for a full-time job. He told me to stay in close touch with Nancy and promised to help. Naively, I believed him. I continued writing him friendly and conversational letters, mentioning my need for a job, like the following one on October 18, 1994.

Dear Mr. President,

Thank you so much for taking the time to meet with me. Since I've seen you, I have had the opportunity to talk with Mel French, Harlan Lee, the assistant chief of protocol, and Craig Smith. I hope to meet with Leon Panetta next.

As I said to you, I have invested almost three years with your campaign and administration and am not very willing to depart yet. I would like to be considered for an ambassadorship or a position in an embassy overseas. I now find myself with no encumbrances, with Shannon away at medical school and Patrick in college in North Carolina.

I feel confident that I would represent you and our country well if given the opportunity and hope you will consider my request.

Please accept my best wishes for your historic trip to the Mideast next week—I don't need to remind you of my willingness to help you in any way that I can.

Fondly,
Kathleen

In 1994, Colonel Oliver North was running for the governorship of Virginia against Chuck Robb. I've since changed my mind, but at the time I thought North would have been a terrible mistake for Virginia. Clinton had come to Virginia to help Chuck, who won, and I wanted to thank him because I thought he'd done a great service for Virginia and I had been his "number one fan." So in November 1994, I wrote to Clinton.

Dear Mr. President –

You have been on my mind so often this week –

There are so very many people who believe in you and what you are trying to do for our country –

Take heart in knowing that your number one fan thanks you every day for your help in saving her wonderful state.

With appreciation,
Kathleen

I spent that Christmas in Stockholm with my friend from the Social Office, Debbie Siebert, and her husband, Tom. Tom had become ambassador to Sweden, so it was a memorable trip. I missed Shannon and Patrick, but it was a remarkable Christmas. While I was there, I made contacts at our embassy and even pursued employment in Europe.

Back in Virginia, I eagerly sought employment. Hoping for Clinton's support, I continued to write letters to him into 1995. One of them paid off and I had a series of meetings with Bob Nash, the head of Presidential Personnel. He told me that he had received a handwritten note from the president and was eager to help me. He soon called and asked me to attend "The World Summit for Social Development" in Copenhagen in March.

I didn't know what to think about it. I attended State Department briefings and met members of the delegation. My role was to be whatever I made of it and I was eager to pitch in, helping delegates, copying notes, going with them to meetings, and following-up. Early on, I was told that an invitation to join a world summit delegation was a real coup, that only very connected people who had worked hard to get Clinton elected or had given a lot of money were invited on such trips. Most of the time, these invitees did not participate with the delegates. As "working staff," they just observed, shopped, and dined on the government dollar. I did not want to be like them. I wanted to participate and work hard. I thought I was possibly being observed by State Department members as something of an audition, in which they would see that I really would do a good job if our government hired me. I wanted to show that I had the goods, so to speak, was worthy of a position in Clinton's administration, and that I could perform the duties for whatever opportunity might arise.

The summit was fascinating, and I saw how delegations work, particularly how minions—people you will never see— work into the night for weeks beforehand, hashing out language and fighting over words like "the" and "and" before the president shows up to sign papers and pose for the photo ops. As the public member, invited by the president, I was included in everything, even the bilateral meetings with the heads of the delegation and talks with third world nations. It was unbelievable, mind-blowing. The one thing that I realized early on was that *everybody* wanted our money. It was a real education for me.

Introduced as a friend of Clinton's, I met Fidel Castro during one of the meetings. In a television interview, when asked what she thought of Castro, Barbara Walters said he was charming, a real flirt, and one of the most intriguing people she'd ever met. When I met him, he was all of that and more. He was very cagey.

"You tell Clinton, we talk," Castro stammered, pretending to speak only broken English, though I knew he understood our language just fine.

Yeah, right. I'll just go tell President Clinton to meet with Castro...

"Please tell your president that we should meet," he said through an interpretor, "someday soon."

Fifteen minutes later, I met Nelson Mandela. He had recently been released from prison and I shook his hand, expecting it to be weathered after all he'd been through. I was amazed and distracted by his exceptionally soft hands. Very soft-spoken, he was a gentle human being and it was an honor to be in his presence.

Al Gore gave a speech at the summit. He was friendly to the whole delegation and made himself accessible to everyone. Hillary, however, was neither friendly nor accessible. Scheduled to speak in a massive auditorium in Copenhagen, she was the star of the summit. The conference center was the biggest place I've ever seen, something like three miles from one end to the other, and you could sense the anticipation throughout the facility: *Hillary's coming! Hillary's coming!*

The people in our delegation worked many evenings into the wee hours of the morning, day after day, and all they wanted was to meet Hillary. But they were essentially told, "She doesn't have time for you." It wasn't going to happen.

"Well, that's awful," I said, always the fixer. "I'm going to have to do something about that."

I found one of her people. "What's it going to take?" I asked. "Ten minutes? Fifteen minutes? It's the least she can do for them, you know. If she can stand up and make a speech for thirty minutes, she can meet these people."

So they arranged it. I stood at the door to this room and cleared everybody who went in. Hillary finally came in and shook a few hands. Then somebody said, "If you don't mind, we'd like to go around the room and introduce everybody." Everyone stood in a large circle around the room and the introductions went around. Standing near her, I was last. When it came around to me I said,

"Kathleen Willey, formerly of your Social Office." I thought maybe she would recognize me. All I received was an icy cold glare. I looked at her and we made eye contact, and I shuddered. *She knows,* I thought to myself. *Oh God, she knows!* I felt chills. Goose bumps stood up on my arms. In that moment, I knew that she knew who I was. She didn't speak. She turned back to the roomful of people and poured on the graciousness. She thanked everyone and left.

Juanita Broaddrick told a similar story. A few weeks after Clinton raped Juanita, she and her husband attended a subsequent political gathering at which the Clintons made an appearance. En route, Hillary said she was anxious to meet a woman named Juanita Hickey (now Juanita Broaddrick), and told her limo driver, "Bill has talked so much about Juanita."[11] According to Christopher Andersen, author of *Bill & Hillary,* she even told her husband, "Bill, now be sure and point Juanita out."[12] Then, Juanita says, Hillary 'caught me and took my hand and said, "I am so happy to meet you. I want to thank you so much for everything you do for Bill."' Juanita started to turn away while Hillary held on to her hand. "Looking less friendly," Juanita says, Hillary reiterated the statement, *"Everything* you do for Bill."[13]

She knows, Juanita thought. Juanita later told me it scared the living hell out of her. Hillary's meaning was clear: *Thank you for keeping quiet for Bill.* "I understood perfectly what she was saying. I knew exactly what she meant—that I was to keep my mouth shut," Juanita said. Hillary "was not going to let [the rape] get in the way," Juanita said. "At that moment, I knew what Hillary was capable of doing. And I could see in her eyes that she wasn't doing it for her husband. She wasn't even doing it for them. She was doing it for Hillary Rodham."[14]

After my trip to Copenhagen, I started working part time for a friend in Richmond while I continued to pursue work in the government. I touched base with Nancy Hernreich frequently. And I kept networking with contacts from the Copenhagen delegation, including Bob Nash and Sheila Lawrence, wife of Larry Lawrence, our ambassador to Switzerland. Nancy suggested I meet with Mel French, whom I'd helped with the 1993 inaugural festivities. She directed the Office of Protocol and it looked like I had found the perfect niche. Again, the job did not materialize.

In October, Bob Nash invited me to join another world summit delegation to the Convention on Biological Diversity in Jakarta the following month. Nash reiterated that this was at the request of the president. During that summit, Tim Wirth, head of the delegation, introduced me to everyone as a "very, very close friend of the president's." Given Clinton's reputation, I didn't exactly appreciate that.

While I was in Jakarta, Newt Gingrich's Republican Congress shut down the government over a budget impasse, and Bill Clinton met Monica Lewinsky.

In January 1996, Nancy called and suggested that I come to Washington and speak with two people working on the president's reelection campaign. I made an appointment with Brian Bailey, who was in the process of opening the new headquarters in downtown Washington, D.C. He told me that he, too, had received a note from the president requesting that he interview me for a position. It began to look promising.

I also met with Congressman Barney Frank's sister, Ann Lewis. She encouraged me and said I could expect to be hired by the campaign. She sent me to Marvin Rosen, DNC finance chair, whom I met with in the spring. Rosen and Richard Sullivan hired me to do fund-raising for the campaign. He told me that I would be on the road for most of the summer and fall, traveling from event to event to coordinate fundraisers. We agreed on the position, salary, and a June start date. We agreed to finalize the details with a phone call later. But later never came.

After that meeting I got organized, agreed to sublet an apartment, and made arrangements for all my pets. I called Rosen about my start date. He did not call me back. I called again, called Sullivan, and called the campaign office. They never called me back. I never worked on the campaign and never got a job with the Clinton administration.

I finally realized that my career chances in Washington probably never existed. I admitted that they had likely been placating me all along. Why was I sent to two world summits? Had I mistaken those appointments as auditions for employment with the State Department? Why would I be hired for a job—and never hear another word?

After all I had done for Clinton, after all I had endured, they jerked me around for two years. In July 1996, I wrote one last letter to Nancy Hernreich, expressing outrage at the way the White House had treated me. "I am appalled at the way in which I have been trifled with," I wrote. Curiously, this letter was not among more than a dozen letters I had written to Clinton that the White House later released.

November 5, 1996, was Election Day. America did not know what I knew about Bill and Hillary Clinton, about how they abused the office and degraded the presidency, nor about how they treated their friends, much less their enemies. I didn't vote for Clinton, but America did. He was elected to a second term.

I had managed, however, to bring back some semblance of normalcy to my world. I was, as it were, back on my feet, intent on paying down my financial debts. But the two years between the death of my husband and Bill Clinton's election to his second term proved only to be the calm before the storm. My history with Bill Clinton, including his assault on me, would soon land me in the middle of a firestorm that would burn through the entire country and once again throw my life into chaos.

CHAPTER SIX

EXPOSED

CLINTON TOOK the oath of office on Monday, January 20, 1997. Not long after that, all hell broke loose—for American politics, for Clinton's presidency, and for me.

In early February, I received a letter from Michael Isikoff of *Newsweek* magazine, requesting "a brief chat to discuss a matter of mutual interest." A few days later, he called me. Frequently. Famously tenacious, Isikoff would not take no for an answer. An article in *The Nation* later confirmed that Isikoff "pressed...real hard."[1] I talked to Dan about it. "Let's see what he wants," Dan finally said.

I agreed to meet Isikoff at a restaurant in Fredericksburg, which is halfway between Washington and Richmond. It was a very cold, clear winter day. I arrived about twenty minutes late. I sat down across from him in a booth and he started to talk. He talked for two hours while I listened. He knew how Clinton had assaulted me in the galley kitchen hallway behind the Oval Office. He told me that he had gotten the information from the attorneys in Paula Jones's sexual harassment case against Clinton.

I did not confirm or deny any of what Isikoff said. I just listened and then drove back to Richmond and went directly to Dan's office. After that, Isikoff was like a pit bull. He called every week and asked me to tell him my story "on the record."

A few months later, Linda Tripp called me out of the blue. I had not spoken with her for more than three years, and I did *not* want to speak with her then. She was very vague, but told me that she had been talking with Isikoff "off the record." It crossed my mind that she might tape our conversation so I confronted her with some old issues from the Counsel's Office, to see if she would talk about them. Linda brought the subject back to the president, telling me that Clinton was involved with a young White House intern and that Linda had gotten herself in the middle of it. Her call waiting beeped and she excused herself to take the other call. In a minute, she returned to my line, but was confused. "Monica?" she asked. We didn't say much after that, and soon hung up.

I never really knew why she called and I was oblivious at the time that I had an inside tip on the biggest presidential scandal in recent memory. Almost a year later, of course, "Monica" became a household name synonymous with scandal, as the young woman was having a disastrous affair with Clinton. And Linda Tripp was indeed in the middle of it, taping the telephone conversations in which she "counseled" her young friend and coworker.

Michael Isikoff never let up. He called and called and wouldn't leave me alone. Finally, Dan and I thought we could control the story if I talked to Isikoff off the record—neophytes that we were! We thought, *This is how to get rid of him.* If I talked to him off the record, he couldn't use it, but he would at least understand that my story wasn't much of a story and he would leave me alone. *That'll be the end of him!* In March, we met Isikoff at Dan's office. We sat in the conference room and I told Isikoff about the incident in the Oval Office *off the record.* I finally finished.

Dan looked at Isikoff and said, "Hardly an impeachable offense, hmmm?"

Wow, would those words come back to haunt us!

Since I had spoken off the record, I thought—and hoped— that it would go away. I was naive.

Isikoff wanted to corroborate my story, so I sent him to talk to Julie Steele. Julie told him the story and, according to Isikoff, Julie said the incident was appalling, that I had adored Clinton and that, now, he was a fallen hero.[2]

Originally, with the trauma of Ed's death I'd forgotten that I had seen Julie the night I was looking for Ed, after Clinton had assaulted me. But when I finally came up for air, she reminded me that I had stopped by when I was driving all over town searching for my husband. It started to come back to me. I had talked with her about Ed and briefly told her, "On top of all that, you're not going to believe what happened at the damned Oval Office this afternoon."

Sometime after Ed's death, Julie and I had lunch with another old friend of ours, Mary Earle Highsmith. We talked about Clinton and what was going on in the White House, and Julie made some reference to what he had done to me in the Oval Office. She ran her mouth for a minute but I didn't really want to talk about it so we changed the subject.

Julie knew what happened to me from day one, and she constantly pressured me to sell my story. She figured I could make a bundle by selling it to the tabloids. One day, she even threw a stack of tabloids down in front of me and said, "These will show you just how easy it's going to be." Over and over, I told her I would never voluntarily tell my story, but Julie kept trying. "This is how it's going to work—quick and dirty," she said. "Take the money and run. Nobody will remember when it's all said and done. Let's get as much money as we can out of this thing. Just do it quick and dirty," she kept saying. "And as Adam's godmother, you could set up a tuition fund for Adam's college education."

I just looked at her. "*What?*" I insisted, "I am *not* going to sell this story to the tabloids." Besides, I am *not* Adam's godmother.

As the Paula Jones sexual harassment case against Clinton raged on in the news, stories flew about his infidelities. The media was dying to substantiate a claim against Clinton, but the Clintonistas quickly dispatched each accusation, saying Paula Jones was "white trash after cash" and making Gennifer Flowers out to be a promiscuous lounge singer. But now a rumor circulated that Clinton had accosted a woman in the Oval Office. If he denied it, he might commit perjury. And if he admitted it, the feminists would string him up.

Isikoff was sitting on dynamite, but he couldn't use it until I agreed to go on the record. He pursued me and wouldn't let up. He called all the time. "Talk to me," he pleaded. "Talk to me on the record!"

"How am I going to get rid of him?" I finally asked Dan. "What am I going to *do* here?"

As we talked about it, I realized what I could do. I decided to call Nancy Hernreich. She mothered Clinton and was one of those women who knew where all the bodies are buried. I figured I could get her to intervene. *Somebody's got to do something*, I thought. *And she's the one to do it.*

Dan agreed. "That sounds like a great idea."

So I called Nancy. "Look," I said. "Bottom line—here's what's going on. Michael Isikoff is all over me and he won't leave me alone. Now do I have to say any more?"

She knew *exactly* what I was talking about.

"And Isikoff is also talking to Linda Tripp," I said. "You need to know this. The president needs to know this. And I just want Isikoff to leave me alone."

The epitome of a lady, Nancy was always gracious and discreet. She never said anything about anybody, just handled everything delicately. "Kathleen, I'm so sorry," she said. "I'm really sorry about that. Let me look into that."

The next day, Isikoff called me again. "So let me get this straight," he charged. "You called Nancy Hernreich to tell her to get me off of your butt? You told Nancy Hernreich that I just won't leave you alone? That I'm looking for a story?"

What? I was stunned. I was only trying to mind my own business, trying to get out of this thing. "How the hell do you know that?" I said. "Just how do you know that?"

"I *know* it," he snapped. "I know it!"

And he was mad. He figured I was warning the White House, reassuring them that I was still on Clinton's side.

Some months later, I found out how Isikoff knew I'd called the Oval Office.

Nancy told Clinton and Bob Bennett about my call. Unbeknownst to me, Monica was in the picture at that time, so Clinton panicked and called Monica. "Do you have a friend named Linda Tripp?" he interrogated her to find out if she had confided in anyone. "Are you talking to Linda Tripp about any of about this?"

Monica still wanted to get her relationship back on track with Clinton so she lied through her teeth and said something like, "Oh, *God*, no! I'd never tell Linda anything!"

When Monica hung up, she immediately went to Linda, accusing her of talking about the affair. "Are you talking to Isikoff?"

Linda denied everything. Everybody denied everything. And Linda told Isikoff.

When Isikoff found out that I had called Nancy to warn her and get her to help getting him off my back, he called my credibility into question. He figured that if I'd been "victimized" by Clinton, I wouldn't have called to warn him. Isikoff demanded to know why I would call the White House if I was angry at Clinton for harassing me. "Let me get this straight," he said. "You're calling Nancy Hernreich to warn them about me?"

Linda

Linda, of course, also corroborated my story. But she changed it. Linda never viewed the incident as an assault, but assumed it would lead to an affair. And, even though Ed died that day and I was a wreck for most of that year, Linda remained loyal to her fantasy that I had an affair with the president. And she still believed that was why I kept my little part-time job while she lost hers.

She told investigators that when I came to her that day, I seemed "happy" or "elated." I've pondered that a lot and there are two explanations. Either I was so full of stress that I fell back on my sense of humor to get me through, or my story of Clinton's behavior so perfectly fit her agenda that she assigned her own happiness to me.

However, there was a discrepancy in Linda's story. Well aware that I was looking for Ed that day, Linda asked me to call her when I got off the train in Richmond and to keep her posted. And yet her earliest iteration of the story was that I seemed happy or elated when I told her of my encounter with Clinton. In time, she embellished her version with my supposed intentions of seducing the president and starting a relationship with him.

Throughout her years at the White House, Linda obsessed about stories of Clinton's philandering, but she claimed that *I* had been trying to entice Clinton and that *I* pursued *him*. According to an article in *The Nation*, she said I arranged to cover evening functions, trying "to attract his attention with outfits such as a particular black dress which accentuated" my cleavage.[3] But as a 34B, I *have* no cleavage! (Just ask former president Clinton, who assured Monica Lewinsky that he would never have been attracted to me because my breasts are too small!)

According to *The Nation*, Linda told the grand jury (though grand jury testimony has never been released) that I called her "many, many times" after Ed died, and that I was "in some sort of shock...didn't cry...didn't dwell or even speak much about Ed." According to this account, I talked about the president and suggested that Ed's death would spook Clinton and he wouldn't have anything to do with me "on a personal level after this because of the tragedy."[4]

To back up her notion that I was pursuing Clinton, Linda told investigators that I frequently called her on my days off to find out Clinton's schedule. I didn't have regular days, but worked two or three days a week, depending on what events were scheduled and where they needed me. Linda said that I would call her to get Clinton's schedule so I could plot and plan to accidentally run into him. Linda talked as though I could find out his schedule the night before. The FBI questioned me on this and I said, "Obviously, the president's schedule was *never* printed the day before or two days before." For security reasons, it was available only in the morning of the same day. Besides, he never stuck to his schedule! Whatever he had scheduled was, at best, a goal. It was the way his day was supposed to go, but that didn't mean it was necessarily going to happen.

I had helped Patrick get an internship at the White House while I was volunteering and when he was there I sometimes got him situated to watch a helicopter take off or similar events. If Patrick had a friend visiting and I knew that Clinton was in the Old Executive Office Building, I'd tell Patrick, "Come with me and maybe you'll get a chance to see the president." I was glad to do things like that for my son, but Linda made me sound like a stalker.

Though she contradicted my story, reports claimed that before 1997, Linda had written a proposal to sell a book that included a married woman who came out of the Oval Office and said the president groped her. Though her book was never published, the report validated my story.

It has since been proven that Linda was very involved with Paula Jones's attorneys and gave them a lot of information, so I suspect that she was the one who told the Jones lawyers about me. If not Linda, it was Julie.

The Owls

Lanasa, one of the two men to whom my husband owed money, would have been happy if I'd ended up in the street pushing a grocery cart. I tried to reason with him. Since I had signed that note for Ed, I offered to settle with Lanasa for half of the amount Ed had stolen. I felt it was the right thing to do. But that wasn't good enough. He wanted all of it and then some. So we couldn't settle. Luckily for me, I had a really smart, bright lawyer, Dan Gecker.

Ed's life insurance went to my children. I lived frugally, and Dan let me pay him over time. He managed to keep me in the house in Midlothian for a while, but I eventually had to sell it. It was okay. It was a big, traditional, New England–style house and I was alone. Even though it was the house where we had made all our family memories, I needed to downsize. I started thinking that I wanted a little house out in the country. I decided to move to Powhatan, the next county over, where it was peaceful. I set my mind to it. I didn't know much about the county but that was where I was going.

I knew a young man who washed my windows when he was a teenager. When he got married, he moved out to Powhatan and he and a man who owns a timber-frame business built a cottage with some friends. I had heard about the house for years. Eventually, he and his wife had to move, and they had just put the house on the market when my brother went to wash the decks and help get the cottage ready to sell.

"Are you going to go in?" I asked my brother.

"Well, they're not there," he said. He was just going to work outside, on the decks.

"Well, look into the windows and tell me," I said. "All I want is a house that's at the end of a mile-long dirt road, sitting in the middle of the woods. That's all I want."

A while later, he called back. "What are you, psychic or something? I think I found your house! It's pretty great."

When I walked in the kitchen door and got about ten feet into the house, I knew it was perfect.

All my friends said I was nuts when I left my suburban neighborhood in Midlothian and moved to the country in March 1997. But it was a good move.

I had ten acres of forest, which gave the dogs Meg and Shawn room to run. They'd encounter squirrels and raccoons, skunks and deer. My cat, Buttons, liked to get outside and explore the woods, but Bullseye preferred lounging in front of the fire with me. He was such a good guy, a real cuddler. There were many lonely nights when he snuggled up with me. He seemed to know that all was not well in the sad years after Ed died. I used the fireplace in the cottage a lot, curling up in front of the fire during cold weather, which I love. I love the beauty of snow and the dramatic ice storms, and the peaceful forest with the owls calling out to me in my perfect little house.

Drudge

In early July, renegade Internet reporter Matt Drudge was "hot on the trail" of Isikoff's story about me. Drudge's sources at *Newsweek* told him that Isikoff was sitting on the story. Drudge didn't have any of the restrictions that Isikoff had, and it didn't matter that I'd told Isikoff off the record. So while Isikoff couldn't report his own story, Drudge could report it as a rumor, and it was a juicy one: The president had groped a White House volunteer in the Oval Office.

And Drudge had substantiation. Hours before he broke the story, he had an AOL chat session with a senior White House staffer. Drudge asked the contact about me, but the White House staffer didn't know who I was, so he asked around. On that Saturday afternoon, the White House learned that I had talked to Isikoff. And they reacted.

Drudge's contact said the information was interesting and wrote, "Are you sure the last name is Willey?"

"Yes," Drudge replied, adding, "I'm holding off my story on it, because of an urgent request...but will move very soon."

The contact continued to dismiss Drudge's information. "*Willey* just doesn't seem right to me. I've been here for five years and I've never heard the name."

"Willey? Midlothian, VA?" Drudge pressed. "Her husband committed suicide?"

"I'll check it out," he typed to Drudge.

When he returned, "the senior staffer turned wordy, and panicky," Drudge wrote. "Okay, I'll give you this bit of information," the staffer wrote to Drudge. "I just asked [Deputy Chief of Staff John] Podesta about it and he knows what it is and asked me to check to see if Isikoff was writing for it in tomorrow's magazine. He's not, but you knew that. You and I did not have this conversation. I just got a lot of people very riled up around here about this Willey thing. We'll talk later. Do not mention this conversation. Do not mention this conversation. If asked, I'll tell people that you had on your web page: 'Possible Isikoff story on Willey' but that it's gone from your page now."

Drudge did not reveal this online conversation until nearly a year later, in March 1998. On the *Drudge Report*, he noted that while the aide replied that the mention of my name got people "riled up" around the White House, "Several hang-up phone calls were received at the *Drudge Report* office in Los Angeles." According to Drudge, subsequent records also show that "White House staffers were so fixated on the story that they logged onto the *Drudge* site more than 2,600 times during the first twenty-four-hour period" after Drudge named me on July 28.[5]

Just days after Drudge exposed me, Isikoff called Julie Steele to review the story and, he later wrote, she "balked." He also asked her for a picture of me with the president and, according to Isikoff, Julie "started to sound nervous." When they talked later that day, Julie recanted the story, said it wasn't true. She said that I had made it up and asked her to lie about it and that, in fact, I hadn't come to her house that night at all.[6] Eventually, Julie even signed an affidavit saying that I had asked her to lie about Clinton's assault.

Isikoff, to his credit, reported both versions—that Julie initially corroborated my story and then that she denied it. Isikoff also later wrote that Julie "voiced no objections to her name appearing in the magazine at the time" and stayed in touch with him, calling to chat and apologizing for not giving him the picture of me with the president. In fact, she couldn't have given the picture to Isikoff because she had already sold it.[7]

When Drudge broke my story, all hell broke loose. But for a few days there was one little silver lining: I had just moved.

I was listed in the phone book at my old house with my old phone number, so everybody in the world descended on my house in Midlothian. That was fine with me, because we had a really contentious closing. The buyer and I had fought over some of my furniture, especially a sideboard that Ed had given me. So when the house finally closed and I turned over the keys, neither she nor I were happy.

When I heard that television trucks and radio station vans and newspaper reporters descended upon my old house, I thought, *Well, isn't that just too damned bad.*

Then a friend called me at the cottage and said, "You gotta call your old phone number!" So I did. The phone company had already reassigned my telephone number and the people who had my old number were being overwhelmed with phone calls, so they changed the outgoing message on their answering machine. When I called my old number, I heard the voice of an irate man who said, "Kathleen Willey does *not* live here! This is her *old* telephone number. If you're calling to talk to her, this is *not* her phone number. *Leave us alone!*" Poor guy.

When I moved out to the country by myself, I didn't list my address in the phone book, just "K. Willey, Powhatan." It was funny because most people assumed that I had an unlisted number, so they went through all these gyrations to get my number from other people, when all they had to do was look in the phone book. But my house was hard to find, so at the time I was sitting pretty out in the beautiful forest of Powhatan County thinking, *They can't find me!*

Paparazzi

Soon enough, of course, they did. And it made me nervous, because I knew they had to work hard to get there. Powhatan is farm country, even if there aren't many actual farms left. It's a community of horse pastures and livestock, with a lot of land between houses and more land between roads. There are no suburbs and no sidewalks. It's not like visitors could stop at the gas station and pick up a street map. Reporters and photographers visited the little country post office in Powhatan Village and asked for information and directions to my house. "We know why you're here, and we're not going to tell you how to get there!" The mailman told them, "She doesn't want to talk to you, so get out!"

It took a while but the news crews eventually abandoned the house in Midlothian and swarmed my cottage at the end of the mile-long dirt road. Most of the reporters stayed up on the road and never passed the "No Trespassing" signs on to my gravel driveway.

But one afternoon, in the high heat of a humid August, I had all my windows open when the dogs heard a noise outside and started barking. I was upstairs in the guest bedroom and I got down on the floor below the window and peeked outside. My beautiful German shepherd, Tess, was lying next to me. We saw a man standing on the gravel driveway across from my yard, smoking a cigarette. He came down to my front door and knocked. I didn't answer. He banged on the door and walked around to the kitchen and banged on that door as well. "Hello? Hello!" He smoked one cigarette after another. He must have thought someone was home since my car was parked in the driveway, so he persisted. But I didn't want to talk, so Tess and I just watched him. Finally, he left the side of my house, walked along my walkway and up the steps to where my car was parked and lingered there. Tess and I walked out onto my front porch. I held her collar. He was twenty-five or thirty feet from us. I asked him what he wanted and he said he wanted to talk to me.

"Who are you?"

He said he had been sent to get my story and asked if I would talk to him.

"I have nothing to say to you," I said. "Did you see the 'No Trespassing' sign at the top of my driveway?"

"I really need a story," he said.

"Well, I really need you to leave."

"My editor is going to be real mad if I don't come back with a story," he pleaded.

"Really," I said with more urgency in my voice, "you need to leave. This dog is trained to attack on command and if I were you I would just turn around very, very quietly and go away."

He finally turned and started to tiptoe on up my driveway. "And take your cigarette butts with you," I added. "She doesn't like them, either!"

So, before long, they all knew where I was and they knew my phone number too. My phone started to ring and it didn't stop. Everybody wanted me to talk. The tabloids called and told Dan I could name my price. They were talking about obscene amounts of money. A product of Catholic guilt, I thought only *one* thing: *I cannot do that!*

Of course, I could have used the money. Here I was, still in the middle of the lawsuits with judgments against me, still afraid I was going to lose my house. And with everything I went through, I racked up legal bills. What's more, with my notoriety, it was harder than ever to find a job. Though I eventually gave a few interviews to try to clear my name, I never made a dime doing them because reputable reporters do not pay for stories.

When the story first broke, the White House denied that I had ever worked there. How could they think they could just say things like that and get away with it? These things are all documented. Of course in the Clinton White House such documents often disappeared, but I was a White House volunteer for years and I had a pass. Hounded by the press, Clinton finally had to acknowledge that he knew me. "Yeah, I kind of remember her," he said. "She was always real nice." It went from that to, "Oh, yeah, I guess she was in the Oval Office."

A reporter asked a question about me and it was the most bizarre experience to be sitting on my sofa and watching her ask whether "Kathleen Willey" was a potential witness in the Jones case. I thought, *This is weird. This is really weird!* And then I watched as Clinton froze and glared at her while answering her question. "There was a request to be left alone and not harassed"—by me, incidentally!—"and we're just trying to honor it."[8]

My mailbox was up at the top of my little hill, where my driveway met the road, and I walked up there every day to get my mail. Invariably, somebody was waiting to pounce on me, so I didn't even pick up my mail, but turned around and came home. Sometimes I even sneaked up there in the middle of the night to get my mail, which made me nervous. One Friday, at five in the afternoon, there was a knock on the door. I opened it to see my mail carrier standing there with a post-hole digger.

"How about I move your mailbox down here, closer to the house?" he offered.

I couldn't believe it. "But then you'll have to drive down here to bring my mail and turn around," I said. "It'll be a pain in the neck."

"I don't mind," he said. "I really don't care."

That Friday night, he moved my mailbox for me. That's how nice some people are.

Some people.

The day after Drudge ran the story, Dan called. "Well, you're going to be in the *Enquirer*," he said. "You got sold out."

"Julie Steele?" I said.

And he said, "Julie Steele."

I knew. I just knew it.

Julie was my best friend of twenty years. That's how desperate she was for money. She had mortgaged her house, had a baby, couldn't get a job, and was in a real financial bind. And David Kendall, a fop who represented Clinton, also just happened to represent the *National Enquirer* at that time. With a streak of luck—and no doubt a little help from her friends—Julie sold my story to the *Enquirer*. The article, published on August 19, 1997, called me a conniving woman who was obsessed with Clinton. Without naming Julie Steele, it said I launched my scheme when Isikoff asked me about the incident and I called Julie, asking her to lie to him. Supposedly, I had come up with the story in order to sell a novel with the same plot, and I allegedly felt that "snaring Clinton in a real-life romantic disgrace would generate huge public interest in the book."[9] This is the only time Julie expressed this book concept. But it did come up again in 1998, when Uncle Bob accused me of seeking publicity to promote another book—this time a nonfiction account. (For the record, *this* is the first book I have ever written and I am doing so *only* to tell what I know about Hillary Clinton because I believe it is relevant to her presidential bid.)

Julie had wanted to sell this story to Isikoff but *Newsweek* doesn't pay for stories. Julie, of course, found out that the *Enquirer* does. Only days after my story broke, they arranged an all-expenses-paid trip to Palm Beach, Florida, for Julie with her grown daughter and her son, Adam, who was seven. The tabloid put them up at a posh resort, The Breakers, and bought the photo and her story. Julie sold me out for ten thousand dollars. Later, *Time* magazine also bought Julie's story for another $5,500. That's what our friendship was worth to Julie—fifteen grand.

The sad thing is that Julie had asked for the picture of me with the president so that she could put it in Adam's room when he was just a baby. After I gave her the photo, she hung it in her kitchen and it stayed there for years. It was never for her son. And it was that picture that I had given to Julie as a gift for her child that she sold to the *Enquirer*.

"Uncle Bob"

I avoided the press as best I could but was under constant assault by the media. Worse, as a result of the *Drudge* story, Paula Jones's attorneys subpoenaed me, wanting to depose me for her sexual harassment lawsuit against Clinton. They felt my incident with Clinton corroborated her story and helped her case. I did *not* want to get involved. That was the last thing I needed.

Dan spoke for me, saying I had no relevant information for the Jones case. He expressed my outrage at being drawn in and made it clear that I continued to have a very good relationship with Clinton. "We made every effort to avoid Kathleen's deposition," Dan said. He called Clinton's lawyer Bob Bennett to get the White House take on the fact that I was being drawn in, and we immediately began proceedings to quash the subpoena. Dan said he spoke with Bennett almost daily and recalls that, "Bob was a good lawyer representing his client well and he wanted to control all aspects of the case."

Bennett was extremely anxious to keep me out of the Jones case, so in a case of strange bedfellows, "Uncle Bob" became my new best friend. While he came across as gruff and a little clumsy, he seemed like a nice guy, the type who has a spot of food on his two-hundred-dollar tie. But Uncle Bob was *very* good. He offered substantial legal help, whatever he could do, and even faxed legal cases to Dan to help him substantiate the argument that I should not be drawn into the case. I did not want to be deposed. I did not want to tell the story that Clinton has assaulted me. Bennett was more than happy to help me to that end, and the implication was that I didn't need to worry about paying him any legal fees.

We asked for a hearing before Judge Robert Merhige in his federal court in Richmond, Virginia. The hearing was in November, and Uncle Bob attended with Dan and me.

Joseph Cammerata and his law partner, Gil Davis, had recently resigned from the Jones case and Cammerata had been called to testify, so we met him at the hearing. But the scene turned into a screaming match between Bennett and Jones's Dallas attorneys. Dan looked at me and whispered, "Why are *we* here?"

In the end, we lost. Judge Merhige ruled that I must be deposed in the Jones case on December 5, 1997.

I started to feel some pressure from Uncle Bob. He casually mentioned that the president thought the world of me and then he said, "Now, this…was not sexual harassment, was it?" When I didn't answer, Uncle Bob pressed, "Well, it wasn't unwelcome, was it?"

I said it was.

Nate Landow

Nate had always kind of stayed in the picture and we called each other now and then. When the story broke, we talked again. It was a pretty day in the fall and he invited me to come up and see him. I liked the idea of getting out of town for a while and Nate's estate was a good place to escape. Besides, he was always busy and didn't hover, so I could relax. I told him I'd drive up and stay for a couple days. "I'll send a plane," he offered. To me, that was like something you'd see on television, *I'll send a plane*. But that was Nate. He liked making all these arrangements. He set it up, called back and told me where to meet the plane.

When I got there, he asked me a lot of questions about what I was going to say about Clinton. "What happened?" he pressed me.

I intimated that something did happen, but I did not give him any specifics.

Nate advised me to try to dodge the subpoena. And he pressured me to lie in the deposition, to just say that nothing happened. He had no problem suggesting that I lie.

"You do not have to tell anybody anything," he said to me. "Only two people in this world really know what happened in there—you and him. You do not need to talk about this. You don't have to say anything happened."

It wasn't out of the ordinary for Nate to fish for information because he's an obtrusive man, the kind who tends to push and give advice. But I felt as though he was strong-arming me. It was overbearing. At that time, I actually felt like it was coming from somewhere else, like he wasn't the only one who was interested. I started to think there was something else going on, somebody he was involved with. I wondered whether Al Gore might have pressed him because he and Nate were close. They had the kind of relationship where Nate could call Gore on his cell phone. Nate had been Al Gore's national finance chair in '88 and was chairman of the Maryland Democratic Party. He was also very influential in the national Democratic Party. Whether it was Gore or someone else, I am positive that Nate was getting phone calls from someone at the White House who told him to talk to me.

Nate had always lived on the fringe, so when his name came up in my case the investigators' interests were piqued. They had been trying to get him for years and I think they thought they were finally going to. Nate was subpoenaed to testify about pressuring me to lie under oath—witness tampering. To defend himself, he lied and turned it all around on me. He claimed that I called him and demanded he send a jet. For good measure, he claimed that I wanted a relationship with him because he was rich and I was broke. I was supposedly pursuing him and he wasn't interested. That's the stance that he took, and it was good enough. They couldn't prove what he'd said to me, so he got out of it.

Nate's explicit pressure on me to lie was merely the beginning of a campaign to ensure that I did not tell the truth in my deposition. Whoever was working hard to protect Bill Clinton waged war against my sense of safety and well-being. The message was very clear: I was not supposed to talk about what happened in the Oval Office. The media feeding frenzy was hard enough to manage, but what happened in the next months would test my resolve more than anything in my long and wearisome saga.

CHAPTER SEVEN

TERROR CAMPAIGN

W HEN THE STORY BROKE, I had been in the cottage—in
my wonderful, secluded piece of heaven—for about five
months. My safety had never been an issue. I had never felt un-
safe there when I was alone. But I suddenly felt very vulnerable
in my own house. And when that happens, it is terrible to live
without a sense of security. And it happened constantly. A lot of
it was little stuff, but some of it got very scary. Through a series
of what some consider minor events, my sense of safety eroded.

After Drudge ran my story, it was on television and everything
hit the fan. After a few days, I finally called the sheriff because people were knocking on my door and I felt defenseless. Once the
deputies got out there and saw where I lived, they realized that I
could have a problem because they were not close. The sheriff's
office was fifteen miles away from my house. Because they were so
far away, the deputies drove by at night to check up on me.

I was new in Powhatan and didn't know anybody, but I
started to hear that, after I would leave a store, strange men
would walk in after me and say, "You know who that was, don't
you?" They would ask the merchants what I bought and how I
paid, looking for any information they could find. The merchants
did not tell me right then because they didn't know me. But the
next time I came in, or if I ran into them a couple of weeks later,
they would say, "Oh, did I tell you…?"

Since I had moved into a smaller house, I was trying to make
room in closets, cleaning things out and organizing my little cottage. I took some clothes to a consignment shop in town. Less
than a week later, I went back in and the woman in the shop said,

"Boy, you should've seen the guy who came in after you left." She thought it was weird that somebody would walk in and ask her if she knew who I was and what I bought. But she didn't know about everything else that was going on, so she didn't do anything about it until she saw me again. I told her my FBI guy would be calling her.

Things like that started to happen a lot. I sensed I was being followed and started looking in my rearview mirror, asking myself if a car had been behind me a while, or thinking I recognized a person from earlier in the day.

The Mechanic

I'd sold most of my furniture with the other house, and was starting to decorate the cottage. I had ordered a rug and was heading out to pick it up. I was excited and in a hurry. My little white Subaru Outback was parked in my driveway at the top of the walkway steps, forty feet from my kitchen door. I hopped in and took off. The dirt road seemed extra bumpy, but I was in a hurry and distracted, so I didn't think much more about it. But when I got to the paved road, my car made a lot of noise. I got out and looked, and one of my tires was pretty flat. I decided to just drive it to the tire shop. I know it can ruin the rim, but it was only a few miles away and I thought I could make it.

When I pulled in, the men at the shop rolled their eyes. "You *drove* it here?"

"Well, yeah," I said. "What else am I going to do?" After all, I was in a hurry.

The mechanic went to work on my tire while I waited for my car. It was late in the morning on a sunny September day, and I sat out in the sun reading the paper. Finally, the guy came out and said, "Can I show you something?"

I followed him to my car. "Have you been anywhere, like in a construction area or anyplace like that recently?" he asked me.

I wracked my brain. *What have I done the last couple days?* "No," I said.

We stood under the lift and he showed me my tire. "I've never seen anything like this before," he said. "There are a lot of nails in these tires, especially the sidewalls."

I was trying to think of where I might have been where someone had dropped nails. People have been known to do things like that. But I clearly remembered where I'd been and I hadn't been near any construction.

And then he said, "It's just got to be a nail gun that did this. It looks like someone has punctured your tires with a nail gun. They are full of nails."

Only one tire had already gone flat, but three of them were punctured, full of nails.

He said to me, "Do you have any enemies?"

"Well, possibly," I said.

As I left, I thought, *What the hell is this all about?* The best I could figure was that it had happened at my house. Somebody had come down in the middle of the night and shot my tires full of nails. And that was only the beginning.

I later found out that at about the same time that my tires were punctured, my best friend's tires were also punctured. She lived in Richmond, on the other side of town, so we didn't see each other often, but we talked on the phone all the time. Now and then we would get together for long visits. Either I was followed to her house in town or she was followed home from visiting me. Either way, "they" knew who she was and where she lived. And presumably, they hoped that terrorizing her would send me another message. To this day, she believes that, as my friend, she was also a target.

Later, when the FBI got involved, I told them about my tires. "The tires went to a recycle center and were ground up before we could recover them," said FBI agent Dennis Alvater. "However, in talking to the professionals in the tire shop, they'd never seen anything like that." Alvater said that, in one of the front tires, there was a grouping of approximately nine nails in an area the size of a fifty-cent piece. In the other front tire, there were approximately four nails in a similar grouping. A rear tire had approximately three nails. "All of the nails were consistent in size and type," he added. Based upon the description and grouping of the nails, the investigators speculated that the person had used an airless, portable trim nail gun. The agent also noted that some of the nails punctured the *sidewalls* of the tires. "You just don't pick up nails in the sidewall of a tire," Alvater said. "The number of nails, pattern, and consistent nail type suggested that the damage was deliberately done. It's not like somebody threw a bunch of nails on Kathleen's driveway and hoped they would puncture her tires."[1]

Telephone Men

I started to hear all kinds of clicks and interference on the phone. Out where I turned off the main highway onto the dirt road, I noticed a telephone box. And all of a sudden, I saw a lot of activity at that box.

Finally, I stopped and asked the telephone repair man, "What are you doing here? Why am I all of a sudden seeing people here?"

"I'm just working on the lines."

I said, "Are ya'll doing something, because I'm getting all kinds of noise and clicks on my phone."

He just said, "No."

I was exasperated. I never told people who I was but, finally, I said, "Let me show you something." The local newspaper ran an article about me that morning. I said, "Look, that's me." I showed him my picture in the paper. "And I'm getting all kinds of interference on my phone. Now, do you need to tell me something? Who *are* you? What are you doing here?"

"Ma'am," he said, "I don't know what you're talking about." There was a Verizon truck parked there, so I decided to let it go.

Shortly after that, I sat in my office writing bills on a really hot, humid afternoon. The phone rang and a number came up on caller ID. I answered and the man said he was calling from my power company, VEPCO.

"Is this Kathleen Willey?" he asked me, verifying my address. And I said, "Yes."

"We're getting ready to turn your power off to work on the line," he said. "We just want to make sure you don't have any invalids or seniors or infants in the house before we turn off the power."

"Nope," I said. "It's just me here." Just cats and dogs, and they were all lazing around in the afternoon heat.

"All right, then, we're going to cut the power off in a few minutes," he said. "It'll be off for about thirty minutes or an hour."

"Okay." I didn't think twice about it.

As the afternoon went on, it got hotter than the hinges of hell and I thought, *I wonder when they're turning the power off.* After a while, I realized the power was never turned off. Finally, I thought, *All right, this is bogus.*

I looked up the number that had come up on caller ID. I called the number and it just rang and rang. Then I called VEPCO to check, but it wasn't them. So I called Dan and I said, "There's something weird going on here…"

Bullseye

On Election Day in November, a month before I was to give my deposition, I opened my front door and let Bullseye out. A sweet old cat, he was thirteen years old. He didn't go out much anymore and, when he did, it wasn't for long. He never went far and he always came right back. But not that day. That day, I watched Bullseye jump off the porch and I never saw him again.

I watched election returns and wondered where he was. The next day, I called a few neighbors to see if they'd seen a yellow tabby, a big guy with a red collar. If you lose an animal, the people around here will look. We're all animal lovers, and they knew how I felt. But all the homes were spread far and wide, surrounded by many acres of woods. No one had seen my cat.

I felt bad for Patrick, because he always thought of Bullseye as his cat. Eventually, I had to tell him and he got really angry at the thought that someone had harmed our old cat.

I was shocked when people later mocked me for being upset about Bullseye. People made terrible jokes about him, as if a cat isn't just as much a family pet as a dog. People would have been *outraged* if he had been a dog! Lucianne Goldberg, for one, made a really snotty remark on a talk show. I was incensed. I tracked her number down and called her. "You know, you don't have any right to make fun of my poor cat like you did today," I said. *"Really!* He was our *pet!"* She backed down and apologized right away.

Judge Merhige

My deposition was coming up on December 5. I was scared. I didn't want to give it.

Adding insult to injury, I had a herniated disc in my neck that had bothered me for years and was exacerbated by the stress in my life. I was going to have surgery about a month later, but on the evening of December 3 my neurosurgeon called with a sudden opening in his schedule. I could have my surgery on the morning of the fifth. I told my doctor that I was supposed to give a deposition that day, but he advised me that I should have the surgery. So I agreed.

Dan informed Judge Merhige and the Jones attorneys, asking to reschedule my deposition for January 10, 1998. The Jones attorneys arrived on December 5 anyway and accused me of performing a stunt to avoid the deposition. Did they actually think I would *invent* a ruptured disc? Did they think I fooled the chief of neurosurgery at the Medical College of Virginia into performing invasive surgery on me just so I could get out of giving a deposition? Judge Merhige called Dr. Young, who satisfied him that I needed the surgery. The judge postponed the deposition. I had another month.

Patrick surprised me and came home for Christmas. We didn't have a Christmas tree or a single decoration, but I was happy and it hastened my recovery. It was my first Christmas in my little cottage in the woods and, although Bullseye was gone, I had Patrick there. For a while, there was peace on earth.

The Jogger

It was Thursday, two days before my deposition. I'd had a fitful night and awoke very early. Still recovering from surgery, I suffered from insomnia. I had to wear a cervical collar around my neck and was always uncomfortable, so I had trouble sleeping and was often awake at first light. A longtime runner, I felt lethargic and out of shape. My surgeon agreed that careful and moderate walks would help my recovery. I started walking in the early morning, sometimes just as the first hint of daylight broke the night.

I walked about an eighth of a mile up my driveway to my gate, where my mailbox had been, and passed my closest neighbor's house. Through the forest, the house is about five hundred yards from mine and in the winter, when the trees are bare, I can see its lights at night.

I walked along the road, the dirt crunching under my feet. It was still early and quiet. The bats and owls finished their night chatter as my dogs and a rambunctious puppy rambled along with me through the cold morning. Just up the road a piece, I turned right, taking a road that had a few houses on it, maybe one every hundred yards or so. I usually walked to the end of the road where it came to a dead end.

I was about half a mile from home when a hint of light softened the eastern sky through the foggy, gray morning. In the distance, I saw a man jogging toward me from the dead end of the road. As I was relatively new to the neighborhood and still hadn't met all my neighbors, I assumed he lived somewhere around there since he approached me from the cul de sac. Dressed in dark sweats, running shoes, and a plain dark baseball hat, he slowed as he got near me. We walked nearer to each other.

"Hey, Kathleen, how are ya?" He stopped before he reached me. My dogs milled around, sniffing the ground.

"Good," I said. We stood talking, several feet apart.

"Hey, did you ever find your cat?"

"No, he never came home and I still look for him all the time. He was a member of the family and I really miss him." Then I stopped and added, "Why, have you seen him?"

"Yeah, that Bullseye, he was a nice cat." He said, "He was a really nice old cat."

"Yes, yes he sure is." I said.

I started to wonder how this stranger could have known my cat's name.

"It's a shame, and I just have no idea what happened to him," I added. "Well, did you see him?"

I started to feel uneasy. *How would he know he was a nice cat?*

So I asked, "Who are you?"

He didn't answer. His eyes were fixed on me and he looked serious. I felt more uncomfortable. After a moment, he spoke again.

"Did you ever get those tires fixed?"

Whoa—how did he know my tires had been vandalized a few months back? I didn't think I'd told any of my neighbors. I felt the hairs stand up on the back of my neck and a sickening feeling welled up in the pit of my stomach.

"Who *are* you?" I demanded.

"And how are your children doing? How are Shannon and Patrick?"

I got chills, felt a lightness in my head. I thought, *Where are my damn dogs?* They were just milling around, oblivious to my sense of danger. And I was so far from home. Where was the nearest house? It was about six thirty in the morning and still quiet. I stepped back from him.

"My children are fine. What's it to you?" I tried to sound assertive to hide the fear in my voice. I didn't want him to know that I was scared.

He continued, seeming a little more at ease. Then he asked about good friends of mine and mentioned their two children by name.

Oh God! The realization suddenly exploded in my consciousness. *He means me harm! He means my loved ones harm!*

"Who *are* you? What do you want?"

I backed away, trying to be careful not to trip and fall and re-injure my neck. I called the dogs. I was shaking from fear. My legs felt like they were frozen in place. They wouldn't move. A flurry of thoughts clogged my mind. *Did he have a gun? Oh my God, this guy is going to shoot me! And who would know? He might even hurt my dogs! Where could I go? Was anyone awake nearby? Would anyone hear me scream?*

As I backed up, he walked toward me. He was closer to me now. He looked at me, hardness in his eyes. He spoke deliberately and quietly.

"You're just not getting the message, are you?"

I wanted to get away. I knew I had to get away from him as fast as I could. I had to get home. I turned my back on him and ran, my neck immobile in the collar, my feet like lead. About fifty yards up the road, I stopped to catch my breath. I turned around to see if he was running after me. He was gone. I never saw him again.

As best I could, I ran all the way home, not thinking about the damage I might have done to my neck. I was desperate to get back to the house, to Patrick. Then I remembered that Patrick had gone away for the weekend.

I didn't know what to do. I brought in the dogs, dead-bolted the doors, and locked all the windows. I had resisted getting a security system, but that day I wished I had one. And I wished I had a gun. I was in danger. My children were in danger. My friends and their families were in danger.

I sat in my living room and thought, *This is a whole new ballgame…and I am out of my league.* He knew my routine. I was being watched. I was frightened to death.

Should I tell? Should I be silent? Would we be harmed if I went to the police? What was the best way to keep everyone safe?

I started to understand. He was there scare me, to let me know that I was being watched. But it was more than that. I realized that Bullseye's disappearance was part of it, that the damage to my tires was part of it. And the noises on my phone. It was all part of their message: *Keep your mouth shut. Don't talk about the incident in the Oval Office.*

I decided not to tell anyone, not even Dan.

Frightened beyond words, I could not sleep for two days. I knew someone was watching me because the jogger knew my routine. I felt more vulnerable than ever. I realized I had no protection. He had harmed or killed Bullseye. He had threatened my children. Who's going to protect *them*? Who's going to protect *me*?

"You're just not getting the message, are you?"

I should lie during the deposition on January 10. Go in there and just lie.

Uncle Bob

Two days later, on January 10, 1998, Dan and Uncle Bob went with me to the federal courthouse in Richmond, Virginia. Judge Robert Merhige told me that this was the first time in his long stint on the bench that he had opened his courthouse on a Saturday. He wanted to avoid a media event and succeeded. There was no one in sight except a marshal for security. Nobody had heard about it.

Trying to mediate a settlement, the judge sent Dan and me packing for two hours, then we met with Uncle Bob back in Dan's office for a quick lunch. The three of us sat there eating when Bennett's cell phone rang. "Yes, sir," he said. Then, turning to us, he said, "Excuse me, my client is on the phone." I thought, *So, Bill Clinton is calling him down here asking him how things are going.* I felt he was calling for my benefit, to let me know that I was on his radar and he was keeping an eye on things. I felt really intimidated by that. Bennett said, "Yes, sure… Yes, sir, I will certainly give her your best."

I gave my deposition in a conference room in the judge's office suite. I had a large audience: Judge Merhige, two Jones lawyers, Bob Bennett, Dan, various law clerks, and the video camera operator. I danced the dance for about two hours. A classic hostile witness testifying under threat of contempt charges, I was as evasive as I could be. Having been a lawyer's wife, I knew how to dance around their questions, to avoid revealing what had happened. I evaded, I said I didn't remember, on and on, blah, blah, blah. Even Dan noticed it. He had never seen me so evasive. Trying to stay within the parameters of the law, I was doing anything I could think of to get out of Clinton's mess. It took the Jones lawyer a long time to just get me to say that Clinton gave me a cup of coffee in the back room. He had to ask me step-by-step questions to get me to admit that he hugged me when I was leaving the private office. He asked if there was any kissing involved.

I said, "There was an attempt." I only answered each specific question, volunteered nothing.

Finally, the lawyer thought to ask, "Did Mr. Clinton attempt to touch your breasts?"

"I think so."

So the lawyer followed up. "And what is the basis for your thinking so?"

I said, "I have a recollection of that."

"Was he successful?" the lawyer asked.

"Yes."

It went like that for quite a while.

The Jones lawyers got totally exasperated. Finally, so did the judge.

Later, even the FBI said I was very evasive. Of course, that's what I wanted to be. They said that I seemed to contradict myself, but I don't remember that. I may have a few times because I was just trying to get out of it any way I could. I did not want to have to tell the story.

Dan asked for a recess. "Let's go talk," he said. We went into the jury room and sat down. He looked at me and said, "Are you ready for this?"

"I don't think I have a choice here," I said. "So I guess I'm as ready as I can be."

We returned to the conference room and Dan asked Judge Merhige to ask all the interns and law clerks to leave.

I did not cave. I told my story.

The judge grew pale. He couldn't believe it.

I looked at Uncle Bob. He was dumbstruck. Totally blindsided. He looked as if someone had kicked him in the gut. He had no idea of the actual facts. Until that moment, he never knew what Clinton had done to me. His face turned red. His eyes narrowed. He began to perspire. The worm had turned. No more Mr. Nice Guy, no more "Uncle Bob." I had broken the code of silence. It was war.

Bennett had the opportunity to cross-examine me and he could hardly collect himself. His re-direct was brief and pained. "Well, so, what you're saying, Mrs. Willey, is that the president made a pass at you? It was really just a boorish pass, wasn't it?"

I gave him an icy glare. "Hardly."

The judge put everyone under a gag order. "This better not leave this room," he said.

But the session had been videotaped. Each of the parties—Bennett, the Jones lawyers, the judge, and Dan—would get a copy of the videotape. And the video operator was sworn to silence under penalty of death.

My brilliant lawyer said, "Your Honor, we don't need to look at it. We'd like you to keep our tape in your safe, with yours."

The judge looked at everyone and said, "This tape better not see the light of day or else I'm coming after people."

After my deposition, I got home when it was getting dark. I'd been invited to my first party in the neighborhood and I found the strength to go. It proved to be a good distraction. Everyone was very casual and welcoming. I liked them. That was the first time I met everybody and actually had a conversation with my next-door neighbor. I had been staying to myself after everything broke in July and I think a lot of my neighbors didn't know who I was. They didn't connect my face with the pictures and didn't know my last name. So I didn't mention the remarkable events of my day and it turned out to be a relaxing evening. I almost felt normal. After all, doesn't everyone swear under oath to a devastating story about the president of the United States before going to a neighborhood party?

"Once Kathleen was deposed in the Paula Jones case," Dan said, "we made every effort to keep information from her deposition away from the media." But Judge Susan Weber Wright, who presided over the Jones case in Arkansas, allowed certain information to become public if filed with other pleadings in the case. According to Dan, "We were notified that substantial portions would be attached to a motion for summary judgment filed by Don Campbell on behalf of Paula Jones," and this meant that the information was going to be made public the following week.[2] The video was attached to the documentation that was going to be released to the public.

It was on the street in seventy-two hours.

After my deposition, Uncle Bob was no longer my friend. In fact, he was clearly my enemy. I never spoke to Bob Bennett again.

Skull

On Monday, two days after I was deposed, I was home alone. Just as the sun was coming up, I opened my front door to let my dogs out. On the porch in front of me was a new horror. A small animal skull was lying on the bricks staring at me. It was bare bone, empty, dry, sitting a few feet from the door. It was the size of a cat's skull.

I thought of Bullseye. Had they had killed my wonderful old cat?

It was payback.

I didn't know what to do with it, and I thought, "I just can't deal with this." I got so mad, I went around to my backyard and I threw it into the woods as far as I could throw. I was really angry—about the cat specifically, but generally about the scare tactics. I thought, *I will not give in to these people!*

But I was afraid to tell anybody. I was fearful that it was Bullseye and I didn't want to know. I didn't want to think that somebody would kill a cat—kill *my* cat—to intimidate me. So I didn't tell any officials about the skull right away.

When I finally did tell them about the skull, the FBI came out and found it. "We looked for shoe prints," said FBI investigator Dennis Alvater. "We looked around in the woods for any evidence of people watching the house. I wasn't able to find anything..." But they did learn that the skull was not Bullseye's. It was a raccoon.

Cats, of course, sometimes drag small rodents to the porch, or bring home similar little gifts. But before this incident and since, not one of my animals has ever brought home any animal bones, and a dog or cat certainly couldn't present a raccoon skull with its face perfectly facing my front door. Besides, my habit is to have all the animals inside the house with me at night. I knew my pets did not put it there.

Later, I watched *The Insider*, a movie about a witness in a case against "Big Tobacco" and the reign of terror aimed at getting the witness to back away from testifying. The witness opened his mailbox and there was a bullet sitting there. It was a constant campaign of weird things going on. The witness felt like he was being watched. He just knew it. Jack Paladino, one of the Clintons' infamous private investigators, played himself in that movie, doing background research on the witness. I watched that movie with the hair standing up on the back of my neck and thought to myself, *Boy, do I know about this!*

Clinton

On January 17, Clinton gave his deposition in the Paula Jones case. It took a couple of weeks, but on March 13 portions of his deposition were released. Clinton testified that he never tried to kiss me and never touched me inappropriately. He denied all of it. He remembered that I was "quite agitated about family problems when we met" and he alluded to my financial difficulties, my distraught state, and my husband's suicide, as if it had already happened before I went to see him. In trying to console me, he said, "I embraced her, I put my arms around her, I may have even kissed her on the forehead." But he claimed that my allegations of a sexual encounter were not true. When Paula's lawyers asked him, "You deny that testimony?" Clinton answered, "I emphatically deny it. It did not happen."[3]

The Jogger

Two weeks after I gave my deposition, I told Dan about the jogger. He was shocked.

The FBI investigated it in February, after I became a cooperating witness. "I absolutely believe that the jogger did occur," said FBI agent Dennis Alvater, but he also said, "We were never able to identify the jogger." Alvater recently said he "always felt Kathleen was one hundred percent honest about that" and pointed out that I passed a polygraph test that included questions about the jogger.

Alvater's partner in the investigation, Jerry Bastin, was a retired FBI agent working for the Independent Counsel as an independent contractor. Jerry said, "We never discovered, to our satisfaction, who it could be. I suspect there's somebody else who knows the identity of the jogger that we did not become aware of, and there are probably other people who knew the identity and did not, of course, come forward."

A year after the jogger confronted me, Jackie Judd, a reporter with ABC, sent Dan a photograph of a man whom she suspected was my "jogger." A lot of people suspected him. His name was Cody Shearer.

Shearer's twin sister, Brooke Shearer, was director of the White House Fellowship Program and she was married to Deputy Secretary of State Strobe Talbott. As Talbott's brother-in-law, Cody Shearer once decided he was going to go save the world from war criminal Radovan Karadzic, one of the awful Bosnians who led the Serbian bloodshed that left hundreds of thousands of people dead or missing. Cody went there making diplomatic passes and setting up meetings with Karadzic's lieutenants. Though he was just Strobe Talbott's brother-in-law, he tried to pull off the impression that he worked with Talbott and the State Department. According to an article by the Associated Press, "The Bosnian Serbs persuaded Shearer to support their goal of partitioning Bosnia." The State Department flipped and went to pains to convince Bosnia's government that Shearer was acting on his own, not for the United States.[4]

While he was there, Shearer became big news in the European press and the newspapers published his picture. Jackie Judd with ABC had a colleague in Europe who saw Shearer's picture in a paper and sent it to her.

Jackie was working on my story and had found out about a private investigator, Jared Stern, who said he was positive that I had told the truth—that the jogger had approached and threatened me. Jackie had been talking with Dan frequently so she sent the picture to him and Dan gave it to me. He caught hell from the FBI for giving it to me without telling the investigators first, because then they couldn't have me do a proper lineup.

Still, after all those months, I looked at the picture and I thought it was Shearer. I had spoken with the jogger for a few minutes, looking into his eyes when he threatened my children. I do not think I would forget such a man's face!

The man in Judd's photo was Cody Shearer, who had direct ties to the Clintons. At some point he had worked for Terry Lenzner, who owned a Washington D.C. investigation firm, Investigative Group International. The FBI investigators looked into it thoroughly. On the one hand, I was told that Shearer had an "airtight" and "ironclad" alibi but another source told me that it was "un-checkable." In fact, when prosecutors for the Office of the Independent Counsel questioned Clinton aide Sid Blumenthal on it, he said that Cody Shearer "was in California during the so-called jogging incident, had the documents to prove it." In fact, Blumenthal claimed that Shearer's seatmate on a "trip back from Los Angeles to Washington happened to be former secretary of state Warren Christopher."[5] David Schippers, chief investigative counsel for the House Judiciary Committee, said he did not think it was Cody Shearer. "I think they recruited somebody to come up from Arkansas," he said. So I do not know who the jogger was. All I know is that I was up against the Clinton machine, which had unlimited power and money. With those resources, I figured any alibi—or any "jogger"—could be arranged.

Monica

After my deposition, I was in the middle of a media storm.

One evening I came down the road toward my house and there was a car sitting on the side of the road, just outside my driveway. I pulled up next to the car. "Are you looking for somebody?" I said. "What are you doing here?"

"Ah, no," they said. "We're kind of lost..."

"Oh really?"

They didn't recognize me, and I drove on through my gate and down my driveway. That's when they realized it was me and they had missed their shot. They called from their cell phones and begged me, "Please, please, please talk to us!" They were from a New York newspaper. "Our editor is going to be really mad if we come back without an interview."

That kind of thing happened a lot, but it was nothing. The media storm was about to become a hurricane. Barely two weeks after my deposition, on January 21, I turned on the *Today Show* and looked into the face of Linda Tripp. A major story had hit the news: Clinton had had an affair with a White House intern and, indeed, Linda was smack in the middle of it. She was close friends with the intern—Monica Lewinsky.

I thought, *Monica? Monica...* It was so familiar. I'd heard that name. I thought back to the conversation I had on the phone with Linda, when someone else had beeped in.

I called a mutual friend who had worked in the Counsel's Office with Linda and me and I said, "Are you watching television this morning?" The press cornered Linda coming out of her house and she looked awful. My heart sank. I felt bad for her. The images of Linda at that time were selected to make her look more ominous.

"Those horrible photos helped the White House defame me," Linda acknowledged in a 2001 article in *George Magazine.* "I wanted to sink into the earth, disappear, come out different-looking. I tried to change my appearance many times to make it less offensive, but I didn't know how. Which is why I decided to have plastic surgery."[6]

Late-night television dished out a steady stream of jokes and said terrible things about her. The press was brutal to her, just brutal. I felt sorry for her. She was always down on herself about her appearance, so that must have been an extremely bad time for her. The press made fun of everything, from her hair to her clothes to her nose. Nothing was off limits.

Linda had two teenagers and her relationship with them up until that time had been like typical mothers with teenage children—not good, just constant battling. But the media was so mean that her children rallied to her. And they really did.

Linda was also trashed for betraying her friendship with poor young Monica. Linda later commented on that. "Friends don't ask friends to commit a crime," she said on *Larry King Live* in 1999. "The notion that I would bastardize my values, my sense of integrity, for a young woman with whom I had worked for a year and a half and commit a crime was not ever an option."[7]

Early in the scandal, Clinton confided in Dick Morris, who later wrote that Clinton said, "'Ever since I became president I've had to shut myself down, sexually I mean,' he told me. 'But I screwed up with this girl. I didn't do what they said I did, but I may have done enough that I cannot prove my innocence.'"[8]

As the scandal steamrolled, Morris conducted a survey for Clinton "that indicated while the voters would, indeed, forgive the adultery, they would not overlook perjury," he wrote in *Re-*

writing History, a Hillary biography. "Misunderstanding my advice, he decided to keep on lying. And he did it in the most emphatic way possible, wagging his finger on national television."[9]

"My own feelings about the Clintons changed as I saw their tactics in defending against impeachment," Morris wrote. "I could not countenance the Clintons' use of secret police digging up dirt on innocent people, a tactic that turned my stomach."[10]

Linda

Clinton's credibility and defense suffered another blow when the press found out about Monica Lewinsky's "talking points" memo. Monica had given it to Linda Tripp on January 14, telling her what to say to the grand jury about my incident in the Oval Office. Monica claimed to have written the "talking points" herself but the notion that Monica wrote the document was widely discredited. Nearly everyone agreed the memo was "far too complicated" for Monica. It also contained information about which Monica would have had little knowledge.

In essence, the memo told Linda to say that nothing had happened to me in the Oval Office. It told Linda, "You now do not believe that what she claimed happened really happened. You now find it completely plausible that she herself smeared her lipstick, untucked her blouse..."[11] Branding me the liar, the memo told Linda that Monica was going to lie, the president was going to lie, and Linda must do the same.

Finally, in 1999, Linda Tripp came clean. Appearing on *Larry King Live*, she set the record straight. "What I would like to get across if nothing else," Linda told King, "is the fact that I became aware, in July of '97 when the Kathleen Willey story was just beginning to surface, that the president did call a meeting at the White House, summoned Monica late at night to that meeting...for one purpose, to get me to sign on to the lie...about Kathleen, not about Monica."[12]

It is likely that Clinton gave Monica the "talking points" memo at that meeting. It is also likely that he was the author.

Linda added that after the *Drudge Report* came out, she was "being solicited to commit a crime." She said, "Remember...I wasn't asked to commit a crime because of Monica Lewinsky. It was all about Kathleen Willey. And Monica to the extent that she was having an intimate relationship with the president was my friend, passing messages to me, from the president: You must lie. You must lie. You must be a team player. You are a political appointee. This how you save your job."[13]

To confirm, King asked Linda, "The felony they wanted to commit was?"

"Perjury for him in the Paula Jones case," Linda replied, "which had nothing to do with Monica. It had all to do with Kathleen Willey."[14]

"I had the information," Linda continued. "I knew I was going to be deposed. I knew I was being set up by the president and his lawyer as a liar, had been already in the media," Linda told Larry King. "Let's not forget what I was facing. I'm going to lie, he's going to lie, we are all going to lie. If you don't lie, perjury, jail, or worse. There were threats."[15]

In fact, Linda received some very ominous messages. Monica "began relaying implied threats from the president about my safety, the safety of my children," Linda told Nancy Collins of *George Magazine* in 2000. "That the Clintons would always know my whereabouts, and...I would never be able to stop looking over my shoulder. That losing my job would be the least of my worries." One time, she said, before the president's deposition in the Jones case, "Someone left a 'body count' on my chair at work...a list naming the people who were dead...in close association with the Clintons."[16] There was a note that read, "Thought you might find this of interest," attached to the paper, but the handwriting was not Monica's.

Joanne

I was glued to the television. Morning until night, I flipped through the channels, dreading it all and thinking, *What are they saying about me now?* After a few days, Patrick came in. "Mom, you're out of here!" he said. "You have got to get out of here. Just go lie in the sun someplace." He bought me an airline ticket.

I had heard about the Turks and Caicos Islands in the Caribbean from Nate Landow. Of course, Nate stayed at the Parrot Cay Resort, which is popular with celebrities, but I found an affordable bed and breakfast. When I arrived, the proprietor, Joanne, met me at my bungalow. "Don't worry, Mrs. Willey, I know who you are," she said. "I have a relative who is with the Secret Service and I assure you, you'll be safe here."

I was dumbfounded. I was in the middle of nowhere and this woman knew who I was? Here I was going to get the hell *away* from all this, and she had family who worked for the federal government? So much for anonymity. It freaked me out!

The islands were a great place, though, and I found peace and tranquility there for a week. Joanne ran a little motel and a few bungalows. Mine was remote, which was perfect. The room was dreary and sparse, but it was quaint, clean, and it was on the water! For six days I relaxed on the beach, read, and walked. I felt like a chip in a vortex and I pondered my future. I breathed in my surroundings, the beautiful breeze and the aqua water — a color I'd never seen before. Joanne proved supremely helpful and friendly, driving me from my bungalow to her dining room for meals twice a day.

On the fourth day, Joann showed up unexpectedly. "You've got a big emergency," she said. "Dan's calling."

Oh my God! I thought, *Why would he track me down? Why would he call me here?* I jumped in her car, wondering what had happened. I had given him the number for emergencies. I got on the phone, out of breath, dry-mouthed, and shaking, trying to steel myself for whatever news I was about to hear.

"Well," Dan said, "we've been invited to the dance."

What a way to put it! I had been subpoenaed to testify before Ken Starr's grand jury.

But there was more.

"Uncle Bob called me today," Dan added. "He said you'll be needing a criminal attorney. He recommended Plato Cacheris."

"Why the hell do I need Plato Cacheris?" I snapped. "He's one of the best *criminal* lawyers in Washington! Why would I need *him*? I have done nothing wrong!"

I felt threatened by the suggestion. To me, his implication was obvious: If I told my story under oath, I would be in big trouble. I would face perjury charges. Dan didn't see it as a threat, but I absolutely did.

"Bob suggested that I was out of my league," Dan later said. "He told me that Plato Cacheris should represent Kathleen," and that Cacheris would do it. But, Dan added, "I told Bob that Kathleen had not committed any crimes and that she certainly could not afford Mr. Cacheris. Bob told me that money was not an issue, that it would all be taken care of."[17]

A few months later, on *Larry King Live*, Bennett's story was at odds with Dan's. Bennett told Larry King that he called Dan and said, "Dan, I wouldn't come down to Richmond and close a commercial real estate transaction. You better get somebody who knows this business." Bennett also told Larry that Dan "asked me for a recommendation, and I gave him a recommendation. I gave him a very fine lawyer, I gave him Plato Cacheris."[18]

Dan eventually talked to Cacheris, a very expensive lawyer, who told Dan, "Money is not an issue here." Regardless, by June of 1998, Cacheris was busy. He was representing Monica Lewinsky![19]

Julie Steele

I frequently went to Dan's office to meet with FBI agents and federal prosecutors with Ken Starr's investigation. As a cooperating witness for the Office of the Independent Counsel, I was interviewed and questioned on many occasions for eight or nine hours at a stretch. They took notes in longhand on yellow legal pads, with no recording devices whatsoever—at least not that I knew of. Those agents probably questioned me for more than seventy-five hours total. It was exhausting.

During all this questioning, they asked me about a relationship I'd had in 1995 with a younger man who was a soccer coach, a couple of years after I lost Ed. I had a hard time in this relationship and I confided this to Julie Steele. He hurt me, and I wanted to shake him up and make him think twice before he treated another woman as badly as he treated me. So, after a while, I lied to him and told him I was pregnant. It was stupid and wrong, the worst mistake I've ever made in a relationship. When the FBI asked me about that relationship, I was ashamed of it—embarrassed about what I had done—and I denied everything. I did not know it at the time, but even if you're just answering FBI agents' questions, it is a felony to lie to them. If I had known that, I would have just told the truth because I wasn't as interested in concealing it as I was embarrassed and didn't see the relevance. Were I Hillary Clinton, I might have said, "I think those questions are out of bounds," as she did during her Senate race when reporters asked her about a rumored affair with Vince Foster.[20] Or I could have mimicked the Clintons' favorite legal response, "I do not recall." But I didn't. I lied. And Julie, who was already being romanced by Clinton's team, had told the FBI about my lie to the soccer coach and the FBI found him. The prosecutors now had to "rehabilitate" me as a witness. Later, I passed their polygraph test, which resolved the issue of my credibility for them, but it didn't help in court. And I was upset again with Julie Steele for betraying my confidence. The episode was the kind of thing women only tell other women, if anyone.

On my way in to one of the meetings with the investigators, I parked my car in the garage and caught a fleeting glimpse of Julie. I called out to her. She could have kept on walking, but she came back and talked to me. We exchanged greetings.

"What are you doing here?" I asked her.

"Oh, I'm here on business."

I said, "I just have to ask you, Julie, why did you sell me out to the *Enquirer*? Why did you do that? You took my secrets, things I trusted you with, every picture we'd ever taken with me and Ed and the kids... What were you thinking?"

"Oh, I don't know," she said. "The story was already out, and everybody knew what was going on. It was no big deal."

It was *one* day after Drudge ran the story! But she blew it off as if she hadn't done anything wrong.

Soon after that, all the lawyers in Richmond were together at a bar meeting. When it ended, Jim Roberts, one of the top lawyers in the city of Richmond, sidled up to Dan. Jim and Ed had known each other well for years. Dan didn't run in the same circles as Roberts did, so Dan didn't know him.

Roberts said to Dan, "One of these days we've got to sit down and talk about this Julie Steele thing."

"Anytime," Dan said. "Anytime..."

"She'd come to see us and we talked to her about signing an affidavit," Roberts told Dan. "And all I can tell you is she got some phone call from Washington and all of a sudden she was in a big hurry to get down here to sign that affidavit."

So when I saw Julie in Dan's parking lot that day, she wasn't there on business. She was there to see Roberts, to sign that affidavit about me!

Julie had blown into Richmond wanting people to think that she was from high society. When I met her in 1978, she wanted me to think that her family owned Ashland Oil. At the time I didn't have any reason to doubt it, but years later I found out that her father only worked there. Just a nobody from Nowheresville, Julie came from Ashland, Kentucky, but she preferred a prettier story.

Her grandmother left her some antique jewelry, and Julie was always making a big deal about going to get the "family jewels" out of the safety deposit box at the bank. I think she probably grew up relatively privileged, but she certainly wasn't anything that she portrayed herself to be.

In fact, Julie's life was not pretty. She told me her mother was an alcoholic before she died, and then her father came out of the closet—and this was back when *nobody* came out of the closet, much less your *father*! Julie was really sick with anorexia. And her husband, John, left her for another woman.

Julie always wanted to climb the social ladder, wanted to be on the inside and involved in politics, but she never quite got there. She begged me to get her a job as a White House volunteer, which I never considered. Still, she perpetuated the image that she was filthy rich. The truth was, she was more like me, a soccer mom. Julie had a little more education than I did—a college degree or close to it—but it was hard for her to find a job. We both went through that. And she had mortgaged her house to the hilt after her husband left her.

So we were friends, girlfriends, and I trusted her, told her everything, and she told me her secrets, too. But she was pure drama. Julie lived in a world of high intrigue, blaming all of her troubles on her gay father, drunk mother, and anorexia. With a stack of self-help books on her bedside table, she was always victim to the designer disease of the month. A few times I got exasperated and didn't talk to her for a few years but eventually I let myself get sucked back in.

One time after I hadn't seen her for a year or two, I was pumping gas and saw her going into a 7-Eleven. She was nearly fifty years old—and pregnant!

"Wow!" I said, "Are you married?"

"No," she said. She had gotten pregnant and decided to have the baby so she "wouldn't be lonely anymore." She told me how dramatically things had changed since we'd had our babies back in the 1970s. She was going through Lamaze and loving every minute of it. But they missed something on the amnio. When the baby was born, his days were numbered. A very beautiful baby, he died when he was three days old. Julie was a mess. She had the viewing in her living room.

She was desperate to get pregnant again and tried everything before finally deciding to adopt. She went to Romania. She told me she literally drove from village to village to find somebody who wanted to give up a baby and found a young girl willing to do that. Money changed hands. Julie brought the infant home and named him Adam.

Michael Radutzky

All the press wanted me to talk to them, to go on their shows, and they romanced me. They constantly schmoozed me, looking for anything to motivate me to do an interview. *60 Minutes* did the biggest schmooze job on me, using my relationship with Julie Steele to get me on their show.

The *60 Minutes* producers went to Dan first. Dan told me that they were in Richmond and wanted to talk to me about doing *60 Minutes*. So I met with the producers, Michael Radutzky and Trevor Nelson. They had spent a month in Richmond and had a notebook full of information. They told me that they had figured out why Julie Steele wouldn't corroborate my story, why she had branded me a liar. Julie had a reason.

Radutzky and Nelson said, "We have every reason to believe" that White House advisor Mickey Kantor, a close friend of Bill Clinton's, had been seen in Richmond a number of times. They said they had evidence that Kantor had found out that Adam's adoption was not legal. They told me that the Clinton people were strong-arming Julie, threatening to expose that the adoption wasn't valid. They assured me that the evidence was strong and Radutzky expressed his own disgust at the Clinton machine.

"No mother should be threatened with the loss of her child," I said to Radutzky. "No mother! I don't care what Julie did to me. That's her *child*."

It was an "aha" moment for me. "Now I get it," I said. "Now I see what's going on." As angry as I was at Julie for selling my picture to the *National Enquirer*, I finally understood why she was lying about me.

I wanted to expose the Clinton administration's tactics in threatening Julie and her son. Judge Starr had asked me not talk to the media until after I testified, so I agreed to do *60 Minutes* after my grand jury appearance on March 10. We set the interview for March 12 at a suite in the Jefferson Hotel in Richmond. It would air on Sunday, March 15. Dan, my attorney, sanctioned the interview, though we had nothing in writing about its scope. We didn't ask to see the proof behind their story that the Clinton people were blackmailing Julie. We trusted the *60 Minutes* producers to air the story as they presented it to us, which was a serious mistake.

Julie

I was caught up in the biggest legal case in American politics and my friend Julie had sold me out to a tabloid and called me a liar. But the story Radutzky told me made me sick. I decided to call Julie.

I said, "I know why you're doing all this. I've just been told that you've been threatened with Adam's adoption. I know that somebody from the White House went to the Romanian embassy.

I know the whole story." I told her I would support her and that I wanted to expose the truth about Clinton's strong-arm tactics.

She freaked out. "How do you know that? Nobody's going to take my baby!"

"I'm just telling you," I said, "I know why you're doing this, and you know what? I don't blame you! If these people are holding this over your head…"

I didn't know it at the time, but by then Julie was already the darling of the White House. She had agreed to contradict my testimony and they loved her for it. And Julie loved being loved. Though she was strapped for money, she suddenly had a powerhouse Washington lawyer, Nancy Luque, who happened to be an attorney for the DNC and was close to Hillary. Julie put up a website at the time to solicit money for her legal fund, but I imagine her legal bills were "taken care of," the same way Uncle Bob had recommended Plato Cacheris to me, saying money wouldn't be an issue.

So I was up against it and they got me. With Luque holding her hand, Julie claimed that I was the one who threatened her child. With her lawyers, she claimed that I had told Ken Starr about the adoption questions and that Starr threatened her, told her that if she didn't tell the truth they were going to take Adam away from her. It was all lies. I know Ken Starr as a prosecutor and as a man. He is a good man who would never do such a thing.

The Grand Jury

On March 9, Patrick and I checked into a Washington hotel, using assumed names. The next morning, the FBI picked us up in their van and drove us to the Alfred J. Prettyman Federal Court Building. Hordes of press awaited us.

I appeared before the grand jury while Dan and Patrick waited in the hall. I testified all day with a lunch break and shorter breaks in the afternoon. A few jurors fell asleep in their chairs. Patrick went out for a short walk and the press swarmed him. During the last break, the jury forewoman took me aside, out of view of the others. "I want to commend you," she said. "I believe you and I think you are a role model."

The next day, I opened up *USA Today* and my picture was on the front page. I was what they call in the business a "get." Every news organization wanted to talk to me.

Ed Bradley

On March 12, I taped the *60 Minutes* show at the Jefferson Hotel in downtown Richmond. Ed Bradley interviewed me and he covered the blackmailing of Julie Steele, but he was much more interested in the details of what Clinton did to me. Dan watched the interview on a monitor with Radutzky and Nelson. When it was over, Radutzky said to me, "Kathleen, you are a national hero!"

But, as Dan says, "The *60 Minutes* producer, Radutzky, significantly misled us regarding the story that they were going to tell. They told us that the emphasis would be on Ms. Steele and the pressure brought on her by the White House."[21] It sure as hell didn't happen that way.

On Sunday morning, March 15, I disappeared to the Florida Keys to be away when the show aired. It was a great place to go. I was in a new relationship, which was exciting, and I tried to enjoy the Florida sun and forget what I left behind. Seeing myself talking to Ed Bradley on national television felt like an out-of-body experience. It overwhelmed me. There was nothing about Julie, not one word about her or the blackmail! They didn't air that story at all. It was all about the incident in the Oval Office.

Dan called me after the show. He was livid. "Where's the goddamn story?"

In hindsight, it's possible that Radutzky's blackmail story was only part of a strategy to get me on the air. He and Nelson had been in Richmond for a month doing their homework and talking to Julie Steele. They may well have seen Mickey Kantor in Richmond, or knew that he had been there, and maybe they had heard a rumor that he was threatening Julie. I don't know what evidence they had to substantiate the story they told me. But to this day I think it was true. I don't think *60 Minutes* producers would lie about something that significant to get me on their show. I don't think they would go that far. I may be wrong, but I don't think so.

A former *CBS News* producer recently told me that "guys like Radutzky do these kinds of things." When a story emerges about a novice like me, a producer will work on the details of the story and while doing so also uncover something else. They bring that side story to the subject they're after—like me—and say, "Look what we've uncovered!" They'll share the information and the subject will fall for it, just as I did. They do their story and then they abandon you. The former CBS producer told me Radutzky has a habit of doing this.[22]

Clinton and his people did not want to attack me too directly, because I wasn't the "usual" kind of accuser. I was a *Democrat*. They couldn't play the "right-wing conspiracy" song and dance about me. And since I was a widow, a White House volunteer, and a Clinton fundraiser, they couldn't paint me as a slut either. They had to treat me more discreetly. But they smeared me nonetheless.

The administration sent their soldiers to saturate the airwaves with attacks on me and my motives. White House advisors launched a quiet campaign against me, anonymously speaking to reporters about my background, intimating that I was so emotionally distraught that I was confused by our encounter.

But Kelly Ann Fitzpatrick and other conservatives argued on my behalf. Appearing on *Hardball with Chris Matthews* the day after my *60 Minutes* interview aired, Fitzpatrick said, "If they start attacking Kathleen Willey, even subtly, as overemotional and so distraught that she mistook the president's comfort and patent trademark hugs and a kiss on the forehead, I seem to think that, even in the darkest moments of despair, when a man fondles your breast, you're not confusing it with a hug and some comfort."[23]

Patricia Ireland also went on the offensive. "I've already seen in the newspapers here an anonymous quote that she 'only wanted to hang around with the president.' We've seen comments that she was a 'remarkably untalented woman for the positions she got.' I mean I think already the attacks are coming," Ireland charged. "I don't think that they're going to undermine the credibility of her demeanor, of her apparent lack of political or financial motivation, and the reality that she did not want to come forward with her story."[24]

Their careful strategy started with Clinton's statements of confusion and disappointment, which made him look like a victim. Like a broken record, Clinton's denial of my allegations was constantly played on television. "I have said that nothing improper happened," Clinton said, looking dismayed. "I am mystified and disappointed by this turn of events and I have a very clear memory of the meeting and I told the truth."

The next day, I saw on the news that the Clinton administration had released the letters I'd written to him. I was shocked! Many months earlier, the Jones lawyers had subpoenaed Clinton for any and all material relating to me but the White House provided only vague excuses and couldn't produce my letters. But once I appeared on *60 Minutes*, voilà! Like magic, they found them.

It felt awful. I kept thinking, *That's not for public knowledge! I wrote those letters to him.* Once again, I felt betrayed. All those years I'd helped Clinton and the Democrats, all those years of my life, all the time, money, effort, and passion that I had devoted to Democratic causes—and they repay me by humiliating me?

The media, no doubt encouraged by the Clinton machine, characterized my letters as "adoring" and "admiring," zeroing in on incidental words, such as when I told Clinton I was his "number one fan" when I thanked him for helping us defeat Oliver North in Virginia, or when I signed my letters "fondly," which I always did. I didn't save that for Clinton. Florence Graves and Jacqueline Sharkey wrote in the *Nation*, "Questions about Willey's credibility surfaced when the White House released a stack of effusive letters she had sent Clinton."[25] Not one of my letters could accurately be characterized as "effusive" but that certainly didn't stop them from attempting to undermine my credibility.

They also misconstrued a telephone message that Nancy Hernreich gave the president from me. As Bill Plante reported on *CBS Evening News*, "Two days after the incident there is a phone call record saying that there's a message from Kathleen Willey telling the president, 'You can call her anytime.'"[26] The White House, the reporter, and many others failed to note that this call was not just two days after the incident, but also two days after my husband's death. That was the day when Nancy Hernreich called me and told me she was sure the president would want to speak with me. I replied, "He can call me anytime."

Patricia Ireland eventually defended my letters to Clinton— sort of. She argued that I could have been assaulted by Clinton and subsequently written the letters. "I think the letters are an indication that she wanted to not burn those bridges," Ireland said, "which in some apparent sense may be the only allies and resources that she thought she had."[27]

"This is every woman's fear in a workplace with a superior male boss," said Kelly Ann Fitzpatrick on *Hardball with Chris Matthews*, "creating some type of a hostile work environment where you feel like you can't ask certain questions, you can't be alone with the boss, you can't show up certain times, you can't wear certain clothes..."[28]

Everywhere I turned, pundits used the letters to malign my credibility and refute my account of the incident. People seemed to accept the interpretation that since I tried to remain on good terms with Clinton after the incident, it must not have happened. But that presumes that what Clinton did to me was so devastating and traumatic, I should have been terrified of him and hated his guts. If he had raped me, obviously, I would likely have felt that way and probably would have left my job at the White House. But Clinton did not rape me. My experience with him showed me what the man is capable of and warned me to be mindful of the potential danger he presented. But he did not victimize me! Clinton violated my person. In fact, he sexually assaulted me, which is a crime. But I was not traumatized by it. He degraded himself in my presence and I was embarassed for him. Unfortunately, starting in their teenage years, many women have experienced similar abuses. It was wrong and slimy and predatory, but it was not devastating. I never saw myself as his victim. And I still needed the man's professional help. Why in the world would I have cut off all communication—to my own detriment?

Few people understood that, at that time in my life, Clinton was the only person who could help me. I was desperate after Ed died. My whole world crashed in on me. I was a soccer mom who didn't finish college and I had just lost my husband. I wasn't trained to do anything other than be a homemaker and work in politics. I needed a job, so I turned to him.

I never asked for this fight. I decided that I was going to act like it hadn't happened because I never wanted anyone to know what he did to me that day. I told only my closest friends. Other than them, it would have gone to my grave with me.

"Kirk"

Patrick called. He was staying at my house while I was in Florida. He told my boyfriend, "I think you need to hear something." Patrick played a message that had been left on my answering machine. It was a man's voice. "My name is Kirk," he said. "And I just want to warn you, there are people out there who want to hurt you. I will call you back tomorrow night." That's all he said.

I couldn't hear their conversation, but I could see that it was serious. "What?" I said. "What's going on?"

"Never mind," my boyfriend told me. I never heard the recording. The FBI was interested in it and took my whole phone because it was digital, not a tape.

The next night, two female FBI agents from Miami drove down to the Keys and brought in elaborate electronics to trap the call and automatically diverted my calls from home to Florida. We sat late into the evening and talked, but he never called again.

I figured he lost his nerve. Whoever he was, he had been hired to rattle me, to let me know that I was being followed. And he broke every rule of the private investigators' code of conduct. I mean, PIs don't notify their subjects and tell them to be careful. Do they?

I stayed in Florida for three weeks while my boyfriend ran his charter business in the Keys. He was out working every day and I relaxed, read, and talked to friends on the phone. I finally became bored stiff and said, "Look, I need a project."

He had built a sailboat, the *Egret*. It was a beautiful wooden boat, his labor of love. "The *Egret* needs sanding," he said with a hopeful tone.

"Well," I said, "tell me what that's all about."

He set me up with a hand-held sander and a face mask and I ground away on that boat for hours on end. It was a great stress reliever, just mindless sanding. I came to understand why people fall in love with wooden boats. You just can't fall in love with fiberglass, but I sure fell in love with the *Egret*.

When I finally left Florida, some people in the airport recognized me. On the airplane, nobody said anything to me, but when the plane landed, the whole crew stood at the cockpit, saying "Bye-bye" over and over as all the passengers deplaned. When I walked by them, they all said in unison, "We believe you."

That really got me. I almost started to cry.

In the months after Drudge leaked my story, my life turned upside down. The world that I had started to rebuild was once again threatened by invasions of privacy and threats to my security. The media firestorm made me a figure of public notoriety, which compromised my freedom to lead a normal life, which I desperately wanted and needed.

But the firestorm would not abate. I had aroused the ire of the Clinton administration and was about to bear the full force of its fury. Through their henchmen and minions, Bill and Hillary Clinton would wage nothing less than a media war to undercut my credibility and the credibility of any woman who dared tell the truth about Bill's sexual advances. That war would reveal the chronic hypocrisy of those who advocate for women's rights, as none of them—not Democrats nor feminists nor Hillary Clinton, an alleged promoter of women's rights—would come to the aid of the women he had assaulted. It was me versus the machine, and I was scared.

CHAPTER EIGHT

SMEAR CAMPAIGN

"EVERYBODY IS FAIR GAME, simply for being on the other side," Sid Blumenthal wrote in the *New Yorker* when the Clintons were moving into the White House. "Humiliating one's prey, not merely defeating one's foes, is central to the process." No doubt this nasty blueprint for political success struck a chord with Hillary. According to Carl Bernstein, who wrote the Hillary biography *A Woman in Charge*, "His was a message that Hillary could embrace, along with its author." She hired him.[1] Blumenthal helped write some of Clinton's speeches and, in 1997, went to work in the White House as assistant to the president.

And assist he did.

By the time Bill and Hillary were up to their necks in Whitewater and Jones and Monica and me, Blumenthal conducted and collected "copious research on almost every aspect of the political, professional, and private lives of Starr, his prosecutors, the Paula Jones gang, the Republicans in Congress...and...the individual mercenaries of the right."[2] He would eventually be questioned in detail as to how he went about collecting that "copious research."

When Monica's story came out, Blumenthal cheered blindly for his team. Like a cult follower, he blamed Hillary's vast right-wing conspiracy. "The right-wing politics that had forced the scandal were alien and unknown to much of the White House senior staff," Blumenthal wrote in *The Clinton Wars*, his eight-hundred-page account of his years in the Clinton White House. "To them, what the right was doing seemed far-fetched, so impossibly convoluted, that they couldn't quite credit it."[3] It was quite a stretch of the imagination that White House aides would swallow the story that my testimony—and Monica's and Paula's and Gennifer's—were creations of right-wing politics, but the Clintons' brainwashed minions chose to swallow it. And Hillary's boy Sid served up the bait.

Blumenthal says, "Part of my duty as a good soldier, first knight, was to try to get the right story out. I felt I had to go into a journalistic mode, but I couldn't be a journalist myself. I could suggest information, ideas, and leads to writers willing to examine them rather than follow the story line as Starr set it out." Thus he admitted—and justified—his dissemination not of facts, but "ideas" and "suggested information," particularly about Monica Lewinsky and me.[4]

Blumenthal said Clinton told him that Lewinsky was a "stalker" who had come on to him. And Clinton had, of course, rejected her. Word of Clinton's characterization of Monica as a stalker happened to leak out and Monica naturally heard it. Needless to say, she didn't appreciate it. But how did it leak out? Starr eventually subpoenaed Blumenthal, demanding to know which journalists he'd spoken with about the Monica scandal—and what he had told them. Of course, he denied giving any reporters any information about any of us.

In his bio of the Clintons, "Sid Vicious" even glazed over the White House debate and decision to violate federal privacy laws and release my personal letters. Busy in Puerto Rico at the time, Sid implied that, while attending a conference there, he danced the conga and drank rum at a Bacardi party.[5]

He was, in fact, in Puerto Rico, but he was actually having frantic long-distance conversations with Hillary in the White House. With my damaging *60 Minutes* interview imminent, they discussed my letters. According to Larry Klayman of Judicial Watch, it was Hillary, in concert with Sid, who approved the release of my private letters—in violation of federal privacy laws. When Larry Klayman of Judicial Watch filed suit against Clinton, he obtained responses to interrogatories from many of the key players inside the White House. In his response to the Klayman action, Blumenthal acknowledged that he had conversations with senior White House staff about the letters but he "cannot recall with whom he had these conversations, nor precisely when."[6]

In an intriguing twist, George Archibald, writing for the *Washington Times*, pointed out that while Hillary denied any involvement in Filegate, her role in the release of my letters is indicative of Hillary's misuse of White House files. According to Archibald, Judge Royce C. Lamberth said "misuse" of materials from my White House file "could prove to be circumstantial evidence of file misuse aimed at the [Filegate] plaintiffs."[7]

Klayman alleged, "Sidney Blumenthal and Mrs. Clinton also participated in, recommended, and furthered the release of the letters." Blumenthal's response to the interrogatory validates this. "On or about March 14, 1998, Mr. Blumenthal left on an official trip to Puerto Rico. While in Puerto Rico, on March 16, 1998, Mr. Blumenthal spoke to Mrs. Clinton by telephone. Mr. Blumenthal recalls that he and Mrs. Clinton discussed Ms. Willey's letters to the president, and that the letters were inconsistent with what Ms. Willey had said on *60 Minutes*. Both Mrs. Clinton and Mr. Blumenthal agreed that the letters should be released."[8]

Urging the press to discredit me, Sid Vicious told reporters that, while my poll numbers looked good then, I would have no credibility by the end of the week. He turned out to be psychic. Blumenthal would have America believe it was a coincidence that the press suddenly had my letters and other private information about my past. It must also have been a miracle that the exact words the president used to smear Monica Lewinsky to Blumenthal were also all over the news.

Clinton's chief advisor Bruce Lindsey was also involved in releasing my files to the public. In responding to a Judicial Watch interrogatory, Lindsey revealed that when he learned from Linda Tripp that I had spoken to Isikoff, he mentioned it to Nancy Hernreich, who told him she had seen my letters to the president. Nancy gave the letters to Lindsey, who kept them in a drawer in his office! Before the *60 Minutes* interview aired, the White House received a transcript, which Lindsey reviewed. Lindsey then called Clinton at Camp David "to advise him of the recommendation to release the letters. The president concurred in that recommendation."[9] Lindsey began preparing to discredit me *a year* before I was dragged into the public eye![10]

Hitch

Author and columnist Christopher Hitchens, a friend of Sid's at the time, reported that he had a conversation with Blumenthal over lunch on March 19, 1998. A journalist who then had twenty-six years of experience, Hitchens was both a social friend and "journalistic acquaintance" of Blumenthal's. Hitchens's wife, Carol Blue, also came to lunch.

According to Hitchens, they discussed me. Blumenthal acknowledged that my "poll numbers were high but would fall and would not look so good in a few days." More recently, Hitchens confirmed, "The way he spoke about Kathleen Willey suggested that she would soon be discredited." At the time, Hitchens thought Blumenthal's remarks didn't seem significant so he "didn't pay very close attention." Hitchens assumed that my fall from grace would take the form of an accusation of a "cash for trash" book. But, Hitchens added, "I particularly remember that he said he could go to jail for what he was doing."[11]

Questioned under oath about discrediting me to Hitchens and other journalists, Blumenthal flat-out denied having done any such thing. In his book, he said of Hitchens's account, "I had no recollection of saying that or anything like it."[12] As a result, Hitchens was further drawn in to the ordeal. In February of 1999, he provided an affidavit about the conversation.

Hitchens wanted to testify against Clinton, not against his old friend. In the affidavit, he didn't include Blumenthal's comment that he could go to jail for what he was doing, but iterated that he and Blumenthal met over lunch and "Blumenthal had stated that Monica Lewinsky had been a 'stalker' and that the president was 'the victim' of a predatory and unstable sexually demanding young woman." In fact, Hitchens said, "Mr. Blumenthal used the word 'stalker' several times" about Ms. Lewinsky, and "advised us that this version of the facts was not generally understood."

In his affidavit, Hitchens also said that, "During that lunch, Mr. Blumenthal stated that Kathleen Willey's poll numbers were high but would fall and would not look so good in a few days." While Blumenthal later defended himself by saying that he regarded Hitchens as a friend, not a journalist, Hitchens added in his affidavit, "I have knowledge that Mr. Blumenthal recounted to other people in the journalistic community the same story about Monica Lewinsky that he told to me and Carol Blue."[13] In response to Klayman's Judicial Watch interrogatory, Blumenthal admitted that he left a message for Jill Abramson, a *New York Times* reporter, about my letters.[14]

About the calls between Hillary and Blumenthal in Puerto Rico, Hitchens would only add, "Yes, I seem to remember something about Puerto Rico also. But I know more than anyone else on this."[15] Tellingly, after nearly ten years, Hitchens doesn't have much affection for the Clintons. "The prospect of a Hillary presidency," he told me, "makes me want to puke."[16]

Bob Bennett

I returned to Virginia to face the music. The White House had gone into damage control mode even before I appeared on *60 Minutes*. Phone calls and faxes were flying the whole weekend of the show. In his reponse to the Klayman interrogatory, Bruce Lindsey said that "members of the White House Counsel's Office," including deputy counsel Cheryl Mills and White House counsel Charles Ruff, met to discuss my letters. Mike McCurry concurs. He responded that he did not participate in meetings, but believed they may have happened.[17]

Before my interview even aired, Bennett campaigned to get *60 Minutes* not to run it. He told Michael Radutzky and Ed Bradley that I was unreliable and called me a "fucking floozy bimbo flake." That's my buddy, Uncle Bob! When that didn't work, Bennett threatened to sue CBS. Then he and Clinton's press spokesman Mike McCurry met with *60 Minutes* executive producer Don Hewitt. Hewitt offered the president a full hour of rebuttal. Clinton declined. Instead, the White House sent Bennett himself out to badmouth me.

I probably won't ever know if Bennett and others pressured *60 Minutes* to leave out the story of Julie being blackmailed. The producers may have decided that the salacious story of Clinton's assault in the Oval Office was more important, a sexier story.

The day after my *60 Minutes* interview aired, Clinton took the gloves off. "Nothing improper happened," he said at a high school, of all places, in suburban Silver Spring, Maryland. "As you know, the story's been in three different incarnations," he said, inferring that my version, compared to Linda's and Julie's, discredited my claim altogether. "I have said that nothing improper happened," he continued. "I have a very clear memory of the meeting. I told the truth then, I told the truth in the deposition. I am mystified and disappointed by this turn of events."[18]

Ann Lewis and Bennett got out and hit the talk shows. Bennett appeared on *Larry King Live* for the full hour. In his typical style, Larry threw softballs at Bennett, who took the baton from Clinton and played the role of the dismayed victim. First, he blamed *60 Minutes* for not presenting him favorably in his rebuttal video and for editing out forty-some minutes of the videotaped interview. He also whined that *60 Minutes* didn't give the American public the whole story, which was that I was apparently motivated by a financial payoff.

"In fairness to *60 Minutes*, I don't know if they paid her," Bennett said. "I don't know if they knew about a book. I don't know, in fairness to them. But I do know this, when the American people heard that show and when they read the newspapers this morning, they may have had a different opinion this morning if they knew on Thursday or Friday of last week there was a book in the works pushing the *60 Minutes* show to market it."

There was only one problem with all his "fairness to *60 Minutes*." None of his allegations were true!

First, CBS did not pay me for my interview. People think I was paid for the interviews and that I made a fortune, but reputable shows do not pay for stories. If I had to travel, they paid my expenses, but that was all. If anything, I lost money by coming forward because of the legal bills!

About a week later, *CBS News* president Andrew Heyward told the *Washington Post*, "The implication that there was some terrifically important salient material we left out is false."[19]

Larry King Live was not the only show on which Bennet suggested I had done the *60 Minutes* interview to promote a $300,000 book deal. "For a period of time right up until the Thursday or Friday before Miss Willey went on *60 Minutes*, her lawyer Daniel Gecker was hawking a book," Bennett told Matt Lauer on the *Today Show*. "They were pushing the upcoming *60 Minutes* show, saying that this would increase the marketability of the book."[20]

Again, there's only one slight problem with this line: I had no book deal. I needed to do something about my financial situation and thought a book might be a legitimate way for me to tell my side of the story. I asked Dan to contact publisher Michael Viner to see if he was interested. He was. But, Dan says, the $300,000 figure came from a comment Dan made to Viner. My debt was about $300,000 and Dan told him that I could improve my position by that amount through a bankruptcy. Consequently, Dan told him that it would not make sense to do a book deal unless it paid significantly more than that amount.[21] He didn't seem to have much interest in such a book and we didn't pursue it. When I did *60 Minutes*, the interview had nothing to do with conversations between Dan and Viner and it *certainly* had nothing to do with promoting a book.

"Similarly, we never negotiated with any tabloids regarding selling a story," Dan adds. One man claimed that we did, but Dan says, "The gentleman who claimed that was completely unknown to me." Dan was barraged by calls from a "reporter" who said, "We will pay," but Dan always made it clear that I had no interest in the tabloids. In fact, Richard Gooding of the *Star* called Dan and said, "She can name her price." I still wasn't interested.

The episode still leaves the most important question unanswered: Did Radutzky have evidence that Kantor was pressuring Julie on behalf of the White House?

60 Minutes was challenged to reveal the footage from my interview, which would substantiate my version, but they refused, saying they would divulge neither sources nor source material. Radutzky is still a producer for the show so I recently asked him, in writing, if he did in fact tell me that he had evidence that the White House was pressuring Julie. He has not replied, nor has his boss, whom I copied on my letter.

A week after the *60 Minutes* interview aired, they presented a follow-up. Ed Bradley said, "We stand by our story." The broadcast ended with further defense of both the interview and my integrity. "As for money, Mrs. Willey never asked for any money nor did we offer any money." Two months later, I got a handwritten note from Ed Bradley. "What you did was courageous and well done," he wrote. "I have no regrets about the interview. I hope you feel the same."

The Clinton machine didn't just try to refute my *60 Minutes* interview. They attacked me from several angles.

My lawyer was even targeted. The day after my appearance on *60 Minutes*, FedEx delivered a subpoena to Dan from the SEC, "seeking financial information," he said. "They were allegedly investigating whether I was guilty of insider trading." Dan owned a few shares of stock in a bank for which he had served not as a member of the bank's official board but as an advisory board member. According to Dan, he'd never before been subject to such an investigation. "I think it was related to the case," he says, "and I told that to the SEC when I was deposed in connection with the investigation."

Isikoff

After I did *60 Minutes*, I finally went on the record with *Newsweek*, but Michael Isikoff never forgave me for not doing so sooner.

Harolyn Cardozo reportedly told Isikoff—and Starr's grand jury—that I talked about becoming Clinton's mistress. She said I called her after my incident with Clinton and talked at length about how I wanted to advance a relationship with him. According to an article in the *Nation*, Harolyn said, "Willey was gushing about her meeting with the president, saying he had given her a big kiss and hug."[22] Considering Harolyn knew how frantic I was to find Ed that evening and how she came to his funeral a few days later, her story is hardly credible. Harolyn, of course, just happens to be Nathan Landow's daughter. I was a married woman when she says I was supposedly trying to "advance a relationship" with the president, yet a few months later Harolyn set me up with her father and gushed, "You could be my stepmother!" I believe she never forgave me for dropping Nate. It has also crossed my mind that she may have been party to the Clinton smear campaign.

The Clintonistas

Many friends in the loop called me with support, but the media storm was frenzied. Everybody wanted me to be on their shows. Even at my Florida hideaway I received dozens of calls. I heard from Jackie Judd, Jane Pauley, Larry King, and Michael Isikoff. The *60 Minutes* guys kept calling—Michael Radutzky, Ed Bradley, and even Don Hewitt—saying I hadn't told them about the letters. But I had.

Then James Carville, Joe Conason, Gene Lyons, Paul Begala, Julian Epstein, and the rest of the Clinton Goon Squad found Julie Steele. She was heaven-sent, and suddenly she was all over the television. They marched her out and paraded her all over the place.

So the media blitz against me began. All the Clintonistas paraded through the shows, and they all had their talking points. It was ridiculous. On every channel, on all the different shows, the nightly talking heads all said the same things. It was as if they'd each gotten their daily memo: "Things to Say about Kathleen Willey." It was a joke.

One day, they all decided to attack my account of Bullseye's disappearance and my conversation with the jogger. They went on the shows and discussed a man who jogged past my house saying, "Hey, Kathleen, did you ever find your cat?" They made it sound as if I lived in a subdivision and was out watering the lawn! It was *nothing* like that, but that was the way they portrayed it. Of course, not one of them had been down to Powhatan to see what it really was like. They were just soldiers following orders. They had their talking points for the evening, and you could tell they did because they were tripping over each other, repeating themselves and all saying the same things.

Sid Blumenthal had described my appearance on *60 Minutes* as, "Groomed and affluent, wearing a long strand of pearls signifying that she was no Paula Jones, Willey related sordid details to the shocked reporter." The implication that I wore pearls as a ruse is ridiculous. It also reflects an elitism that should never have escaped the liberal press, yet it did. Along with referring to me as a "divorced former airline stewardess," (further evidence of the basic chauvinism at work in the Clinton mind-set), Blumenthal and the Clintonistas often referred to me as a socialite, though I was, in fact, a housewife—a quintessential soccer mom.[23]

One piece of information that may have helped them paint me as a "socialite" was the fact that my daughter went to a well-known girls' school in the west end of Richmond. The west end had the best homes in town. It was the place to live. Other than my daughter, everybody attending the school probably lived within a five-mile radius of the campus, and their parents lived within a five-mile radius, and so did their grandparents. The church and country club were close by, and it was a very enclosed world. Few of them ever ventured south of the river where we lived. Shannon's peers acted as though they couldn't possibly figure out how to find Midlothian because it was out of their sphere. Shannon felt like she didn't belong there and decided on her own to transfer to another school. Still, her stint at that west end school helped brand me as a socialite, which helped them label me with an elitist connotation and imply that I was ideologically opposed to the Democratic candidates to whom I'd given so much of my life.

It was easy for the Clintonistas to brand me this way. They had the bully pulpit. Everyone listened to their erroneous descriptions of me and the other women. We were David against Goliath. How could we refute them with the power that they wielded in condemning us? For the most part, I was very careful about not putting myself out there and subjecting myself to their many ways of maligning my character.

Contrasting what they did to me, they constantly denigrated Paula Jones as trailer trash. Betsey Wright had an interesting observation about her old boss. "Bill Clinton has spent his whole life scared that he's white trash," she said, "and doing whatever he could to try to prove to himself that he isn't."[24] I think Clinton always lived with that childhood image of himself as the little fat kid from the wrong side of the tracks, which is probably still with him today and also part of the reason he is the way he is. Some things you just can't get away from, no matter who you are. I suspect this sort of inferiority complex is at play in his marriage with Hillary and in their denigration of Arkansas natives, particularly women. In any event, the characterizations aimed at the likes of Paula Jones reveal Bill and Hillary's ideological hypocrisy, as they constantly belittled sexually abused women, working-class women, and non-affluent women.

Over many years, I had helped these Democrats, and many others. Not one—not a *one*—gave me any support. Not from a local level, not Chuck Robb, not Virginia's lieutenant governor Don Beyer, nor Bobbie Scott who is in Congress. These are people whom I had helped and they trashed me.

Am I pissed off at the Democrats? Yes, I am!

More, I am disillusioned. Everything the Democrats stood for—everything Clinton stood for—amounted to nothing after what I went through. It is impossible to respect a man like that or his ideology. All it amounts to is hypocrisy.

Later, Alan Colmes interviewed me and I told him I was no longer a Democrat. He acted appalled. "You mean, because of just one thing, all of your political beliefs have changed? Just this?"

"Well, yeah," I said. "A little bit."

"You mean you're not a Democrat? You're thinking like a Republican now?"

I said, "You know, no Democrat came to my aid."

So now that I am older and wiser, I am a "Democrat in recovery."

The Feminists

The feminists were the biggest letdown. As a politically active Democrat, I believed in women's rights, though I was never a militant feminist. Still, I thought I was both "liberated" and strong. I stood up for myself and spoke out against injustice. I became appalled at the way the feminists refused to support me. That really disillusioned me. I kept thinking, *Of course the conservatives are supporting me, but where are the women?*

In the end, even NOW president Patricia Ireland was despicable. She gave Clinton a pass, dismissing his behavior by saying, "All of us knew he was a snake when we voted for him."[25] When Juanita

Broaddrick's rape allegation emerged, Ireland said the media should "stop wasting time on unprovable charges."[26]

Ireland actually advocated for me when my story first came out. "If what Kathleen Willey says happened, we have moved from talking about a womanizer or a philanderer to talking about the behavior of a sexual predator," Ireland said to Lisa Myers.[27] She also said, "If it's true, it's sexual assault... Now we're talking about, really, sexual predators and people who, in positions of power, who use that power to take advantage of women."[28] Later, however, she rallied her troops against impeaching the president for perjury and obstruction of justice regarding his assault on me. "No matter how offensive the president's behavior was, it does not rise to the level of an impeachable offense," she said. "And the no-holds-barred attack by the ultra-conservatives on women's issues is a far more onerous threat to women and our families."[29] I tried to call her, but she wouldn't take my calls. Of course she wouldn't. What could she possibly say? She calls herself a feminist and this is how she regards a woman who has been sexually assaulted by the most powerful man in the country?

Madeleine Albright echoed Ireland's comment about me. "Yeah," she said, "*if* it's true..."

Singing the same chorus, feminist icon Gloria Steinem "suggested that if the allegations are true, Bill Clinton is a sex addict."[30] Later, she declared that Clinton hadn't committed harassment because he "took no for an answer." Her verdict misses the point. Clinton did not *harass* me. He assaulted me, which is not just a civil offense but a criminal one. Steinem, however, couldn't care less. In an even more revelatory comment, she added, "The truth of the matter is that [Clinton's] behavior toward women is considerably better than any president I know of."[31] Once again, a free pass.

Then there was Betty Friedan, who said, "She should have slapped him across the face." What kind of feminist blames the victim? And does she really think that when a woman is assaulted by a man, she should slap him across the face and that should be the end of it? Is this really the message she wants to convey to our sisters and our daughters?

"Jesse Jackson, who had been praying with Clinton in the midst of the Lewinsky scandal, chimed in with an excuse for Clinton, rather than a defense," wrote Candice Jackson.[32] "Sex is not the one string on the guitar," Maureen Dowd reported the Reverend Jackson said of the scandal. "There are nine more commandments."[33]

Then James Carville blathered, "He's a good man who did a bad thing." Carville added, "You can't take him to task for his personal behavior." *Excuse me?* That's personal? The president of the United States, who has to send men off to war, behaves like that in the Oval Office? Seduces young women in the Oval Office? Assaults married women in the Oval Office? This is not personal behavior. At the very least, it is unprofessional. At worst, it is abuse and assault. Obviously, advocating it—on any level—is wrong.

Clinton's henchmen trashed me, just as they trashed all of the women. All of us. And they ought to be ashamed of themselves.

Many more feminists couldn't even bring themselves to comment. The president of the National Women's Political Caucus said she "wanted to remain circumspect." The president of the National Women's Law Center "declined to pass judgment." So did the president of the Women's Legal Defense Fund.[34] Senator Dianne Feinstein only said that, "The word of the president is a very important thing."[35] Even Anita Hill, whose claims of sexual harassment almost derailed the nomination of Supreme Court justice Clarence Thomas, said that since Clinton advocates for women on the grand scale, nothing I had said should derail his presidency. "I don't think that most women have come to the point where we've said, 'Well, this is so bad that even if he is better on the bigger issues, we can't have him as president.'"[36] Her statement affirms the "feminist" view that women should make or withhold a claim like mine—and hers!—based on the ideology of the perpetrator rather than on what the man actually did to a woman, or *women!*

Nationally syndicated radio host Monica Crowley points out the hypocrisy of these so-called feminists. "If feminist groups such as NOW were really serious about their professed objective about 'female empowerment,' they would have rallied to Bill Clinton's female accusers, supported them in their David and Goliath struggles against this powerful man," Crowley recently railed on her program. "Instead, they rallied to him. They put politics first and looked the other way."[37]

Many people could have intervened in this ugly saga to keep Bill Clinton from harming women. But one woman above all of them was in a position to make Bill behave.

That woman is, of course, Hillary.

When news of the Monica Lewinsky affair broke, Hillary had been married to her wayward husband for more than twenty years. But Hillary charged to Bill's defense. "Certainly," she said publicly of the allegations, "I believe they're false. Absolutely."[38] She went on the *Today Show* and told Matt Lauer, "Bill and I have been accused of everything, including murder, by some of the very same people who are behind these allegations. So from my perspective this is part of a continuing political campaign against my husband." Thus she invented the vast, right-wing conspiracy.

Just as Hillary did against Monica Lewinsky, Candice Jackson says she "defended her husband publicly and attacked every woman who leveled charges against him or disclosed consensual affairs with him." Hillary condemned all of us, denied our credibility, and expressed only contempt for us. "She is married to a man who mistreats women on a regular basis, and that marriage is the cornerstone of her own political success... Not only will she excuse Bill's behavior, she will lead the smear team in discrediting and ruining women who come forward against him."[39] And she will do more than that.

The self-anointed queen of the feminists, Hillary smeared and stepped on every one of the women her husband seduced, accosted, and assaulted. Her position on women's empowerment is nothing more than empty hypocrisy.

As Monica Crowley adds, "Hillary has spun herself successfully as a feminist icon, but even a cursory look at her career shows that she is the exact opposite. Hillary is not the feminist icon she holds herself out to be, but is instead a poster girl for *anti-feminism*. Here's why: everything she has achieved has been derivative of a man. She was a well-connected attorney in Arkansas because she was married to the governor. She was co-president for eight years because she was married to the co-president who got elected under his name. She is a U.S. senator because she was married to her co-president. She is a serious candidate for president today because of the man to whom she is married. This is not to say that Hillary Clinton is stupid. On the contrary, she's a smart, savvy, and clever woman. But her entire adult professional life has been defined by an even smarter, more savvy, and more clever *man*. She's all about 'female empowerment,' but she has gotten to where she is on the formidable coattails of her husband."[40]

I agree. The fact is that Hillary hasn't got the goods—the experience—to be president. She may be a woman, but she is not the sort of woman who has earned the right to be called president. "Voting for Hillary Clinton as a way of breaking the glass ceiling in American politics shatters the glass in the name of biology," Candice Jackson adds, "but not in the name of meaningful advancements for women."[41]

If the media suspected that Bush acted toward women like Clinton did, they would string him up. But the feminists gave Clinton a pass because he furthered their agenda. They lined up to express their doubts about me. These "feminists" gave deference to their man because they liked his politics. And, essentially, it came down to one issue: abortion.

Dick Morris has put it most succinctly. "If you're going to be a sexual predator, be pro-choice."[42]

Real Women

When I was still in the phone book, I had anonymous phone calls from women who said, "He's done this to me," and, "The same thing happened to me." Some said he'd done almost the same thing to them in the Oval Office.

I said, "Well, why don't you come out and tell your story?" Not one of them would go public, which is understandable, given what they saw happening to me. They didn't tell me who they were, but I think a lot of them were White House women. My caller ID on these calls came up "Caller Unknown," which is typical for Washington, D.C., callers.

And I often met women, especially women my age, who told me they had been assaulted in the workplace by a former boss.

One woman came up to me in a department store. "I just want to tell you that the same thing happened to me," she said, "and I never forgave myself." She said it happened to her in Richmond, when she was young and had just started working. She said, "It was awful." She broke down in tears, and said that for years she blamed herself. She didn't know what to do and couldn't tell anybody because this kind of behavior by male bosses was somewhat acceptable. It was just one of those things that happened. If you were a working woman, a secretary or even a teacher, you were expected to put up with it, as if that is just the way men are.

When I was a young woman, the attitude was, *Honey, this is just something you have to put up with.* In fact, in TWA's flight school, they taught us that, as flight attendants, it was part of the job to handle sexual harassment and assaults like a lady. "You're going to get the mashers," they said. "You're going to get the overbearing drunk guys who are going to make a pass at you. You have to figure out how you're going to handle it." It was just part of the job. We had to be ladies and handle them with dignity. It was our responsibility.

The thing is, being a woman my age, an early baby boomer, we put up with that kind of attention for years. Women often blame themselves and wonder, *Did I do something? Did I look like I was pursuing him? It must be my fault. I must have invited that.*

Men got away with that for a long, long time.

As wrong as it is, the women of my generation just assumed that ninety-eight percent of all men were predators—that they were all on the make. That was how we survived. If such a man was your boss and you needed to get ahead, then he was inevitably going to take advantage of his power over you. Women were in many situations where they had to give in to get ahead.

In the middle of my media storm, a very well known television interviewer called me numerous times. "No good deed goes unpunished," she said. She gave me woman-to-woman advice and offered to rebut the release of my letters. She also talked with me about sexual harassment. "Boys will be boys," she said. A pioneer in the television industry, she doubtlessly had to deal with it more than once. While she talked to me, we discussed how our interview would go. She said I would talk about what happened to me. "Then," she said,

"I want to talk about what happened to me." She didn't name names but told me that early in her career one of her first bosses had chased her around the desk. "This is how it's going to be," he told her, "if you want to get ahead in this business."

Though we've passed laws and now require "sensitivity training" in the workplace, harassment still occurs. When my daughter was at Harvard, I noticed that the men genuinely seemed to respect their female classmates as equals. Shannon, in fact, helped me understand how much our culture has changed in this regard. When she was in medical school and I told her what Clinton had done to me, she said, "Mom! That is sexual harassment! He can't get away with that!" But when I went through the incident in the Oval Office, everything in my background—not to mention his power—told me that, yes, he *could* get away with it and he *would* get away with it. In my day, men always got away with it.

Every year, I speak to a class of college students at the University of Richmond. Lately, the students I speak to were just ten or twelve years old during the Clinton scandal, so they don't remember it. It's history. I tell them what happened and they want all the dirty details of what happened in the Oval Office. I skirt that. "Read a book or google me," I say. "I don't want to talk about it, but basically it was a pretty rough scene, a very unpleasant scene." Each year the young women become more vocal, more engaged, and more angry about what women have to put up with. Unfortunately, I can't say the young men in the audience have grown as much. Many of them make their attitudes perfectly clear. They sit and listen, but automatically dismiss my story because I am a woman.

Unfortunately, with the Clinton ordeal, our feminists lost all credibility on sexual harassment. We don't talk about it anymore. But obviously women today still have to deal with it—and not just the women who happen to find themselves alone in a room with Bill Clinton. If a man like Clinton can abuse women with impunity, we really have not made as much progress as we'd like to think. And if his wife knows about his behavior and she still accepts and enables it, and we keep her in power because we think she serves our greater political goals, the future for our daughters and granddaughters is so much less than it might have been.

Annie

While the feminists remained elusive and my Democratic friends stayed silent, the Clinton machine continued to smear me in the media. To get away from it, I spent a lot of time in Florida with my boyfriend.

I was going back down to the Keys and needed to make arrangements for all my pets. I had used a pet sitter, Karen, in Powhatan. But Karen was busy and couldn't sit for me, so I found a great kennel owned by a sweet woman named Annie, here in Powhatan. Since I had only recently discovered Annie's kennel, I never mentioned to anyone where it was or its name. If I had told anyone that I was going to Florida, I just said I was dropping off the dogs and cats.

I left them there early one morning on my way to the airport. I took the dogs—Meg, Shaun, and Tess—and the cats—Buttons, O'Malley, and Blarney. Getting them all to the kennel was an ordeal.

I left there and flew to Florida. While I was in the air, a woman called the kennel. She told Annie that she was my pet sitter and that I had asked her to pick up the dogs and cats because I was coming home early. Annie told the woman she needed to talk to me first, that she wouldn't give her my animals until she talked to me.

As soon as I exited the plane, Annie called. That scared me, because whenever the kennel called, I would think, *Oh God! One of them is sick or dying…*

The first thing she said was, "Everything's okay. I just want to ask you something."

When she told me about the phone call, I thought that I must have crossed signals with Karen. Questions flooded my mind. How could Karen know that's where I took them? Did I even tell her I was taking them to that kennel?

My mind was racing. I was trying to make sense of something that just did not make sense. I had to talk to Karen.

I called her. "Look," I said. "Did we get our signals crossed?"

No, she said. She hadn't called.

"Are you sure?"

Karen said, "No, it was not me."

And I started to figure it out.

My God! I thought. *How did they know? And who are "they"?*

I was so freaked out that they knew where the kennel was. Someone had followed me. That's the only way they would have known where my pets were. It was another reminder of Bullseye.

That's when I said, "We'd better call the FBI."

The FBI followed up with it and tried to trace the call.

Annie had an early version of caller ID, the kind that plugged into the side of her telephone. That morning when I dropped everyone off, Annie mentioned that the battery had died. "I've got to put a new battery in there because when the battery dies there's nothing on the thing." Sure enough, the battery had died. When she told me about the strange phone call, I thought, *Well, they broke in there and took the battery out.* It was either that or they just blocked the caller ID with *67. PIs are not stupid.

Annie said the woman had a very Southern accent, almost as though the woman was acting. It surprised me that a woman would do such a thing. Women are nurturers and caretakers. Messing with somebody's children or pets is not a woman's way of doing something. It had to be a challenge for a PI to find a woman to pull a stunt like that. That makes it a pretty short list of suspects.

I don't think they would have taken my dogs and cats. I don't think they were going to show up. They would not risk arriving in an identifiable car with a license plate and a person who could be described. I think they just wanted to let me know I was being followed and to scare the hell out of me.

It worked. They scared me. I walked around with the feeling I had when I couldn't find Shannon or Ed before Ed's body was discovered. I felt a knot in my stomach. I was breathing fast, panting, almost as though I was going to have an anxiety attack. *What's next?* I thought. *Are they going to take all my animals away, the way they took Bullseye? What are they doing? And who are they?*

FBI Agents

One Saturday morning, I went out to my car to look for something. Under the driver's seat I found what appeared to be a cordless phone. It wasn't a cell phone but something between a cell phone and a car phone. I had never seen it before and didn't know what it was or where it had come from. I called Dan.

"You know, it's the strangest thing," I said. "I found this phone thing in my—"

"Get that out of there," Dan said. "They put bombs in those things. Get it out! Throw it out into the woods!"

It took the FBI agents about two hours to get to my house. They scoured the woods. Dennis Alvater of the FBI said they confiscated the phone and traced it, but felt it was "kind of a nonissue." While they couldn't determine where it came from or how it got into my car, he said, "When we were finished looking at that, it was not very sinister in nature." We never found out where it came from.

With the escalation of these incidents, the FBI asked the Powhatan sheriff to keep a close eye on me, so the sheriff's new routine included making the rounds down my dirt road. It always made me feel good!

I went in to my little post office. "Did we tell you about this guy?" they asked me. While I was in Florida, a scruffy-looking man driving a beat-up car came into the post office very early one morning. "I was really nervous about this guy," said Doug, the postman. The man's car had an out-of-state license plate and Doug thought that the state possibly started with the letter "M." The guy had demanded directions to my home and wouldn't divulge who he was. The postal workers wouldn't help him and he left angry. It could have been anybody. It could've been a tabloid reporter or some nut. But he made the postal employees nervous—and me too. So I said, "Okay, Doug, well, you should be hearing from the FBI shortly."

A few weeks later, we were in Florida when a suspicious package arrived from Minnesota. We didn't recognize the return address.

"Don't touch it!" I screamed, frantic. "Don't open it!"

I was ready to call the bomb squad. But it was a gift of fishing tackle from a recent charter.

That's how I was, though. I walked around in a constant state of terror, afraid for myself, my family, my friends, and my animals. Those fears continued for at least two more years. I installed an expensive alarm system in the cottage and a heavy chain across the driveway entrance. The FBI checked my phone several times for mysterious clicks and dead air. And I learned how to use a gun. I was determined to protect myself.

Gentlemen Callers

One night, very late, the phone rang. I was groggy and stumbled to answer it.

"Hello." I finally said.

An irate man was screaming at me. "You fucking bitch! You have ruined my life! I'm going to kill you!"

That woke me up! I thought, *Well, do I call my FBI agent now? Wake him up in the middle of the night?* The caller ID showed a name with a Powhatan number, so I thought, *He's just got to be some drunk wacko.* I decided to hope for the best and wait until morning. It was still hard for me to accept that I might be in danger. It was foreign to me. Much of the time, I felt like I was being silly, but I never knew what to take seriously and what to ignore. First thing the next morning, I called the FBI agent on my case.

"Geez, Kathleen," he said, "you get the weirdest phone calls!"

Witness tampering is a big deal. And when you're a cooperating witness in a federal investigation, the FBI is on top of these things, so people have to be careful about what they say—or what they scream into a phone in the middle of the night.

I pictured black Chevy Blazers full of FBI agents, guns drawn, descending upon some guy on his farm in Powhatan County. They did go see him. And they scared the bejesus out of him!

The guy had a fight with his girlfriend and her telephone number was close to mine. He transposed a couple of numbers.

I was still in the phone book and got other calls from people who wanted to express their support and sympathy. One night, a younger-sounding man called. He seemed as if he had smoked a couple of joints before he dialed.

"Yeah, hey, how ya doin'?" he said. "Like, I've been reading in the paper about you and, so, anyway, what'd that son of a bitch Clinton do to you, anyway?"

I played along, waiting to see where he was going.

"It's a terrible thing ya'll have to go through," he said. "I just wanna tell ya I feel real bad for you."

"Well," I said. "Thanks a lot. I really appreciate that."

Then he said, "Hey, what're you doing later tonight? Wanna go out for a drink?"

I said, "What?"

"You doin' somethin' later tonight?"

Nah, I thought, *potheads aren't my type!*

It was so funny. And I have to say that, despite all the difficulties and pain and fear during those years, some funny things happened too.

Blarney

After staying in the Keys for most of the spring, I returned home to Virginia for the summer. When I went out in public, people recognized me and every single person who stopped me was kind, comforting, and supportive. To a person, they were compassionate. Their words meant so much to me, but I still felt uneasy in public. I was constantly checking my rearview mirror, looking over my shoulder. I knew they were following me, but where were "they"?

On the Fourth of July, I went out to a baseball game and party. I'd been gone all day and came home after dark. Once inside my house, I realized the door to my deck was open. A second-floor deck, it had no access to the yard. As I went to close the door and turn on the outside light, I saw my black and white cat, Blarney, on the deck. He was dead. A beautiful, longhaired cat with poochy white cheeks, Blarney was the prettiest cat I had ever owned. He was young and strong, healthy, and not quite full-grown. He was a sweetheart. And he was dead.

I called the FBI once again. "Well, now I've got a dead pet on my porch."

The veterinarian did a necropsy on Blarney but could never find the cause of his death. There was no reason why this one-year-old cat should have died. There was no pneumonia, no heart attack, no stroke, no feline leukemia, nothing. No reason. Cats don't just up and die, but they could find no reason for this cat to have died.

It scared me. It was so traumatic and painful that I buried it deep inside myself. I was emotionally overwhelmed, and part of me needed to shut down. I kept thinking, *These people are not doing this to me. This cannot be.* I don't think I was naive. Rather, it was more like denial. I refused to believe that people existed out there who did things like that, who would take Bullseye and Blarney and kill them. How could they do that? But there were just too damned many bad things happening, and I had to start believing. It was an awful realization.

That same day, my best friend's new kitten died suddenly, too.

As I ended the summer, I looked forward to the close of this long and grizzly saga. It could not last forever, and I looked forward to its resolution. And it was coming. Bill Clinton would give his deposition in mid-August, which would open the final chapter in the drama. Ken Starr would release his report in September. Everything was moving toward a conclusion. I eagerly awaited its arrival.

CHAPTER NINE

OBSTRUCTION OF JUSTICE

O N AUGUST 17, 1998, Clinton gave his deposition before Ken Starr's prosecutors. This was the famous deposition in which Clinton parsed words beyond belief—as in, it depends on what the meaning of "is" is. Not only misleading, his testimony was also untruthful and he flat-out lied, especially with regard to me.

Bob Bittman and Jackie Bennett, Jr. questioned Clinton for the OIC and Starr. Near the end of his deposition, the prosecutors asked him about me. Clinton said, "You know what evidence was released after the *60 Minutes* broadcast that I think pretty well shattered Kathleen Willey's credibility. You know what people down in Richmond said about her. You know what she said about other people that wasn't true. I don't know if she's made all of this available to the grand jury or not. She was not telling the truth. She asked for an appointment with me. She asked for it repeatedly."[1]

For the record, I asked for an appointment. I didn't ask for "*it*"! When I heard what he'd said, I was shocked. I thought, *What does that mean*, "what they're saying about her down in Richmond"? That seems very sophomoric to me.

Still under oath, Clinton denied calling me at Doug Wilder's campaign headquarters after the Kluge fundraiser, and he denied calling me from the Williamsburg Inn, when he had cleared everyone out so I might bring him "chicken soup." Then the prosecutors told Clinton that they had documented his phone calls to me from Williamsburg and they produced records proving that he had called me. When they presented the phone logs, Clinton's eyes darted from side to side and he looked like a caged animal. His famous red face made an appearance. Angry and agitated, Clinton requested a five-minute recess and I was later told that he went outside into the hall and went ballistic, screaming and hollering at Uncle Bob.

When the *Starr Report* was delivered to Congress, the OIC told me that I was still part of Starr's continuing investigation into witness-tampering incidents, so they did not include my evidence. But faced with the facts in the report and the DNA test results on Monica's blue dress, the president spoke to the nation and delivered his famous "I have sinned" speech. He admitted his affair with Lewinsky but insisted he "did not lie."

Naively, I expected to be mentioned, even hoped for an apology. But he did not acknowledge me.

Once I understood what was in play behind the scenes, of course, I knew he would never apologize to me. While most of his advisors were telling Clinton to be contrite and apologize to the American people, Hillary was in his other ear, nagging at Clinton to continue the fight. According to Christopher Andersen, who wrote *Bill & Hillary*, she advised Clinton "the day of his mea culpa to the nation confessing his improper relationship with Monica Lewinsky. She reportedly told him, 'The worst thing you can do now is roll over and play dead. Bill, you have to come out and hammer Ken Starr.'"[2]

The Clintons left for vacation in Cape Cod, taking the famous walk to the helicopter with Chelsea between her parents. On the first day of Monica's grand jury testimony, the president rushed back from his family retreat, returning to D.C. because of an emergency. He announced our attack on the Sudan and Afghanistan in light of new "revelations." What a coincidence. To this day, I think this was the single-most cowardly and shameful act of the Clinton administration.

Lisa Krapinsky

"Will you take a polygraph test?"

When the Independent Counsel's Office asked me to take the test, I said, "Sure, no problem."

But my lawyer, Dan, of course said, "I don't like it."

It was the only time I didn't take his advice.

It turned out that the polygraph examiner and I had been born in the same hospital, in a little berg right outside of Philadelphia. The questioner was a nice guy from the Richmond FBI office. But Dan had heard that this particular examiner was not well trained. I went forward with it anyway, because I was committed.

The test was degrading. I knew it was a good idea but it was also a testament to the fact that my credibility was in question, that I couldn't prove what I claimed. It was my word against his, and he was the president and I was just me. I felt so vulnerable. They put me in a very sterile room without anything on the walls that could stimulate me in any way. It was a perfectly cream-colored office with a desk, the machine, and the man. He asked my permission before he strapped me up. He sat down in front of me and asked questions.

During the examination, he asked me about talking to Julie the night after the incident. Because of my state of mind that night and the next day, I hadn't originally remembered that I had been there, but Julie eventually reminded me. In light of that confusion, the question the examiner asked was poorly worded. An ambiguous question produced an ambiguous answer, and my response to that one question came up as "inconclusive."

About three or four FBI agents huddled, standing around talking about me. They had a discussion as if I weren't there and I heard them say, "She did this and she…" It was so intimidating. I said, "Hello? Wait a second! What'd I do wrong? What do you mean by that?" They decided to stop the test and I agreed. I realized why people don't take polygraph tests—because you can't use them as evidence in court but you can still shout out the results to the whole world, even if they tell the jury to disregard it and even if the test reads wrong. It was terrible and I felt discouraged. I thought, *Now what? I don't need this. They're already trying to make a liar out of me!*

Dan was angry. I was completely frazzled.

Though the media, of course, reported that I failed the polygraph, a source at the FBI said I really did *not* fail the test. He said they tested me on several key components of my testimony and the results of *one* test, involving Julie Steele, were inconclusive because of an "inappropriate question." The source explained that the question referenced Steele and asked if I related all of the details involving the incident with Clinton. Although the test concluded that I *did* tell Julie about the incident involving Clinton, I had an inconclusive response to "all" and "details."

The FBI asked me if I would retake the test. I said, "Well, yes, I don't think I have a choice." I think Dan thought I should just leave it the way it was, but I couldn't leave it as "inconclusive."

Five days later, I went to retake the test at the FBI headquarters in Washington.

The OIC made arrangements for me to spend the night in Washington so that I would be rested. They registered me at the Hyatt Hotel under a false identity, "Lisa Krapinsky." When I arrived at the desk to check in, the officious desk clerk asked if I had a reservation.

"Yes," I replied. "It's under the name Lisa Krapinsky."

"Is that with a *C* or a *K*?"

"Umm..." I stalled, thinking. I didn't know!

"Ma'am, is that with a *C* or a *K*?" he repeated. "Your name?"

"Uh, well, I'm not sure."

"You are not sure?"

"Well," I finally asked him, "how would you spell it?"

It started with a *K*.

At nine o'clock the next morning I went to FBI headquarters with Dan. Dennis Alvater, the FBI agent on my case, and Jerry Bastin, a retired agent working as a contractor for the Independent Counsel, came with us. The place was swarming with large men in jeans who were carrying big guns. In the testing room next to mine, a well-known spy was going to be examined. He had a reputation as an escape artist, so they transported him in chains and he had on a blindfold.

As I waited to go in, I met all the agents. They were all Irish, including my examiner, Jim Murphy. He was the number one FBI polygraph expert in the country and that was good enough for me. Murphy asked my permission, then put the wires across my chest and hooked me up. This time he sat behind me. Not being able to see him was very intimidating. He asked me the questions and then said, "Okay, we're done. I'll be right back."

But he didn't tell me the results. I waited, dying to know. I didn't know where he'd gone, and I thought maybe he'd dashed out to the bathroom or something. Finally, Murphy came back and we walked out to the hallway. Then they had me wait in a small lunchroom while Dan talked to the agents. Finally, they all returned with big smiles. Murphy looked at everybody and said, "It's a good day. She passed with flying colors."

I was totally relieved and I dissolved into tears.

We had dinner at The Palm with Chris Matthews, his assistant Barbara Daniel, and producer Rob Yarrin. I told Chris "off the record" about the test results.

As we walked back to the car, past the White House south lawn, the presidential motorcade drove by and we saw the president in the back seat of his limo. I always wondered if he saw us, because we held up a copy of *Time* magazine with the headline, "Impeachment" emblazoned across the top.

Later, the *Richmond Times-Dispatch* ran an article under the banner headline, "Willey passed polygraph/lie detector test on second try." Bill McElway wrote it. The guy was just looking for trouble. The man couldn't seem to get *anything* right.

The Intruder

The FBI and my county sheriff ordered me to notify them at any time, day or night, of anything suspicious. I wouldn't hesitate. But I had also learned how to operate a gun and I had one in my home.

My dogs Meg and Shaun did their jobs as barkers, but they were getting old. It was rare that they ever stayed out at night. Before I went to bed, I let them out, with Tess, my German shepherd. I went back out on the kitchen porch a while later and called them to come back in. They didn't come. It was strange. They hardly ever left the yard. But they didn't come. So I walked around the porch thinking how weird it was. Usually I heard them rustling in the woods. I called again. It was a cold night and there was a little frost on the porch railing. It was very late and I was getting impatient, calling them again.

The deck was above a walk-out basement, and the outside light was on down there. Suddenly, I noticed a shadow move beneath me. It extended from the basement patio out on to the grass. I thought it was one of the dogs and said, "Come on, Meg." But it was a long shadow. And then it receded. It moved slowly backward, away from me, away from the lawn, back toward the basement door under my deck. I thought, *Geez, there's somebody down there! My dogs are gone, and there's somebody down there, going toward my basement.*

I kept my wits about me and tried to sound casual. I called the dogs again, then muttered, loud enough, "Where are those dogs?" I went back in the house and closed the kitchen door with a little noise. My boyfriend was sound asleep, but I went upstairs and very quietly leaned down and whispered into his ear, "I think there's somebody outside." He woke up quickly and went into reconnaissance mode, grabbing the gun. I said, "For God's sake, be careful!"

I went outside again, still acting as if I was calling the dogs. I didn't see anything. I walked around to the back of the deck. I wanted the man to know I was there, but he was gone. The dogs had come back by the time my boyfriend came outside. Tess went into reconnaissance mode, too, and never left my boyfriend's side. They went up the driveway but didn't find the intruder. I don't know where he went, but we never saw him. The trash can was down, outside the basement door, and people sometimes go through the trash, but there was no sign that anybody had done that.

The FBI came down the next morning and scoured the woods, searching for a hideaway where he may have sat and watched me. They didn't find anything.

David Schippers

Henry Hyde asked his old friend to serve as chief investigative counsel for the House Judiciary Committee. A staunch Chicago Democrat, David Schippers had voted for Clinton twice. He had also led the Justice Department's Organized Crime and Racketeering Unit under Bobby Kennedy, and convicted the likes of Sam Giancana. I figured he was a man who knew his way around.

Schippers talked about me in a recent interview. "All she'd had was people pushing her around, so she was a little leery," he said. "But she finally agreed to talk to us."[3]

Schippers didn't want me to be seen with him in Washington, so our initial meeting in February 1998 was at a coffee shop in the Sheraton Hotel in Fredericksburg, halfway between Washington and Richmond. Schippers had a legal assistant with him, and a couple of FBI agents. I had Dan. I had gotten lost and must've been forty-five minutes late, so the minute I arrived they started questioning me. We went from breakfast through lunch. Later, Schippers told me that he and his cohorts tried every trick in the legal book to trip me up, but I didn't stumble.

"Number one," Schippers asked me, "why did you write those letters after the injury?"

I had written the letters with my attorney, I told him, "Because I was destitute, I needed some kind of work, and I decided to forget what happened there, to start over, and hopefully they would help me find a job."

At one point, Shippers paused and looked at me. "Why did you finally tell this story in your deposition?" he asked me. "Why didn't you just lie and say nothing happened that day?"

I told Schippers that when I was going in there, I didn't know what I was going to do. I was terrified. Finally, I said, "Because I had to. I was asked a question and I was at the point that I just had to answer it. There was no more dancing around it."

"Her lawyer confirmed all this," Schippers says. "When they were in the deposition and they got to the Oval Office business, her lawyer asked for a recess and asked Kathleen, 'Are you ready for this?' and she said she was going to tell the truth."

"It was one of the hardest things in my life," I told Schippers, "because I was terrified."

"Let me tell you something," Schippers replied. "Going in there and telling the truth was your insurance policy. If you had gone in there and lied, you'd be dead today. You would have disappeared. But after you told the truth, you became too dangerous to trifle with. No one could hurt you after that!" Schippers wasn't trying to scare me. He was just telling me the facts.

To this day Dave Schippers maintains, "If she hadn't gone into the deposition and told the truth, if she had lied, they'd want to get rid of her. Kathleen is darn lucky she wasn't murdered."[4]

He also points out that, "When the skull was left on Kathleen's porch the day after [the] deposition, the only people who knew were Clinton and his people."[5]

When Schippers told his colleagues my story, they reacted angrily. "That son of a bitch should have his teeth knocked out," they said.

Schippers later recounted a scary dynamic during Clinton's deposition in the Jones case as well. According to Schippers, after Clinton went into the deposition, he figured he had it locked. "Monica was locked in, she'd given a false deposition," Schippers says, "so we went in to Clinton's deposition and we said, 'What if we have tapes of Monica?' That's when Clinton went to his secretary and said, 'I was never alone with her, right?' But then, they started making calls, thirty-five calls, looking everywhere for Monica. They were killing themselves to find her. I maintain that, when the Clinton people were making all those calls, trying to reach Monica, I would bet that if they had found her, they would have killed her. In a heartbeat. Something would have happened to her. But she was in custody at the time."[6]

"I firmly believe," Schippers said, "that one of these days Monica Lewinsky is going to wake up and thank Linda Tripp for one thing—for saving that dress—because if that dress didn't show up, Monica was going to disappear too."

Dave Schippers scared the hell out of me.

But he had a definite realism. "The dress was Monica's insurance policy," Linda Tripp later pointed out, "just as my documentation [the tapes] was mine."[7]

The House Managers

Schippers asked me to testify against the president before Ken Starr's grand jury in March. "I want you to be a witness," Schippers said. He later recalled that my face fell. "Believe me, we will protect you," he added. "Whatever happens, we will protect you."

I agreed. As a cooperating witness, I would be one of three witnesses against Clinton in the impeachment hearings.

"As far as I was concerned, the Kathleen Willey case was one of the worst ones I had heard of," Dave Schippers said, "other than what happened to Juanita Broaddrick."

After Christmas, Dan and I went to meet with the House managers. Two FBI agents met us in the parking lot of a mall in Northern Virginia, and from there we followed them to an underground garage of one of the House office buildings. We were whisked upstairs to Congressman Jim Rogan's office.

By now, the throngs of press suspected that I was somewhere in the building, but they did not know where. We waited as the House managers arrived. Congressman Lindsey Graham, dressed casually in a blazer, khakis, and open-necked shirt, came first. He looked around the room at everyone and spoke about Clinton. "This guy's a real trip, ain't he?"

When the other managers arrived, I began answering questions. They wanted to see how I handled the pressure. We left Washington unnoticed that day, having outsmarted the press.

For days I watched history in the making. And for days I was left hanging, not knowing whether or not I would be a witness in William Jefferson Clinton's impeachment trial. One day, the House managers said I would be a witness. The next day, I wouldn't.

Throughout the scandal, I had watched and listened to Senator Susan Collins, a Republican from Maine. I thought I could talk to her "woman to woman" about my saga and I decided to call her. She invited me to have dinner at her Capitol Hill home and she brought in Chinese takeout. Her chief of staff, Steve Bailey, joined us in her dining room. She asked me hard questions and I answered honestly. I felt that she was ultimately fair. In the end, Collins voted not to convict the president in the Senate, but she mentioned me in a statement that she entered into the congressional record.

Every day, Dan and I talked to David Schippers and met with House representatives Asa Hutchison, Lindsey Graham, and other members of the impeachment committee. Hutchison, however, said they decided my allegations were not clearly related to the articles of impeachment approved by the House.[8] Still, we prepared for my testimony in the impeachment trial, and Dan appeared before the House managers to answer questions. And we waited.

I was told that Trent Lott told the House managers that they could have three witnesses. But he did not want me to be one of them. Terrified of unseating a popular president, Lott was afraid I might be too effective.

Then, Judge Ken Starr also asked David Schippers not to call me as a witness. Starr was still investigating the issues of witness intimidation and obstruction of justice and didn't want my appearance to jeopardize that investigation. The other issue for Starr, I suspect, was that my testimony contradicted Linda Tripp's. Tripp was an important witness for Starr and, if I impugned Linda, it could jeopardize that case against Clinton. Linda, however, would eventually vindicate me.

David Barger, Starr's federal prosecutor and lead investigator in the state of Virginia, recently told me that logic strongly suggests that the Clintons were involved to some degree in everything that happened to me, the jogger and all of the other scare tactics, since they were the ones who ultimately would benefit the most from either my not testifying or changing my testimony. Whether either of the Clintons had direct knowledge or whether someone directed those things to be done to scare me without their knowledge is something we may never know. Clearly, someone who was looking after the president's interest was trying to send a strong message to scare me. The investigators had found the skull. They interviewed the mechanic and owner of the tire store. They read "Blarney's" necropsy report. Annie, at the kennel, told them about the woman caller who tried to take my pets out of the kennel while I was away. They talked to merchants who said that strange people followed me into stores and the mailman who talked to the man in the beat up car at the post office. And they had Jared Stern's inside information about the investigation of me which purportedly came out of the Oval Office. In the end, the investigation was not successful in determining for criminal purposes exactly who was behind these scare tactics.

"We did a lot of work on all of those things, and we never concluded anything definitely about any of that, and that's a bit surprising," Jerry Bastin, a retired agent working for the Independent Counsel, recently told me. "Some of the things we checked should have shown some indication, but they just led nowhere, which makes you think it was very well done, a specially done kind of thing or it wasn't connected to your situation. One or the other. If it had nothing to do with your situation, then probably it was just coincidental. But when you add coincidences together, they usually mean something. The difficulty we had was that we never were able to definitively show who had done any of these things and for what reason."

His partner, Dennis Alvater, added, "I'm very disappointed we weren't able to do more and to satisfactorily substantiate more with our investigation."

I met with House representatives Asa Hutchison and Lindsey Graham and other members of the impeachment committee. Hutchinson, however, said they decided my allegations were not clearly related to the articles of impeachment approved by the House.[9]

Clinton was impeached in the House, but he was not convicted in the Senate.

Bill and Hillary Clinton stood on the White House lawn with Al Gore, where Bill gave quite a performance. His arrogance and self-righteousness were almost too much to take. America had witnessed crime without punishment. In abusing me, and in the ensuing coverup, Bill and Hillary Clinton and their minions had committed crimes, ruined peoples' lives, and degraded the presidency with impunity. It was a sad day.

As Linda Tripp told Larry King in 1999, "Based on what I know to be true—the chilling perjury and the obstruction—I wish that had at least been identified as being true."[10]

A friend who works for the FBI told me the Clinton modus operandi is reminiscent of the old joke about J. Edgar Hoover. Hoover would walk into his office and simply say, "My television doesn't work." He would never tell anybody to go fix his television or even say he *wanted* it fixed, but by the end of the day, when he went home, his television worked perfectly. "These are not dumb people," my friend said of the Clintons. "I mean, we're dealing with some very bright, politically crafty individuals and what they would directly tell somebody to do, they certainly wouldn't put anything out, certainly would not put anything on paper, certainly would not have themselves be recorded in any way." He added that there's a good possibility that someone in the White House was pulling strings or implying that they would like some things handled. The FBI, however, was never able to prove it.

Linda

After the media abused Linda about her looks, she had a makeover and cosmetic surgery. Then there was a picture of her looking like a model with her hair blowing. Though it was all done up, she looked incredible. Every time I saw her subsequently, she still looked pretty good.

In 1999, she went on *Larry King Live* and vindicated me.

Larry asked her, "Do you know Kathleen Willey?"

"Of course," Linda answered.

"And?"

"She's an honest person," Linda said. "She's telling the truth."

"You have no question in your mind?" Larry asked.

"Absolutely not," Linda said.[11]

I could not believe what I was seeing.

Some time later, I found out she had breast cancer, and I called her lawyer. I wanted her to know I'd heard about it and that I had called. I felt like it was something that I needed to say—no matter what she'd done. There probably weren't many people making phone calls like that.

After she had battled cancer, Larry King had her on his show again. Her hair was growing back. It was really short, not frizzy but naturally curly, and it was brown—not blonde, like it had always been. She looked great! And she looked like Linda, my former friend. She looked happy.

Her father had been a career army officer and her mother was German, so Linda grew up in Germany. In recent years, she had gone back to Germany and met up with an old boyfriend, her childhood sweetheart. They reconnected, got married, and now live in Virginia. It looks like her life is finally back on track.

Julie

After the Paula Jones case, after the grand jury, and after Clinton's impeachment, my story still had not been heard and I had not been vindicated. I had one postmortem hope to clear my name. Julie Steele was indicted for obstruction of justice and perjury, the only person ever indicted in connection with the whole scandal. Our day of justice had arrived. Julie was on trial.

Dan had informed the OIC investigators that Radutsky and Nelson told us the White House threatened Julie, coercing her to lie about me, so their investigators had to pursue yet another angle. "Certainly as investigators, we considered the possibility that Steele was threatened based on the information provided by Gecker," FBI investigator Dennis Alvater said. "Steele's recollection of the incident involving Kathleen, on critical issues, was inconsistent with the information developed."

Alvater's partner, Jerry Bastin, a retired FBI agent working as an independent contractor for the OIC, remembers it similarly. "What I always thought and what I today remember is that, somehow, something or somebody convinced her to do what she did, to stonewall the investigation," Bastin recently told me. "She seemed to be a person that they could work with. In other words, she could be told in a certain way that things have to be *this* way..."

"The investigation showed that her testimony was legitimately subject to perjury and obstruction of justice considerations," Alvater said. "We had *no* desire to indict a fifty-year-old housewife and mother on a peripheral issue," he added. "It was a tough decision but they decided to go forward with it, based on the evidence. If she chose to cooperate and to reveal any threats that were directed toward her that would have moved the Independent Counsel's investigation forward. Do I think she was threatened by the White House or anyone associated with the White House? She never gave that up. She went to trial as opposed to giving us that information. Were we able to prove that? No, we weren't able to prove it. I think it's a good possibility that it happened. But it also seemed that Julie took a very big risk going to trial. If she was threatened, she may have been less concerned about the Independent Counsel than she was about the people making the threats."[12]

Preparing for her trial, the FBI looked into everything. I was shocked. Before then, I had never realized what they could do. All my privacy was gone. One day, the agents sat me down in my kitchen and showed me records of every phone call I had ever made, from both my home phone and my cell. It verified all my conversations with Julie and confirmed the dates. The agents showed me the list and said, "So, here's where you called Julie on this day, and she called you here…" Everything I had said was all documented in those phone records. If I called the grocery store or the bank, it was on that list. If I called an old friend or a man I was dating, it was on that list. They showed me every call that came in to my house, too, to see if anything stuck out to me. And something did.

I saw the name "Monica Lewinsky." She had called my house the day the story broke on *Drudge*, but I didn't know it until the FBI showed me those phone logs. The press had been calling nonstop that week, so I screened all my calls. But caller ID never identified calls from Washington. Unless it was a cell phone, D.C. calls all came up "Caller Unknown," and during those days, I received dozens of Caller Unknowns a day. Only the FBI could identify those callers, and Monica was one of them.

Clinton had been nervous about me during that time and had told Monica that they shouldn't see each other anymore. But she was badgering him about me, asking him if he was attracted to me. She was like a typical seventeen-year-old, "What's she got that I haven't got?" Of course, the president of the United States did not say, "No, Monica, that would have been wrong," or "No, Monica, I'm married and she was married." According to Michael Isikoff, Clinton told Monica that the allegation that he had accosted me was ludicrous because he "would never be interested in a small-breasted woman like Kathleen Willey."[13] It might have embarrassed me, but I got a laugh out of it—and more than a little kidding.

Nancy Luque, Julie's powerhouse Washington attorney, gave the opening argument, promising, "You will hear from Julie Steele, and you will hear her words..." In his opening remarks, the prosecutor chronicled everything he had and it was very damaging.

Julie had become the darling of Bill and Hillary's cause and had just come back from Arkansas, where she testified for Susan McDougal. They were buddies. So Susan and her lawyer, Mark Geragos, showed up front and center on the first day of Julie's trial to support her. They vowed to come every day. It was a circus. But after they heard all the damaging opening remarks, they left during the lunch recess and never came back.

Julie always had frizzy blonde hair that was so big it almost looked like an afro. She had no sense of style or makeup, so she always wore bright purple blush. She looked like Clarabelle. But they had given her a complete makeover. I've never seen her look so good.

Some time after Clinton assaulted me, Julie and I had lunch with Mary Earle Highsmith, a mutual friend of ours. During that lunch, Julie brought up the incident. So I told the FBI about Mary Earle and they subpoenaed her from Colorado to come and tell the story. "Yes, I knew about it," Mary Earle told the jury. "Julie had told me about it."

But it's my opinion that the prosecutors made some mistakes. I thought they should have revealed more of Julie's financial situation because she was mortgaged to the hilt and desperate for money. If she turned on her best friend of twenty years, she would do anything for money, even lie, cheat, and steal. I don't think the prosecutor wanted to appear to be "piling on," so he didn't divulge the dire extent of her financial situation.

I too could have done a better job in the trial. Of course, they tried to make a huge deal of the fact that the first polygraph test was "inconclusive" until the judge shut them up. But when I was on the stand, I forgot some details that would have helped my testimony. Julie's lawyers threw some zingers at me, and I wasn't prepared for them. I remembered things later that I should have mentioned, but it was too late, of course.

The FBI agents had asked me about everything, all about Julie, and I was brutally honest in response. I told them about her troubles, including her anorexia. She had been very sick and almost died once of complete kidney shutdown. Her illness was well known. After all, she sat there in the trial, shaking her scrawny, two-inch-diameter ankle! It was pretty easy to see that she was sick. But the defense attorney attacked me for betraying my girlfriend and telling the FBI about it.

"Mrs. Willey, did you tell the FBI that your friend Julie Steele was anorexic?"

"Yes," I said. "I'm sure I talked with them about that."

What I should have remembered was that telling the FBI was *nothing* that Julie would have objected to. She even *asked for* an interview about her anorexia with a local reporter. She had endeared herself to a writer who wrote all the touchy feely stories for the "Flair" section of the newspaper, and he wrote a feature article about her trek through anorexia. Julie loved notoriety and certainly didn't mind advertising her plights—whether it was anorexia or her adopted child. This reporter bought it all. After she had Adam, the same reporter went to her house and did a story about her adopting a Romanian baby, with a picture of him in the den where he spent his entire day swinging in the baby swing.

Julie's lawyer had another trick up his sleeve, the last blow. He ended her defense with a flourish. "And finally, Mrs. Willey, at the risk of offending the court, I will write this down...and I ask the bailiff to hand this to you... Did you run into Mrs. Steele at the grocery store and did you call her this name, this four-letter word that starts with a *C* and ends in *T*?"

I looked at the piece of paper. "Yes, that's what I called her," I said. Actually, I called her a *lying* C-word, but I forgot to add "lying" when I testified.

There was a ripple through the courtroom.

When we walked out of court, all the reporters were corralled behind a rope line, but Tom Squitieri with *USA Today* had somehow gotten close to the door, so he was the first reporter I encountered. I liked Squitieri's reporting and thought he was a good guy. As he approached us, before he even told me who he was, I said, "Tom Squitieri?"

"Oh," he said. "You know me?"

That kind of endeared me to him and we actually became friends. But he was still a reporter. He called later that night and said, "So, what was it you called Julie? A *coat*?" he asked me. "Did you call her a *coat*?" He said all the reporters went outside during the recess and were coming up with words—*coat, coot, clot*. "Gee, how many four-letter words can we come up with that start with *C* and end with *T*, without offending the court?"

It became a joke and a lot of people heard about it. Still, I have to say, I hate that word. It is about the worst thing someone can call a woman. But Julie Hiatt Steele deserved it.

Some time later, before I boarded the plane out to L.A. to do the Larry King show, I was on the phone with Dan. His mom was a really good woman, a single mom and very proud of him. I was getting on the plane and he was giving me advice about the interview—like don't curse and don't use any four-letter words about my "dear" friend Julie. "Oh, and by the way," Dan said. "Mom says, that name you called Julie? She had it coming!" I loved that.

Despite the problems with my testimony, Julie's defense was weak and Luque never delivered on her opening argument promise to put Julie on the stand. But after a five-day trial, it ended in a hung jury.

It started with one holdout, a government employee who had decided that if it was okay for Clinton to lie, it was okay for Julie to lie. He wasn't going to budge. Then a couple more people went over to his side. The jury voted nine to three to convict her on all counts. They also stated that the evidence was very persuasive and they "strongly advised" the trial judge to retry her. I told Starr that I would be willing to go through it again if he decided to try her again. But he chose not to.

One of the more intriguing aspects of Julie's case was the issue of her legal representation. By all accounts, she was strapped for money. Yet she had a big-name Washington lawyer, Nancy Luque, who had worked for the Democratic National Committee and was close with Hillary. Knowing how needy Julie was, I'm sure that Luque's team had to babysit Julie throughout the trial. I'll bet she drove them crazy the whole time, because she loved being a media star.

Everything was in flux for a while, but when Starr decided not to retry Julie it was all over. He cited "resource allocation" as his reason for not pursuing it.[14] Then Julie couldn't get the lawyers to return her phone calls. They put it behind them and they were done with her.

It has never been revealed who paid for Julie's defense. One story claimed that it was done pro bono. But then Julie set up a website for her "legal defense fund" to help pay her "crushing legal fees."[15] Parading in front of the cameras, she bemoaned her $800,000 legal bill and claimed to be in the process of putting her house up for sale. Ten years later, Julie's website is still soliciting money and she's living quietly somewhere in North Carolina. Was she paid off?

Julie didn't testify during the trial as promised, but afterward she testified before the press like an evangelist, when she was not under oath. After everything I'd sworn to in court and after all the cross-examinations I'd endured, Julie stood up in public and said whatever she wanted. Even after she was nearly convicted, even after the papers reported that the jury voted nine to three to convict or retry her, she stood before the press and lied.

Then she appeared before a Senate subcommittee, and Maxine Waters praised her as a wonderful woman and a patriot. Julie lapped it up, reveling in the notoriety. She absolutely loved it.

Federal prosecutor David Barger told me they considered retrying Julie, but Judge Starr chose not to. When they looked at the political climate and the public's attitude, they figured everybody was done with it and wouldn't want any more tax dollars spent on it. So they didn't. Luque tried to sue the Starr investigation on Julie's behalf for their "unreasonable prosecution." They lost.

Julie had a game she played about "the white CNN truck." She just *knew* they were going to be showing up at her house and she said she didn't want to be interviewed by them, because it was "just too upsetting for Adam." This from a woman who would have crawled in the gutter to get to a CNN truck! But then she started calling the Chesterfield police—and I know they knew she was a whack job—and she claimed the police were helping her jump over the back fence to get away from CNN. Now find me a policeman who's going to help a woman jump over a fence! If she was being threatened, they would have put her in the car and driven her out of there. They're not out helping ditzy women jump fences to escape from CNN trucks. They're out doing actual police work!

Then she took up with Richard Gooding, who worked for the *Star*. She had many versions of the story that I had told her about the Oval Office incident, and she planned to profit at my expense. She almost went to Europe to sell the same story to the London tabloids for serious money—$100,000.

Chris Matthews

As the months went by, the Clintonistas were grinding my reputation into the dirt. And I was still looking for jobs and trying to have a life. Judge Starr's office had requested that I remain out of the spotlight, so I had stayed away from the media for a little more than a year, but once the trial was over I was free to speak. Finally, I thought, I could rehabilitate my reputation.

I decided Chris Matthews might be someone who could help me because he had been a real supporter. I contacted him and we talked. "Clinton's guilty as hell," Chris told me. "Guys like Clinton are protected." I knew he understood my story, the terror of the jogger's threat, the harm to my pets, and the degradation the Clintons had dished out. He invited me to come on *Hardball* to tell my story.

Chris was my first interview after that year and that was a big deal for him. He was excited. He even bought a new shirt and showed it to me. I appeared on *Hardball with Chris Matthews* for his entire hour.

After a few background questions, he asked me about the jogger and quizzed me about his identity. I told him I couldn't answer the question because the Independent Counsel was still investigating it. But he was insistent. He asked if I'd been shown pictures of the man. Yes, I had. He asked if I had an idea who the man was. Yes, I did. He asked if he was someone close to the Clintons. Yes, he was. And then he said, "Okay, so it's Cody Shearer."

As Chris uttered those last two words, I could hear his producer Rob Yarin yelling into Chris's earpiece in the middle of the show, "No! What are you *doing*?"

But Chris did it. He uttered the name. He had broken every rule known to journalists. He had gotten caught up in the hype and he blew it. I later learned the OIC investigation determined that Shearer supposedly had an airtight alibi, which made his gaffe that much worse.

One of the people watching *Hardball* that night was Pat Buchanan's brother, Hank Buchanan, who has been described as "unstable." When Hank heard Chris say the name Cody Shearer he thought, *How dare he threaten Kathleen Willey. I'm just going to go take care of him myself!*

Hank Buchanan looked up Shearer in the phone book. Then he got a gun. A few days later, Shearer was having a dinner party and Buchanan broke in, brandishing the gun and making wild threats. The Washington police arrested him and took him away.

Cody Shearer, of course, went after Matthews. He confronted Chris at a railroad platform in Philadelphia and threatened to sue him and MSNBC from here till tomorrow.

Chris was angry with me. Though he should never have revealed what I had told him behind the scenes and off the record, he blamed me. I had told him the jogger was average height, but when Chris met Shearer, he thought he was short. Chris badgered me, as if I'd misled him because my description of the jogger didn't match Shearer. Chris turned on me, awfully. He started bad-mouthing me, looking for someone—besides himself—to be the fall guy for his mistake.

"Chris, I didn't do anything!" I said. "You did it. You broke every rule."

"How did you describe the jogger?" Chris challenged me. "How tall is he?"

"I said he was about medium height."

"Well, I know he's not! He's a real little guy!" Chris yelled at me.

"What are you talking about?" I said.

"Have you ever met Cody Shearer? He's a really short guy! He only comes up to my chest!"

"Well, Chris, has it occurred to you that you're a tall guy and I'm pretty short?"

Chris charged that the jogger's description obviously didn't match Shearer because Shearer was much shorter than average, and I had said the jogger was "average." But Chris is tall and I'm only five-three!

"To me, it's kind of average height to be anywhere from five-seven and taller."

He blew it. He was frustrated that I wouldn't name the guy, so he did it. And he went off on me. I tried to patch it up with him, even calling him at home. But Chris wouldn't talk to me. "What are you calling me for?" he yelled. "What do you want with me?" Unfortunately, I've only spoken to Chris once since then, which I feel is a real tragedy.

The Machine

After everything I'd been through, I was pretty shy. But at the same time I felt like I needed to vindicate myself, tell my side of the story. I had been slammed in the press for more than a year. So I agreed to go on *Larry King Live* for the entire hour and I did some print interviews. But it was hard.

"I felt that she was very badly maligned by so many people, on many levels," said Dennis Alvater, one of the FBI agents on the obstruction of justice case for the OIC. "Kathleen's motives, background, credibility, and information were thoroughly examined. She was examined, interviewed, and documented more than any other witness, other than, perhaps, Monica Lewinsky."

The Clinton machine also attacked Ken Starr. What they did to him was awful and he finally resigned. David Schippers gave an eloquent speech in the House about Starr. Without reading notes, Shippers was compelling. In fact, Alice Starr thanked him after it was over.

Robert Ray was appointed to replace Starr and finish the Independent Counsel's investigation. Ray was their boy, with political aspirations. He wanted to run for the Senate from New Jersey and was looking to score points. He undoubtedly thought that, once the thing was over, the Clintons would be out there supporting him, but that didn't happen. They didn't want him, either.

I later learned that Ray considered trying me for perjury, which he couldn't do because I had an immunity agreement. But he was going to try to surpass that.

That's what my life was like after it was all over. Dave Schippers recalls what I went through after the impeachment. "All these people who were going to help her," Schippers says, "who 'had her best interests at heart,' they turned their backs on her, wouldn't help her at all, after it was all over."[16]

Ray concluded the investigation. Everything that had happened to me, all the evidence of scare tactics and intimidation, all came to naught. Ray reported some of my testimony but the terror and intimidation were not part of it. Bullseye and Blarney, the kennel, the man under my deck, the jogger—it was as if none of it had ever happened.

Everything I had done to help the investigation and all I'd been through—the invasion of my privacy, the interrogations, the polygraph tests, and all the time and *work* I'd given to this investigation—was barely mentioned in the Independent Counsel's report. Even Dennis Alvater, one of the FBI investigators on my case, said, "I really resent the fact that the Kathleen Willey portion of the Independent Counsel investigation was barely mentioned and was practically reduced to nothing more than a footnote in Bob Ray's final report." I felt as if Ray just did not care what Clinton and his wife and their friends had done to me. However, we wrote a rebuttal, which Ray did include in the final report.

In 2006, a more sinister side of Ray became apparent. While married, Ray was arrested for allegedly stalking his former lover in New York. "His ex-girlfriend, Tracy Loughlin, had told police that Ray—a former GOP Senate candidate from New Jersey—had obsessively followed her and blanketed her with unwanted calls and e-mails after their breakup."[17]

Larry Klayman

After all the time I had spent sanding down the *Egret* and helping to paint it, I finally asked my boyfriend, "Am I ever going to get to ride on this thing? Take me out for a sail!" At last, we went out on that beautiful boat with her bold red sails.

When we got back to the dock and got in the car, my cell phone had thirteen messages. I thought, *Wow, something's up.* I had messages from Lisa Meyers and Jackie Judd. Numerous media people wanted statements from me.

Larry Klayman had filed a complaint, to which I was not even a party and about which I had been unaware. But he won. *We* won. The federal judge, Royce Lamberth of the Federal District Court in Washington, decided that Clinton was guilty of invasion of privacy for releasing my letters and that, in doing so, Clinton had committed "a criminal violation of the Privacy Act." In his ruling, Judge Lamberth said that when Clinton and his aides released the letters, they surely knew of his 1997 finding that the White House was bound by the Privacy Act.[18] A violation of the Privacy Act is a misdemeanor punishable by up to one year in prison. Clinton is the only sitting president who has ever been found guilty of a federal misdemeanor. For me it was another small victory, another vindication!

I decided not to do interviews that day because I didn't want to. I'd had a nice sail and I was in a good mood. It was already midafternoon, so they couldn't get a crew down to the Keys and back to Miami in time for the six thirty news, so they wanted me to come to Miami. They offered to send a car, but I said no. I didn't want to get dressed up and drive three hours to talk about Bill Clinton.

The Clinton administration went to great lengths to protect Bill's all-important image. My character and testimony were repeatedly maligned in the press and I was constantly reminded of the pervasive power of the Clintons. And at the end of it all, my testimony was reduced to a footnote in a report that had no effect. An anticlimactic ending to what was a tiring journey.

When Clinton left office, the thought of a third Clinton term was barely a blip on anyone's radar. In a few years, however, Hillary would set up shop in New York and begin working toward ensuring that she had a place in history as more than just the wife of one of the most promiscuous presidents in history.

Bill Clinton is clearly an offensive and disreputable person who is capable of much when up against the wall. He is a competent person, even if he is incompetent at keeping his hands to himself. But he is surrounded by people who have done *nothing* to help him change his behavior. Hillary, more than anyone, has enabled him to continue to abuse women. What's more, there is reason to think that Bill was not the one responsible for waging war against me and the other women who were subject to his sexual advances. Rather, it is Hillary who almost certainly saw their political careers on the line and who reacted accordingly — with a clear and strong determination to suppress anyone who dared jeopardize her shot at the presidency, and to suppress them by any means possible.

CHAPTER TEN

A THIRD CLINTON TERM?

THE CLINTONS ARE GOOD at what they do. They are insulated, protected by layers of people who are willing to be layers. Their cabal has long had relationships with private investigators, from the earliest days in Arkansas. And from that beginning, it was Hillary who engaged these private investigators. After all, what woman had more reason? Bill always cheated on his girlfriends and Hillary was no exception. And she knew it. She didn't like it, but she didn't leave him either.

It is fascinating to note that the very first "investigators" that Hillary dispatched were her own father and brother. When Bill and Hillary left Yale and committed to marry each other, Bill went to Arkansas to teach law and Hillary went to work in Washington. But "Hillary eventually got wind of what was going on in Little Rock and sent her father and brother down from Illinois to work on Clinton's congressional campaign," says addictions specialist and author of *The Clinton Syndrome* Jerome Levin, Ph.D. "Everyone in Clinton's circle assumed that Hillary's father and brother were there to spy on Bill and to reign in his sexual proclivities."[1]

According to former Arkansas state auditor Julia Hughes Jones, Hillary kept tabs on Bill's womanizing, not so she could get him to stop or to fight with him about monogamy, but so she could head off any repercussions. "Every time he was out and Hillary knew where he went," Jones said, "she would call behind him to see what she needed to do to take care of it."[2]

According to Thomas Kuiper, who wrote *I've Always Been a Yankees Fan*, "Hillary sent out a group of investigators known as the 'Truth Squad' while Clinton was Arkansas governor, to discourage many of Bill's former lovers from going public."[3] One wonders how they might have "discouraged" these women.

One detective Hillary hired to track down Bill's women was Ivan Duda. According to Ed Klein, who wrote *The Truth About Hillary*, Hillary tasked Duda with "damage control over Bill's philandering." Telling him that her husband was headed for the presidency, Hillary said, "I want you to get rid of all these bitches he's seeing...I want you to give me the names and addresses and phone numbers, and we can get them under control."[4]

In 1987, Clinton was considering running for the presidency when his Chief of Staff, Betsey Wright, compiled a list of Clinton's affairs. Gary Hart was a rising political star until a scandal revealed he'd had an affair—ruining his career—so Wright was more than a little worried that Clinton's rampant infidelities might similarly damage her boy's political future. Dr. Levin says Hillary and Wright were "deeply worried that his 'zipper problem' would lead to disaster." Their plan was to gather the list of Clinton's women and plan for attacks on his character by devising preemptive strikes, "pre-cut responses to the accusations, regardless of what they might be." Levin says the roster was jokingly referred to as the "Doomsday List."[5] To the women, I'm sure, it was no joke.

But there was one problem. According to Dr. Levin, "Clinton had been with so many women that, not only could he not remember their names, he had no idea how many there had been."[6]

Hillary joined Betsey in the effort to find and discredit the women and hired a private detective to follow her husband and verify her suspicions of Bill's philandering. Of eight women the investigator found, Hillary only had hard evidence to prove that Bill was sleeping with Gennifer Flowers and Dolly Kyle Browning.[7]

Hillary biographer Carl Bernstein reported that "Betsey's operation became known as the 'The Defense Department,' and Wright was sometimes referred to as the 'secretary of defense.'" Betsey accumulated boxes and boxes of files she'd developed on all the Clinton scandals, including files collected by San Francisco private investigator Jack Palladino.[8]

In 1988, faced with all the evidence, Clinton decided not to run for president. But with help from the "Doomsday List" and the "Truth Squad," he and his team were somehow assured that his "woman problem" would disappear. In 1992, Clinton decided to run.

When Joyce Milton started writing *The First Partner: Hillary Rodham Clinton*, she was an admirer. In the process of doing her homework, however, Milton connected the dots between Hillary and private investigators. The book names several operatives of the Clinton squad, of which Hillary was in charge. According to Milton, in 1992 Hillary helped enlist a private security agency to silence a rumor that Clinton had sex with a black prostitute and fathered her child.[9]

I think we should be very concerned as to how Hillary's private security agency might silence such a rumor.

A Nest of Spooks

In January of 1999, Jackie Judd reported on *ABC News* that private investigator Jared Stern had "become a key witness in the investigation of whether there was an attempt to scare Kathleen Willey."

"I've been told that you were doing some work regarding Kathleen Willey," Judd confronted Stern. "Is it true?"

Stern was tight-lipped. "It is true. The specifics of it I don't want to get into."[10]

I didn't care. When I saw Jared Stern on television, my mouth dropped open and I started crying.

Jackie Judd found sources who said Nate had asked his lawyer to detail my story in a "chronology," and the lawyer hired Stern's firm. Judd reported that Stern's assignment included pulling my phone records, finding out what medications I was taking, and conducting a "noisy investigation" so I would know I was being watched.[11]

Stern's lawyer at that time, Ed Bouquet, told Judd, "I think that he perceived a situation where he was being asked to do something that he wasn't comfortable with." Judd added, "Bouquet claims Stern was so uncomfortable that he called Willey and left a message—using an alias—warning her that someone wanted to do her harm."[12]

So Stern was the man who called as "Kirk," the man who left a message on my answering machine in Powhatan while I was in the Florida Keys. But, to this day, Stern is cagey about his motives for calling me. He points out that it was *his lawyer* who characterized his feelings as "uncomfortable," *not* Stern himself. When I recently asked him why he felt compelled to warn me, his answer was, "No response." When I asked why he called, his answer was the same.[13] I started to wonder if Stern felt uncomfortable at all. Maybe he didn't really call to warn me, but for some other reason.

Stern said that when he left the message on my answering machine he did intend to call back but began to feel concerned about "the enormity of the matter and possible repercussions. And," he added, "the theory that the FBI or OIC may be recording your calls visited me." He was right about that!

Jackie Judd revealed that my old friend, Nate Landow, was behind Stern's involvement. Nate's lawyer, Saul Shwartzbach, hired Prudential Associates, the firm Stern worked for.[14] Stern is vague about who else was involved. He will only add that, "There may have been other contacts."

Stern won't even say what his job was in 1998, but only confirms information that is already public knowledge, including that Bob Miller, the president of Prudential at that time, gave him the assignment regarding me. He says Miller called him "late one night and asked me to meet him at the bottom level of a parking garage. I went and met him. He said he had something very important that needed to be handled so we discussed the matter and tasks." Stern said the garage was not near their office, but on Jefferson Street in Rockville, Maryland. Stern wouldn't tell me why they met there instead of at their offices.

But another man who was a contractor for Prudential during that time, who refuses to release his name, said that Miller and his "Democrat buddies" gathered at a clandestine club that was known as the "Progress Club." In fact, the Progress Club Foundation is still listed in directories at 1610 East Jefferson Street in Rockville, Maryland. It appears today to be a philanthropic organization but, ten years ago, according to the contractor, this private club had no signage and was "real hush-hush." Though Rockville police busted the place for gambling once or twice, the contractor only knew that the club was a "Washington incarnation" and its politicos were a "Clinton crowd."[15]

"I know that Bob Miller had things done for his Democratic Party buddies for decades because he had this nest of spooks—former CIA agents and contractors—that was disconnected from the federal government, so there was [a] buffer," the contractor said. "Bob Miller was the information backflow stopgap. He was the king of implied threat regarding these secret tasks and preventing disclosure to the public." After Miller died in 1998, the buffer between his Democratic buddies and the "nest of spooks" was gone and, as the contractor told me, "That was the end."[16] Presumably, that is when the place went legitimate.

Miller likely walked out of a meeting with Clinton insiders at the Progress Club, met Jared Stern in the parking garage across the street, and gave him the assignment regarding me. Stern would only discuss the basics of that conversation. When I asked him if he had any knowledge of White House involvement in my case, he replied, "I have no response."

But Stern did divulge that he and Miller discussed a "pretty standard checklist" for opposition research. Speaking only generally, he elucidated that a "checklist of civil litigation related opposition research could include background checks, surveillance, pretext contact with the person to extract information, documentation of current and/or past activities or relationships..." Stern said he suggested some strategies or tactics to Miller, who said, "They have someone else handling that." But, Stern added, "I don't know who 'they' were." When I asked Stern if he knew who had handled the intimidation side of my case, he said, "No response."[17]

Further, when asked what "strategies or tactics" he might have suggested, Stern answered, "No response." However, based on this conversation with Miller, Stern did validate that the jogger approached me. "I knew," Stern says, "because Bob Miller told me it was being handled by someone else. I don't know if that meant someone else within our firm or other."[18] And Stern won't clarify what "it" meant.

"I know that there was a jogger that…threatened Kathleen Willey, but I don't know who it was," said the unnamed former contractor for Prudential, who added, "I have heard firsthand tape recordings of Nathan Landow, screaming profanity-laden threats, insults, and demands at someone. I won't tell you who…"[19] Stern, for his part, won't confirm the existence of such tapes—or even such a conversation.

Stern adds that Miller never explicitly said the assignment was related to Saul Schwartzbach's or Nathan Landow's tasking. Stern further insists that, "Nathan Landow's lawyers—Saul Shwartzbach and Joe Caldwell—nor Mr. Landow ever asked me to do anything illegal."

But when I asked Stern whether Bob Miller asked him to do anything illegal, he replied, "No response."[20] Big surprise.

So what did Miller ask Stern to do?

Stern would only say that, "Among the discussed tasks was investigative research." Whether this would include "opposition research" or conducting a "noisy investigation" is open to interpretation, but it raises the possibility that Stern did not call to warn me. That phone call was likely part of an assignment.

The former Prudential contractor described three possible reasons why Stern might have called. First, he said, it might have been to warn me of clandestine activities underway that were counter to my well-being. Second, it could have been a pretext authorized by Bob Miller to gain my trust and extract details from me about what information or evidence I had provided the OIC, such as tape recordings of Nathan Landow or President Clinton. Finally, he added, it could have been a combination of both.[21]

If Stern had called to warn me, why wouldn't he admit that? Indeed, I now have little reason to think that Stern's phone call was motivated by compassionate concern. Certainly it wouldn't help his reputation as a private investigator. And Stern was no novice PI. He joined Miller's firm in 1990 and worked in various capacities—as a surveillance trainer, manager, and director of operations. In fact, he is now president of Prudential Associates, a "risk-management and security-consulting" firm, after purchasing the company from Miller's widow three years after working on my case. According to his biography on Prudential's website, Stern is a former Marine who has conducted intelligence operations overseas, possesses extensive intelligence acquisition experience, has jungle warfare experience, and has conducted specialized military operations in high-risk environments.[22] Unless I was in danger of being murdered, I doubt that a consummate professional like Stern would defy orders and call to "warn" me out of the goodness of his heart.

Private investigators with CIA training might employ techniques from their experience in intelligence operations. One such concept is the "stalking horse" tactic, which comes from an old hunting technique. It is hard for humans to sneak up on their animal prey, but if another animal approaches, the prey won't flee, so hunters will walk behind their horses to get closer to the prey. In spy jargon, the term "stalking horse" refers to an operative who appears neutral so that he can get close to a subject, but his pretense actually disguises a more sinister motive. In my case, it is possible that Jared Stern called to "warn" me in order to get close to me so he could find out what I had said or was going to say to federal investigators. As the former contractor suggested, Stern may well have called under this "pretext" to find out what I knew about Nate or Clinton.

One PI suggested another strategic concept that might have been at work. "False-flag ops" are operations in which an agent engages in an activity that is counter to one group or country's interest, and makes it look like the activity was done by another person, group, or country. In other words, the operative cloaks his activity behind known or obvious objectives of another entity, as if disguising the action under the "flag" of another group. If this tactic was at work in my case, it may mean that PIs like Bob Miller and his gang were trying to make it look like Nate was behind the investigation, while it was someone else altogether.

Asked whether he was aware of Stern's secret project, the former contractor explained that he was "aware of it, but not of all the details. Things were very compartmentalized," he explained. "The former CIA guys and spook contractors were always working on something secretive."[23] In a large investigative firm, each investigator gets individual orders on a "need-to-know basis." As one investigator told me, "We are all just soldiers." The contractor added that Prudential staff at the time were "all spooks." Bob Miller was former military intelligence, while others were mostly CIA and CIA contractors.

I can only speculate, but I think it is fair to say that despite initial reports, Stern did not have my interests at heart when he called me that day.

I later learned that Prudential operatives also obtained my telephone records. A man named Russell, who was close to Bob Miller's family during the investigation, provided me a copy of a report of every telephone call I made one day after my *60 Minutes* appearance. By email, Russell told me the records were extracted from my telephone records. When the FBI showed me my telephone records, I was stunned at my lack of privacy. When I found out that the private investigators were able to retrieve the same information and pass it along to their clients, I felt sick.

Jared Stern said he didn't exactly quit the investigation or refuse the assignment, but the project "ended at some point." In fact, the end seems to have coincided with the death of Bob Miller, who succombed to cancer. Stern didn't like Miller, personally or professionally, and when Miller died Stern had to undergo yet another round of OIC questioning. Overall, Stern says, "the OIC investigation was...burdensome."[24]

But the unnamed Prudential contractor revealed further tantalizing information that has never been publicly divulged, until now. He said that during my investigation, I was not Stern's only target, but that there were others, particularly another "political operator." He would not confirm whether these were more tasks from Landow and his lawyers or if Miller handled these endeavors without Nate's awareness. Further, while OIC agents ferociously insisted that there were grounds for criminal prosecution, none occurred, and the former contractor suggested that Stern's *other* investigation might have had something to do with why the OIC did not act against Bill Clinton.[25] True to form, Stern will not divulge who else he might have been working for at the time. But when asked if he is concealing anything about these events now, he answers flatly, "Yes."

Clearly, from every angle, there are significant and important elements of the Prudential investigation that are still unknown. The OIC uncovered a great deal of information in several investigations, but most of that remains confidential and under grand jury seal. No doubt the Clintons hope it stays that way. But I hope we find out before it's too late.

While he tries to "maintain a healthy level of near-debilitating paranoia," Stern adds that when Clinton was president, he was more concerned for his own safety and career. Today, as president of Prudential Associates, Stern is obviously mindful of the firm's reputation and won't cooperate in clarifying his firm's role in my case. But what Stern did say was itself revealing. When asked if he had been threatened by any part of the Clinton machine or the Democratic Party, Stern said, "I have no response." And when asked how he feels about the prospect of another Clinton presidency, Stern said, "Sick to my stomach."[26]

Democratic Operatives

In 1978 Clinton was the Arkansas state attorney general, running for governor, when he made a campaign stop at a conference of nursing home administrators. Juanita Hickey, who owned a nursing home, met him at the conference. She was impressed by him. He suggested she call him if she came to Little Rock. When she went there for another conference, they planned a meeting at the coffee shop of the conference hotel. But then he called and asked if they could instead meet in her room, because there were so many reporters in the lobby. She agreed. After all, he was the state attorney general and was going to be the governor. She got coffee ready and he came to her room. Then he raped her.

In time, Juanita remarried and became Juanita Broaddrick. When she finally told her story to Lisa Meyers at NBC in 1999, the network held the story, claiming to need more time to corroborate it. Candice Jackson, author of *Their Lives*, says that when Juanita's story finally aired, a few pundits minimized her allegation on the simple grounds that it could not be proven, while most of the Clintonistas kept their overt attacks to a minimum.[27]

But, Jackson said, Juanita's business was audited by the IRS for the first time in thirty years. "I do not believe this was coincidence," Broaddrick declared. Her marriage also suffered. As Jackson wrote, Juanita's husband had been "totally against my coming forward and I think the unwanted publicity into our private lives gradually destroyed our marriage." They divorced in 2004.[28]

Deeply traumatized, Juanita did not and does not want to talk about the rape. Though we are friends, she would not discuss the experience or its aftermath with me for this book. Her voice trembled as she told me it's still too difficult. Obviously, Juanita continues to experience trauma as a result of Clinton's violence and subsequent events. As Candice Jackson points out, "Most rape victims don't have to stomach their attacker being heralded as the best thing to happen to women since the right to vote."[29]

Juanita does.

Dolly Kyle Browning, subpoenaed as a material witness by House investigators in Clinton's impeachment scandal, swore under oath that she had a sexual relationship with Clinton from the mid-1970s until 1992. Drawn in to the Paula Jones case as well as the OIC investigation, she too had problems with the Clinton henchmen. A lawsuit filed by Larry Klayman on her behalf alleged that, "Plaintiff Dolly Kyle Browning has been intentionally and maliciously threatened by Clinton and his agents, including [Bruce] Lindsey... They threatened to "destroy" her if she told the media about her sexual relationship with Clinton... In addition, Clinton, acting through Lindsey, threatened and intimidated Mrs. Browning into severely limiting her public statements about her relationship with Clinton. Most significant to the instant motion, Clinton and Lindsey also knowingly used threats and intimidation to prevent Mrs. Browning from testifying in the Paula Jones civil rights/sexual harassment lawsuit."[30]

Sally Perdue's 1983 affair with Clinton became news in 1992. According to Candice Jackson, Purdue later said a "Democratic operative named Ron Tucker grilled her and then threatened her not to talk about her liaison with Clinton." Perdue said they offered her a federal job in return for her silence, "[but] if I didn't take the offer, then they knew that I went jogging by myself and couldn't guarantee what would happen to my pretty little legs... Life would get hard."[31] Purdue bravely turned it down. She was fired from her job, her car was damaged, and she received anonymous phone calls and hate mail. There is evidence that a private investigator was involved in her case.

Elizabeth Ward Gracen had a brief affair with Clinton in 1983 and, in 1998, it came to light. According to Candice Jackson, Gracen got an anonymous call telling her "she'd better shut up about her affair with the president or she could lose her job or be audited by the IRS." Instead, "Gracen took the advice of her lawyer and told her story to the press." Jackson explains, "She chose the route other Clinton women have chosen: going public, even years after their sexual encounters with Clinton, in order to raise their public profiles enough to feel a bit safer."[32]

The next scandal to emerge almost derailed Clinton's presidential bid. Gennifer Flowers went public with the fact that she'd had a long-term affair with Clinton. She was the "first Clinton woman whose story garnered widespread media attention and attracted vicious public attacks from Clinton and his cadre," wrote Jackson.[33] Along the way, Gennifer experienced some of the tactics that would later be used against others. Her mother received threatening phone calls. Her apartment was ransacked. According to an article in *Investor's Business Daily*, when she told Clinton about the invasion on her home, Flowers said, "There was just a tone in his voice. And I thought, you probably had this done to me."[34] As her fear grew, her lawyer suggested she should tape her conversations with Clinton, which she did. The Clintonistas slimed her in the press and, Jackson writes, "Flowers's word was mud by the time Clinton and his gang finished trashing her."[35]

But she had the tapes. When the Clintons found out, they went into high gear.

"We have to destroy her," Hillary said.

And then they did.

According to Candice Jackson, James Carville declared, "We're going to have to go to war."[36] Gail Sheehy, author of *Hillary's*

Choice, quoted Hillary as saying, "I would 'crucify' [Gennifer]."[37] Notably, Hillary was ready to crucify Gennifer but she let her husband off the hook. And it wasn't just Gennifer whom Hillary attacked. Reputed to lead the assaults on all of the women who accused Bill, Hillary insulted us, destroyed our credibility, and labeled us as money-grubbing nuts, sluts, liars, and trailer trash. And, all the while, she knew we were telling the truth. And she knew that she was not.

On the attack, the Clinton operatives amplified their "cash for trash" smear and denounced Gennifer Flowers on talk shows, Candice Jackson reported, and denigrated her in the media for years. Later, when she tried to rejuvenate her singing career, Clinton supporters were everywhere, and "an unfriendly public shut her down."[38]

It took six years, but Gennifer was finally vindicated when Clinton had to confess the truth under oath. According to Candice Jackson, many journalists surprisingly called and apologized to her. But throughout her ordeal, as in my case, no feminist organizations helped her in her public battle against Clinton.[39]

In 1993, "Troopergate" gave America another woman: Paula Jones. Once again, according to Candice Jackson, Hillary "came out swinging to defend her embattled husband."[40] Belittling the troopers' claims as "trash for cash,"[41] the Clintonistas sang the chorus, labeling Paula a bimbo, trailer trash, and—their favorite sound bite—"white trash out for cash."[42] In a monumental insult to millions of Americans, James Carville hit all the talk shows with his most famous cheap shot at Paula Jones: "Drag a hundred-dollar bill through a trailer park and there's no telling what you'll find."

Enduring such blatant insults in the press, Paula eventually got a nose job and a makeover, and looked really good. But the experience took its toll. She and her husband divorced in 1999. Although Clinton finally settled the lawsuit for $850,000, Paula didn't see much of it after all of her attorneys "hashed out entitlements to legal fees," reported Candice Jackson, who said that, by 2000, Paula still owed money to lawyers.[43]

Then there's the Clintons' use of the IRS to harass their enemies. I'm sure that it is because I suffered financial problems that this burden was not visited upon me but, according to a *NewsMax* article, the IRS under Clinton investigated Gennifer Flowers, Paula Jones, Elizabeth Ward Gracen, and Juanita Broaddrick. The article appropriately asks, "Who ordered the IRS to audit Clinton's critics and accusers?"[44] Of course, I can't answer that question. But Thomas Kuiper relates a story in *I've Always been a kees Fan*, his remarkable book of Hillary Clinton quotes. Kuiper says Clinton told his staff that he wanted everyone in the Independent Counsel's office audited.[45] When several people counseled him against this tactic, Clinton slammed his fist down on the table and said, "I can do any goddamned thing I want. I'm the president of the United States. I take care of my friends and I fuck with my enemies."[46]

In fact, conservative activist and San Francisco radio talk show host Melanie Morgan told me, "Every year that the Clintons were in office, I was audited—every single year! There was always *one* thing that they found wrong with my tax return. Always one thing. I haven't had a problem since." But she adds that, if Hillary becomes president, "You can expect to see a lot of conservatives and Republicans audited by the IRS and persecuted."[47]

Linda Tripp affirms that the Clinton operation's tactics were out of bounds. It started with the smear campaigns against her and others. Appearing on *Larry King Live* in 1999, for example, Linda said that when Clinton made his "I did not have sexual relations with that woman" speech, Linda got chills. "I knew that, without evidence, that that's precisely what Monica would become," Linda said, "a woman with an unstable background and a stalker reputation." Regarding the subsequent attacks on herself, Linda said she was not surprised. "I knew I would be destroyed," she said.[48]

But Linda Tripp actually had more vital issues to worry about than her public image. "There came a point in time," she said, "where I felt that the biggest safety net for me was to become visible."

"You have a fear of your life?" Larry King quizzed her.

"Oh, absolutely."

"Based on what? I mean…"

"I know these people are..." Linda paused. "I'm not paranoid. I'm not delusional. I'm just normal, believe it or not, and I have reason to believe that I should at least be somewhat concerned."

"'These people,' meaning?"

"This administration," she answered, "the people who surround themselves or who are in [the] president's inner circle are not..."

"...would do you physical harm?" Larry supplied.

"They are not honorable people," Linda answered. "You know, I don't think that the president or one of his henchmen is going to be behind a bush with an Uzi. Do I think it's possible that I may, down the road, walk in front of a Mack truck and have an unfortunate accident? I think it's possible."

"Have you ever had a direct threat?" Larry King asked.

"I have. I believe I've had a direct threat."

"By phone or...?"

"In July, when the president had his Linda Tripp meeting with Monica, she carried what I believe to be threats from the president. And, later in that month, when I spoke with Bruce Lindsey, I believe I received implied threats."[49]

"Hillary's legal team kept a phalanx of detectives on the payroll through the impeachment imbroglio to find incriminating information about their enemies," former Clinton strategist and author Dick Morris wrote in *Rewriting History*. "The fact that they were paid for by private funds, and were not government officials, is a detail. They worked for the president and first lady, and their job was to spy on American citizens."[50]

Morris refers to Hillary's defense of her husband's administration as a "scorched-earth"[51] policy.

It worked. Many of our lives were scorched.

Terry F. Lenzner

Initially, the White House would not confirm whether it had hired Washington, D.C. private investigator Terry Lenzner. In 1998, the *Washington Post* reported that the administration would only say that "no private investigators were looking into prosecutors, reporters, or Clinton critics." But a day later, Lenzer confirmed that he worked for the Clintons and, though he would not discuss his work, he defended it, saying, "There would be nothing wrong if he was investigating prosecutors."[52]

Terry F. Lenzner owns Investigative Group International (IGI) and has a long, intertwined history with the Clintons, especially Hillary. Before she married Bill, Hillary worked on the Senate Watergate committee, for which Lenzner was an investigator. Hillary and Terry also served together on the board of Legal Services Corporation with their mutual friend, Mickey Kantor.[53] An op-ed in *Investor's Business Daily* concluded, "More than likely, bringing Lenzner into the White House fold was also Hillary's idea."[54]

Some reports claim that Lenzner began working for the Clinton camp as early as 1991. But when the 1992 campaign heated up, Lenzner met Harold Ickes, Clinton's deputy chief of staff, and before long, IGI was working for the Clintons' legal defense fund. According to a *New York Post* article by Sam Dealey, "The Clinton campaign hired [Lenzner's] firm in 1992 to do 'opposition research,' a euphemism for dirt-digging."[55] In fact, Joyce Milton wrote that David Kendall, Clinton's personal lawyer, hired Lenzner and IGI to investigate Paula Jones, Ken Starr's prosecutors, and GOP lawyers Victoria Toensing and Joseph diGenova, among others. "IGI agents didn't stop there," Milton wrote. "Accounts have Lenzner's operatives snooping into the backgrounds of Kathleen Willey, Monica Lewinsky, and Linda Tripp." When Dick Morris alleged that IGI was, in effect, the Clintons' "secret police," Milton concluded, "Judging by the revolving door between IGI and the administration, this is not an exaggeration."[56]

Milton said several Clinton staff members had worked at IGI. Raymond Kelly became Clinton's Secret Service chief. Ricki Seidman joined the Justice Department. And Terry Lenzner's daughter became an intern to Clinton's senior advisor, George Stephanopoulos. This revolving door went both ways. Former FBI general counsel Howard Shapiro signed on as Lenzner's lawyer, and former FBI official Larry Potts became an IGI executive.[57]

What's more, the IGI list includes a couple of very familiar names, namely Cody Shearer and his twin sister Brooke. According to Sam Dealey, Lenzner and Shearer were old tennis buddies and, Dealey wrote, Shearer was also a close friend of Sidney

Blumenthal's."[58] An intriguing player, Brooke had been Hillary's close friend and political ally since college. Married to Clinton's deputy secretary of state, Strobe Talbott, Brooke also happened to have a private investigator's license. In fact, in the early years, she was known as the "Dumpster Diver" because she'd dig through people's trash to get the goods on them. Notorious for investigating Republicans, Larry Flynt also called Brooke "a very good friend of mine," according to Dealey.[59] Brooke presumably tired of rummaging through other peoples' garbage and left IGI to run a fellowship program at the White House before joining the Department of the Interior.[60]

Her infamous brother, Cody, presumably innocent of being the jogger who threatened me, was nonetheless an IGI "subcontractor." One of the ironies of the mess was that everyone *knew* Cody Shearer was a covert operator who was tightly woven into the shady side of the Clinton administration. He was also a loose cannon. Pressed under oath in a deposition, Lenzner had to admit that he had hired Shearer as a subcontractor on at least one job. In 1992, Cody Shearer "was charged with digging up dirt on President Bush and Vice President Dan Quayle." Interestingly, the *Investor's Business Daily* column alleged that Shearer is friends with some of Al Gore's associates and has a relationship with Gore's fund-raiser pal, Peter Knight.[61] I have to wonder if Shearer is also tight with Gore's other fund-raiser pal, Nate Landow.

IGI's offices are located just four blocks from the White House. Following the model of the old "Truth Squad," IGI came to be known as the Clintons' private CIA. Outside the government, it could operate more freely. IGI's other political clients included Ted Kennedy and the Democratic National Committee—with which Nate Landow also has a tight history![62]

When IGI was accused of investigating Ken Starr's lieutenants for Clinton's lawyers, Lenzner landed in front of Starr's grand jury. It wasn't the first time he had been called to testify about his activities and clients.

Starr also called Sid Blumenthal as a witness. As "Sid Vicious" wrote in his purported tell-all, *The Clinton Wars*, "I had been subpoenaed...to explain my relations with Terry Lenzner,

Jack Palladino, and Anthony Pellicano—all private investigators who at one time or another had worked for Clinton's lawyers." Blumenthal denied having had any contact with the PIs and testified before the grand jury that he had never received information from them, neither directly nor indirectly. And he supposedly did not know anything about the president's lawyers' relationships with these notorious investigators, either.[63] Contradicting himself, though, he also wrote, "tensions grew between McCurry and the lawyers, who acknowledged that they had hired Lenzner—Bob Bennett had used him for years on the Jones case." But, he adds, "He was not investigating anyone's private life."[64]

Yeah, right.

I recently asked a former *CBS News* producer if he had information that any of Clinton's notorious private investigators were involved in my case. He told me he thought Lenzner's group was probably one of those involved in the terror tactics against me, but he wouldn't divulge any more information. In fact, he wouldn't let me use his name. But when I told him that it was an awful time for me, he said, "I have no doubt that it was an awful time for you. I am sure you were terrified."[65]

Palladino & Sutherland

"Do you think Gennifer is the sort of person who would commit suicide?" Private investigator Jack Palladino found every old friend that Gennifer Flowers ever knew and posed such questions. Looking to discredit Flowers, he also went "around the country talking to people who knew me," Flowers told Lorraine Adams of the *Washington Post*. "I had calls from people—girl friends, guy friends, people I had known. It wasn't necessarily people I had known well." According to Adams, "The Clinton campaign reported that it had paid Palladino $93,000 in 1992 to probe the allegations and private lives of women who claimed to have had relationships with the candidate."[66]

Only recently, a memo from Jack Palladino to the Clintons in early 1992 became known. In this memo, Palladino confirmed that the purpose of his work was to "impeach Flowers' character and veracity until she is destroyed beyond all recognition."[67] That sounds a lot like the philosophy of Hillary and Sid Blumenthal, with their "destroy your enemies" approach to politics. There is little doubt that the Clintons—Hillary—hired Palladino to go after Gennifer.

Palladino also worked on Sally Perdue's case. Her 1983 affair with Clinton became news in 1992 and, less than a week later, Michael Isikoff reported that Clinton, "had retained San Francisco private investigator Jack Palladino to discredit stories about women claiming to have had relationships with the Arkansas governor," and to "douse a number of stories that threatened to revive the issue."[68]

Reporter David Helvarg also said Palladino started investigating "bimbo eruptions" for Clinton's 1992 campaign. Working from their Victorian mansion in San Francisco's Haight-Ashbury district, Palladino and his wife Sandra Sutherland run Palladino & Sutherland, working with a crew of West Coast operatives. In a 1998 *Mother Jones* article, "All the President's PIs," Helvarg wrote that Palladino and Sutherland "have worked for clients ranging from Hell's Angels to Black Panthers to international bankers. While investigating American Express in Europe in 1989, Sutherland posed as a journalist to try to develop leads."[69]

According to Helvarg, there was some question as to why Charles Ruff—Clinton's chief White House counsel—paid Palladino $130,000 to snoop for the Teamsters in 1994 during the contested election of Ron Carey as Teamsters president. Neither Ruff nor Palladino, who has a reputation for intimidating the targets of his investigations, have disclosed the nature of that work.[70] According to a 2005 *NewsMax* story, "A notation in the campaign's Federal Election Commission filing shows that Palladino was paid from campaign coffers."[71]

Of course, Paula Jones's lawyers wanted to question Palladino about his work for the Clintons regarding Gennifer Flowers and "numerous other women who were alleged to have had affairs with Bill," but Helvarg said Palladino dodged the subpoena.[72]

I have every reason to believe that Palladino was deeply involved in my case as well. Many of the scare tactics used against me were just his style.

In the nonfiction movie *The Insider,* a big tobacco executive and his lawyer make a veiled threat to a former employee who is secretly considering blowing the whistle and exposing the company on *60 Minutes.* After the employee leaves the meeting, the lawyer says to the company president, "I don't think he's getting the message."

It gave me chills. That is exactly what the jogger said to me.

Is it just a coincidence that Jack Palladino was a consultant on that movie?

Melanie Morgan met Palladino and his wife in Corte Madera, California, in 2003. Speaking to an audience of mystery writers at the annual Book Passage Mystery Writers Conference, the PI team described their investigative techniques, media exposure, and contributions to books and movies. Melanie, who was writing a cold-case murder mystery, also happens to be a journalist of thirty-plus years and co-host of a conservative talk radio show in San Francisco. At the time, though, Palladino just knew her as another mystery writer.

After they gave their talk, Palladino and Sutherland sat at a table signing books. Melanie approached, interested in hiring Palladino to help with her murder mystery. Looking for investigative tips and resources, Melanie struck up a conversation with him and Palladino gave her some leads and contact information. They had a fun repartee and she found him to be a nice guy, gregarious and outgoing. Melanie established a rapport with him and Palladino jumped up and paced while they talked. He seemed to enjoy the limelight, so she finessed a little more information out of him.

Melanie spoke out of earshot of most of the people around them. "Aren't you ashamed of yourself," she chided Palladino, "with the business you did for Hillary Clinton?"

Palladino looked up and "kind of gave me a lazy smile, and his wife, who is British, shot her husband a look," Melanie says. "Her eyes cut over to him and I could tell he was debating whether to answer me or not." So Melanie added, "You know, come on, that stuff with Kathleen Willey was pretty outrageous. What was that?" She smiled at him. "You guys ran over her cat? What was that all about?"

"Well, I'm not really going to comment about that but let me just say this," Palladino replied. "The only regret that I had about that whole thing was that Hillary did not pay me in a timely fashion."

Then his wife chimed in. According to Melanie, Sutherland looked to be in her late fifties and she had a sharp tongue. "You could tell she was the boss of the operation," Melanie says. "She started making some nasty comments about Hillary Clinton, and the two of them were laughing and snorting over the fact that they had to bring a certain amount of pressure to bear."

"Yes," the radio commentator inquired artfully, "I've read that Hillary has a lot of problems about paying people to whom she owes money, including the ghostwriter for her book."

"Yes, we noticed that problem as well," they told her.

Keeping the rapport going, Melanie smiled at him and asked, "You didn't really kill her cat, did you?"

Palladino indicated his work was "more like Dumpster diving." But Melanie noted that "he smiled when he said it and looked at his wife, and alarm bells were going off, like 'Shut up!'"

"He definitely acknowledged that there was something that had transpired there with Kathleen Willey and her cat," Melanie said, "and that his biggest regret was that he didn't get cash up front from Hillary Clinton!" Palladino and Sutherland were eventually paid, Melanie says, "But my distinct impression was that they had to threaten to go public with it."

"I saved Hillary Clinton's *ass*," Palladino told her. "You'd think she'd be more grateful to me."[73]

The Pelican

When Gennifer Flowers came forward with taped conversations between herself and Clinton, his team accused her of doctoring the tapes. To refute her, they had private investigator Anthony Pellicano evaluate the tapes. Not surprisingly, the notorious thug determined Gennifer's tapes had been doctored.[74] According to Dick Morris, Gennifer Flowers "submitted the tapes to another service, Truth Verification Labs, which found them to be completely authentic."[75]

But discrediting tapes is tame work for Anthony Pellicano. Also called "The Pelican," he is a notoriously bad guy who is known, according to *World Net Daily*, "for dirty tricks and rough tactics on behalf of celebrity clients." A member of the "Shadow Team" through Clinton's two terms as president, Pellicano is reputed to have been deeply involved in the efforts to discredit both Gennifer Flowers and Monica Lewinsky.[76]

In a 1992 profile in *GQ Magazine*, Pellicano boasted about the dirty work he had performed for his clients, including blackmail and physical assault. He claimed to have beaten one of his client's enemies with a baseball bat. 'I'm an expert with a knife,' said Pellicano. 'I can shred your face with a knife.'"[77]

This is not a nice guy.

In 2002, as the story goes, Pellicano hired Alexander Proctor to threaten a *Los Angeles Times* reporter who was working on a story about actor Steven Seagal and possible links to the Mafia. According to *World Net Daily*, "Proctor allegedly…placed a dead fish with a rose in its mouth on the windshield of her car and made a bullet-sized hole in her windshield. He also placed a sign with the word 'stop' on the windshield, court documents show… Proctor said Seagal hired…Pellicano to intimidate the woman into silence. Pellicano…wanted to make it look like the Italians were putting the hit on her, so it wouldn't reflect on Seagal."[78]

These are precisely the kind of terror tactics that were in play against me. It is also, by the way, a perfect example of the "false-flag ops" that may have been involved in Prudential's work on my case.

Proctor told an informant about the Seagal case and Pellicano went to jail for thirty months. *The New York Times* reported that Pellicano pleaded guilty of "illegal possession of hand grenades and plastic explosives."[79]

In 2006, Pellicano finished his term on the weapons charges. Thanks to the feds, though, according to *World Net Daily*, he was "transferred to San Bernardino County Jail, which is sometimes used by the federal prisoners. He was booked on charges that were at that time under seal…[and] is the target of a 110-count federal racketeering indictment…"[80] *The New York Times* reported that a separate grand jury is investigating reported illegal wiretapping and that authorities seemed to "hope that the prison term would extend much further."[81] Pellicano is still in jail, which is where the guy belongs. Unfortunately, his incarceration came after the Clinton years.

During Clinton's administration, Hillary commissioned Pellicano to spy on their perceived "enemies," presumably me and the other women whom Bill Clinton abused, reported *World Net Daily*. "During two terms of the Clinton administration, Pellicano was one of several private investigators used by the White House to conduct 'shadow operations,'" *World Net Daily* said. "But it was Hillary Clinton who hired the 'Shadow Team'—some believe to do work that employees of the federal government could not do."[82]

"In the political life of the Clintons, it was [Hillary] who pioneered the use of private detectives," reported former congressional investigator Barbara Olson (who was killed on 9/11). "It was she who brought in and cultivated the professional dirt-diggers and smear artists."[83]

The "First Husband"

When Clinton assaulted me, Andrew Friendly knocked on the door, then he pounded on the door, then he yelled for Clinton to answer. But Friendly never came in. If the president of the United States does not answer a knock, shouldn't someone enter and make sure he is okay? But Friendly never did, and neither did anyone else. Clinton had obviously told them to stay out.

I have often wondered how many times Andrew Friendly knocked on that door for the Monicas of the world—and whatever the hell else was going on in that place. And I wonder how many times those stewards—those sweet, friendly men who served the president in the Oval Office—had to clean up after Clinton and the likes of Monica Lewinsky.

Clinton never seemed to understand where he was when he lived and worked—and had sex—in the White House. He treated the people's house as if it were a "cool pad" back in Hot Springs, Arkansas, or a frat house at college. He just didn't get it.

Addictions specialist Jerome Levin, Ph.D., who voted for Clinton twice, wrote the fascinating book, *The Clinton Syndrome*. Like many Americans, Dr. Levin believed the "misplaced prosecutory zeal" that invaded Clinton's privacy was worse for the country than Clinton's "sexual practices, whatever they may be."[84] Unfortunately, in Clinton's case, "whatever they may be" included sexual assault and rape. Just because a sex addict happens to be a popular president, we cannot allow him to attack women with impunity.

Nonetheless, Levin *did* hold Clinton accountable for making his sex life a public issue, and affirmed that it was Clinton's addictive behavior that led to his "inability to keep his private life private." Clinton's compulsive desire for approval, which seems to manifest itself in his sexual addiction, "crossed the line from the private to the professional," Levin wrote, "and therefore (because he is the president) has entered the public realm."[85]

Like any other addiction, sexual addiction eventually reaches the breaking point. The alcoholic hits bottom. The gambler goes broke. Drug addicts overdose. And sex addicts self-destruct.

According to Levin, as early as his engagement to Hillary, Clinton's overindulgence in sexual activity became a serious problem for him, not because his behavior had changed but because his life had changed—he had become engaged. And, according to Levin, Clinton "was cheating on Hillary with a girlfriend that he was also cheating on."[86]

In a few years, the consequences of his addiction began to spiral. The Paula Jones case, for example, was indicative of how seriously addicted Clinton had become. Levin argues that it was madness that Clinton refused to settle with Paula Jones so he could stop the inquiry before it snowballed. But Clinton could not admit that what he did to Paula was out of line or that Paula might have felt differently than he did about what happened in that room, so he certainly wasn't about to apologize for it. According to Levin, this mistake was irrational and "revealed his inability to admit that his sex life had been out of control."[87]

Levin further points out that, on the road to self-destruction, Clinton was already under the microscope when he assaulted me and seduced Monica Lewinsky. Given that he was already in serious trouble, these advances were extremely irrational. Levin observes that, in conducting this behavior, Clinton further "opened the door and invited both personal and political destruction."[88]

Of course, John Kennedy also had many affairs and some of these were risky, Levin recalls, such as "sharing women with various gangsters." And Levin adds that, "Kennedy's sexual behavior had a profound influence on Clinton, even foreshadowing Clinton's behavior in many ways." But the difference between Clinton and other presidents who had extramarital affairs—including Kennedy—is that *those* presidents were not sex addicts. "True leaders are programmed to lead," Levin argues, "not to self-destruct." Clearly, the self-destructive nature of Clinton's sexual addiction subverted his ability to lead. That is the distinction between Clinton and other presidents who had extramarital affairs. While Lyndon Johnson, Dwight Eisenhower, Franklin Roosevelt, and John Kennedy all had affairs, Levin says, they differ from Clinton in that their "private indiscretions were not self-destructive and did not compromise their leadership."[89] Clinton's certainly did.

After my accusations about Clinton came out, several women who worked in the White House were reportedly upset, refusing to accept his denials. John Harris, author of *The Survivor*, wrote, "One woman, a senior White House official, had heard from two colleagues who had experiences uncomfortably similar to what Willey described: innocent conversations that pivoted (into) instant fervid advances."[90]

Robert "Buzz" Patterson wrote that President Clinton once even groped a female steward on Air Force One. Upset, the woman demanded an apology. Remarkably, Clinton did apologize to her. [91]

The stories about Clinton's degradation of women go on and on. The undeniable fact is that Bill Clinton is not just promiscuous, not just a womanizer, but a habitual *abuser* of women, a sexual predator and, in fact, a misogynist.

There is something that kicks in for him when he's around a woman to whom he is attracted. Something overtakes him, manifest in his beet red face, his distraction, his detached consciousness of the person in front of him, and a hyperawareness of his surroundings. He seems tuned only to the risk of moving on his urges, sizing up the place, the time, the woman's reaction. This is the weird, dark side of Bill Clinton.

Consider the striking similarities between Clinton's 1991 abuse of Paula Jones and his assault on me two years later. Just as I did, Paula tried to make conversation but felt like Clinton was distracted. Just as I did, Paula tried to retreat when he tried to kiss her. Just as I did, Paula said she needed to leave but Clinton said, "Oh, you don't need to go right now." And, just as I observed, Paula said Clinton's face got "beet red." As Candice Jackson said of Paula, "Partly because of the...power differential, she didn't leave the room at that point, not wanting to offend him too badly."[92] My feelings in that moment were similar. Other feelings aside, I was ashamed for the president, and I did not feel not inclined to humiliate him further, even when his behavior was so base.

San Francisco radio talk show host Melanie Morgan once briefly encountered Bill Clinton. In that moment, she also saw his dark side. Clinton was arriving in San Francisco's Pacific Heights neighborhood for a fund-raiser at Gordon Getty's home. To prepare for his arrival, Melanie and a friend organized a unique protest. They emblazoned a neighborhood awareness campaign with a special logo that said, "WARNING: SEXUAL PREDATOR ALERT," with added text about notification requirements for neighborhood sexual predators. Melanie's friend went door-to-door to deliver the information to residents in Pacific Heights. The notoriously liberal *San Francisco Chronicle* actually covered the protest. The Associated Press picked up the story and it went all around the world.

Clinton's limousine arrived at the Getty residence where he encountered a throng of protestors shouting, "Shame! Shame!" They held a fifteen-foot banner that said, "I Believe You Paula, Kathleen, Gennifer, Dolly, Elizabeth, Monica, Juanita..."and another that said "I BELIEVE juANITA," (a reference to Juanita Broaddrick and Anita Hill). Melanie Morgan stood in front of the signs with a megaphone, rallying her troops.

Clinton's smoky-glass window was rolled halfway down and Melanie got a clear view of him as the rage welled up in his face. "Clinton looked at the signs the protestors behind me were holding and then he looked at me," she recently told me. "I will never forget the look in his face when he read the banner. His eyes narrowed and he gave me a stare of such hatred and focus and intensity that I could imagine him raping a woman at that moment. I absolutely believed all of the women's stories. There was no question in my mind when I saw that look directed at me that he was entirely capable of it. I kept staring at him as his face raced to a purple rage and I must say that, for a moment, I was scared."[93]

David Gergen said in a *Frontline* interview, "Watching Bill Clinton erupt is like watching Mt. Vesuvius. It is something to behold. He gets very red in the face and it goes very quick and it leaves."[94] A *US News and World Report* story also said of Clinton, "His rage built on itself, and some of his aides thought he might even get violent..."[95]

It is interesting to consider that Clinton's sexual arousal and aggressiveness appear to be related to his anger response. It certainly seems plausible that Clinton's deep-seated emotional issues would include a significant amount of anger around his mother's abandonment of him at a young age. Compound this with her overt sexuality in his presence and all the other complex dynamics that turned him into a sexual addict, and it is likely that, in his psyche, sexual arousal might well be associated with anger. Further complicating his internal dynamic, Clinton, a sex addict, likely has a few issues *with himself* over his behavior with women. Of course, I am no psychiatrist or sexual abuse expert. But, taken together, these clues might indicate that Clinton's anger issues are wound together with his sexual abuse mechanism, all of which expresses itself in the aroused man's beet red face. Twisted in his mind, perhaps inappropriate arousal triggers his anger. Alternatively, deep, subconscious anger might result in inappropriate, uncontrolled arousal. Either way, the ugly association of anger with arousal sounds dangerously close to a frightening and violent interpretation of "sex," namely rape.

Despite whatever crazy, psychosexual mechanism is at work in his mind and body, he is very savvy at the psych-out. He is a master predator. And that is precisely the problem with having Bill Clinton anywhere near the White House—as president or first spouse. He is and always will be a sexual predator. Period.

We have no reason to think otherwise, no evidence that he has received treatment, nor any other indication that his behavior has or will change, *especially* if he has the full powers of the presidency to enable his pursuits—again.

As the child of an alcoholic, Clinton was predisposed biologically and socially to develop his own addiction, Levin says, adding that an "inappropriate early exposure to sexuality taught him to prematurely associate sex with excitement, secrecy, conflict, and intense arousal." Clinton's highly sexual mother perpetuated this dynamic and later added to it, promoting her smart and competent son to the role of her hero. As a teenager, Levin says, Bill filled his mother's need for a father-figure for Roger, his troubled younger brother, and served as a substitute "husband to his flirtatious [and near-sexual exhibitionist] mother." As a teenaged male, Bill was the man in his mother's life. Levin concludes, "There was something unhealthy in this—excessive and somehow erotic." Levin explains that feelings of grandiosity and special status combined with Bill's successes, causing him to suffer a condition called "terminal uniqueness"—the belief that he is special, absolutely different from other people, superior to them, and therefore powerful.[96]

For a brief moment in history, Clinton supposedly participated in "counseling" for his sexual addiction. That moment was fleeting. Though it is obvious that nothing has changed, Hillary's presidential campaign would have us believe that it is resolved. But a man with such a deep problem would require extensive intervention and likely even intensive inpatient treatment before he could overcome his lifelong pattern. What's more, his wife would have to contribute to such a recovery, and we have no evidence of that either.

When Clinton gave his famous "I have sinned" speech admitting that he had lied about Monica, he claimed to have had prayer breakfasts in the White House every week with Jesse Jackson. But Jackson himself seemed to refute the impact of those prayer sessions on Clinton. As Jackson himself put it, "There is nothing that this man won't do." According to Jackson biographer Marshall Frady, Jackson once said of Clinton, "He is immune to shame. Move past all the nice posturing and get really down in there on him, you find absolutely nothing…nothing but appetite."[97] So while he might have had weekly spiritual moments with Jesse Jackson nearly ten years ago, it is highly unlikely that his confessions changed Clinton's behavior in any way.

Make no mistake: Bill Clinton is still addicted to sex.

When the Clintons relocated to New York so Hillary could become a senator, her husband started making the rounds, immersing himself in the New York social scene. He dropped in on a party, making a big entrance with his entourage of Secret Service agents. He spied Barbara Walters across the room and sent a Secret Service agent over to her—just like he used to dispatch the Arkansas state troopers! The agent told Barbara that President Clinton would like to talk to her and asked if she wanted to join him. Being a woman of great dignity, Barbara Walters told the agent that if Clinton wanted to talk to her, he could come on over.

Clinton also spied Monica Crowley at the party. A beautiful young woman, Clinton tried to get near her and witnesses saw him giving her the "full Clinton eye-sweep." But the staunch Clinton-hater proved too agile and avoided him completely.

The former president of the United States just wasn't getting lucky that night, but apparently desperate for female attention, he was still on the prowl. In the end, he was the last to leave the party—after hitting on the waitresses.

Yes, Bill Clinton is still on the make.

Now that his wife is running for the presidency, however, Bill is doing a better job of keeping his sex life out of the news—for the most part. "Clinton is rarely without company in public, yet the company he keeps rarely includes his wife," wrote Patrick Healy for the *New York Times*. "Since leaving the White House, Bill and Hillary Clinton have built largely separate lives… In choosing to keep their public lives separate, people around the Clintons say, there is a political calculus at work." Indeed, Clinton "has told friends that his number one priority is not to cause her any trouble."[98]

It would seem their "political calculus" also includes distancing Bill Clinton from his role as Hillary's *husband*. Further, it looks as if Bill might have tried to solve his problem, for the time being, with a "geographic cure." According to Levin, Alcoholics Anonymous describes a *geographic cure* as "physically running away from one's problems without ever facing them, without ever relinquishing denial and getting help for one's addiction."[99] This sounds like precisely what Bill Clinton is up to.

While Hillary is busy pursuing the presidency, Bill Clinton is often out at night, "Zipping around Los Angeles with his bachelor buddy, Ronald W. Burkle, or hitting parties and fundraisers in Manhattan," Patrick Healy wrote for the *New York Times* in 2006. In fact, Healy said several prominent New York Democrats got concerned after a tabloid photograph showed Clinton leaving a Manhattan restaurant late one night after a dinner that was attended by the Canadian politician Belinda Stronach.[100]

Worth about $600 million, Stronach also happens to be a smart and elegant blonde who is twenty years younger than Clinton. After a brief foray into Canadian politics as a Member of Parliament, Stronach announced in April 2007 that she would return to the family business as vice-chairwoman of Magna International, an auto-parts company. Rumors about Clinton and Stronach persisted for quite some time. According to Julian Coman, writing for the *UK Telegraph*, Stronach and Clinton are close friends and though she "firmly denied rumours of a romance with the former president," they maintained their friendship for a couple of years. "She has told friends that her bid for office was inspired by Mr. Clinton, who has been a good friend since the two met over a round of golf in 2001," Coman wrote. "They have since been to the Toronto races together and have been spotted having dinner at an elite Toronto restaurant." Stronach has not volunteered much more than that Clinton "is a great communicator," but Coman said her friends divulged that "she was 'intrigued' by his 'charisma and brainpower.'" Rumors have also swirled that Clinton and Stronach traveled together.[101] This doesn't sound like a platonic "friendship," particularly since Bill Clinton is half of the equation.

While the presidential candidate's spouse is spending a good deal of time traveling outside the United States and overseas, we Americans should be concerned about what forms his "womanizing" might take in other countries. Since Hillary could very well become president, we must consider the damage her spouse may well do as a predator in the White House again. We have even more cause for worry because Hillary has recently suggested that when she becomes president, Bill might assume an ambassadorship. Since it is highly unlikely that he has overcome his addiction but has instead employed a "geographic cure," we must consider the danger this poses for the United States. Not *if* but *when* Clinton loses control of his addiction again, when he self-destructs, when he assaults or rapes another woman, this time in a foreign country, or when he has an affair with the wife of some important international figure who might not appreciate it, his "sexual escapades" may well become a foreign-relations disaster. And when his wife is the president of the United States, such an issue could hardly be construed as a matter of the man's "private sex life."

The problem for America was *and is* that Clinton, like all addicts, thinks he is above the rules that govern everyone else. According to Dr. Levin, "because of this belief, such individuals are prone to lying and justifying their actions with self-righteous rationalization."[102] Now *that* sounds like our boy!

Levin raises another issue that will be a concern if Hillary becomes president: Clinton's pattern of flirting with risk. With respect to my case, for example, Levin iterates, "Not only was the time and location risky, but…he had no reason to believe that she would keep her mouth shut." While his "total lack of consideration for this distraught woman is almost inconceivable," Levin adds, his actions were just as irrational.[103]

Gennifer Flowers described some of the very risky behavior in which Clinton engaged during their affair, stating, "Bill was always a risk-taker." In her book *Passion and Betrayal*, Gennifer recounts a story about Governor Clinton, who wanted her to make love with him in a bathroom in the Governor's Mansion during a party, when Hillary and fifty guests were just outside.[104] This behavior only adds to the considerable odds that, once his wife is president, his sexual addiction will again cause him to self-destruct.

A Freudian term explains the apparent dysfunction in the Clinton marriage. The "Madonna-whore complex," also known as the "mother-whore complex" is a syndrome in which a man initially pursues a woman who might fill his need for intimacy unmet in childhood. After he marries her, however, he begins to see the wife as a mother or "Madonna" figure, and she then becomes sexually off-limits because, in his mind, it would be incestuous for him to be sexually attracted to a woman whom he beholds as a mother figure.

Admittedly, it requires a stretch of the imagination to see Hillary as a "Madonna" figure, but it's pretty easy to see her as a maternal persona in her relationship with Bill. In fact, Hillary has often been described as Bill's advisor and disciplinarian. While Bill is famously "boyish," Hillary has always assumed the parental role over him. Hillary is not so much a nurturing maternal figure, but more an ill-tempered, scolding woman whose personality is strikingly reminiscent of the very angry grandmother who raised the young Bill Clinton in his mother's absence.

With a sexually charged mother, it is reasonable to assume that Bill would grow up with some "issues." Such a man may well love his wife but, in time, no longer regard her as a *sexual* woman but, instead, a *maternal* woman, in whom love and sex no longer mix. Interestingly, Monica Lewinsky revealed that Clinton "confided to her that his romantic affairs 'multiplied' after he married Hillary Rodham."[105]

Detached from feelings of love, then, sex is reserved for "dirty" women. Prostitutes, the other half of the "Madonna-whore" equation, meet this job requirement. However, so do all women whom he perceives as beneath his wife. In Bill Clinton's case, that includes subordinates, volunteers, interns, "white trash," and any other casual acquaintance who happens to be female. Interestingly, other women who nurture him or otherwise behave maternally toward him might also be "Madonna" figures and, therefore, sexually off-limits. This might explain why Clinton apparently never victimized the very beautiful Nancy Hernreich, who actually spoke baby-talk to him.

By all accounts, Bill never developed feelings of love or affection for the women he engaged sexually, but universally objectified women in these relationships. As governor of Arkansas, for example, "Clinton would spot a woman he wanted and, in an incredibly dehumanizing way, would send a bodyguard to bring her to him," Levin says. "Clinton began trying to control women by objectifying them…[and] did not attempt to establish any type of a relationship with these women, nor did he even engage in the niceties of seduction. Rather, he chose to further degrade them by simply exposing himself and asking for oral sex."[106]

Clinton's own words validate his sexual objectification of women. After a long affair and supposedly loving friendship with Gennifer Flowers, Clinton said of her in 1992, "What does that whore think she's doing to me? She's a fucking slut."[107] Even in a reference to Ted Kennedy's car accident at Chappaquiddick, Clinton said, "He couldn't get a whore across a bridge."[108]

Apparently, calling us "bimbos" was putting it nicely! *That* degrading term was just for public consumption.

Providing further evidence of Bill's opinions about women, Arkansas trooper L. D. Brown gave a deposition in 1997, describing Clinton's "womanizing" as Arkansas's governor. Paula Jones's attorney asked Brown, "You said that Clinton's extramarital sexual partners were 'purely to be graded, purely to be chased, dominated, conquered.' What did you mean by that?"

"Well, grading, as degrading as it may sound, is something that he and I both would do," the trooper admitted. "Pretty much every pretty woman that we would see, eight, nine, ten, seven, six, whatever."

"Well, you're saying that as far as Clinton was concerned," Paula's attorney asked, "they were purely to be graded, chased, dominated, and conquered?"

"Well, in the sense of a game, in the sense…that any of these people that I'm talking about, say, Jane Doe 2, it was not a love relationship. It was a sexual relationship alone."[109]

According to Dr. Levin, "The sex addict…views others as existing only to serve him." Specifically speaking of Clinton, Levin adds, "He does not even appear to care about the other person's feelings at all. Time and time again, Clinton has shown total disregard for the women as people and has treated them as objects."[110] As further evidence of this, Juanita, Paula, and I all observed that Clinton seemed *emotionally* detached from what he did to us and, eventually, even Monica realized this about her "affair" with Clinton.

While Bill Clinton has demonstrated his view that all women—except, of course, his wife—are whores, Hillary evidently shares this opinion. According to Christopher Andersen, rather than expressing anger at her husband about the women, Hillary said to Betsey Wright, "These women are all trash. Nobody is going to believe them," she said.[111] Another time, she said to president-elect Clinton, "What the fuck do you think you're doing? I know who that whore is. Get her out of here."[112]

Cleverly, Hillary's presidential campaign presents a narrow view of the man who will again be her White House roommate. They show us the former president, the world leader, the great orator. They circulate footage of him on his international tsunami mission, suggest that Hillary will appoint him to an ambassadorship, and publicize his altruistic 2007 book promoting volunteerism. But where is Hillary's *husband*?

They don't want us to remember that he is her spouse, the husband who will sleep with her in the White House residence, who will help make decisions from a nearby desk, and—worst of all—who will again have access to the interns, volunteers, and staff. Make no mistake: If Hillary wins the presidency, we will get them both. They are a team, and all of this will come up again. Just as he needed her to put out his fires, she needs his influence and his political wisdom. He will be there as her partner and, still, as a predator.

The Enabler

Hillary could not have been very surprised that her fiancé had a problem keeping his pants zipped. Bill Clinton had many "girlfriends" in college and, once he became engaged to marry Hillary, his sexual addiction went to the next level. "Hillary was already, in a way, enabling Bill in his sexual behavior simply by not leaving him," says Levin.[113]

According to Carl Bernstein in his 2007 Hillary biography *A Woman in Charge*, Clinton had many "short, sexual, casual, one-dimensional" relationships with women when he was at Yale. By 1974, Clinton was campaigning in Arkansas and had a woman in every town. Bernstein wrote that he had "girlfriends in Little Rock and several towns in his campaign district."[114]

Aware of all the red flags, Hillary consciously chose to dismiss them. She married the philandering Bill Clinton in 1974. Why?

By all accounts, they are a formidable team—much better together, much more effective and powerful—than they ever would have been individually. There is a yin and yang to the Hillary-Bill partnership, the essence of which seems to be that he is so charming and she is not. In fact, her nastiness seems to be the valuable asset that she brought to their winning equation. "She possessed the one necessary quality that was not native to his soul: a kind of toughness," wrote Bernstein, putting it charitably. "Without it, he could never have gotten to the presidency." Bernstein said former Clinton pollster Stan Greenberg "described this quality as a 'fierceness'…summoned by Hillary in pursuit of their shared goals because Clinton, unlike his wife, was preternaturally 'conflict averse…and by nature uncomfortable attacking.'" Dick Morris puts it a little more bluntly, saying, "She has a quality of ruthlessness, a quality of aggressiveness and strength about her, that he doesn't have. A killer instinct."[115] Riding on the coattails of Bill's likeability, Hillary's tough skin got them out of jams. Sounds like a political match made in heaven.

From the get-go, Hillary chose this partnership—their mutual political ambition—over a monogamous marriage. She knew what she was getting into. She traded fidelity for the plan. No doubt she recognized early in their partnership that Bill's promiscuity would be a political problem and that it would not go away. She doubtless also realized that her discipline, her problem-solving nature, and her stomach for the fight would keep him afloat, just as she would rely on his charm to keep her in the political game.

But their marriage, by all accounts, has been "less than ideal." They've both been miserable, each paying a high personal price for their lofty political idealism.

But Hillary Clinton is no martyr. If Hillary cares that her husband chases anything in a skirt, if she's repeatedly devastated and surprised that the sex fiend she married continues to be a sex fiend, her sad predicament should not be mistaken for sacrifice.

After all, she didn't just partner with her political alter ego, she *married* him. Their political simpatico has a precise parallel in their personal relationship, in which they are a perfect match—a perfect *dysfunctional* match: He is the addict and she is the enabler.

While it started out subtle enough, Dr. Levin says, "Eventually...her enabling would be overt."[116] In *The Clinton Syndrome*, Levin wrote that, "Most addicts, including sexual addicts, are helped by enablers who continue in relationships with someone who is actively addicted for compelling, unconscious emotional reasons despite the fact that the relationship is grossly detrimental to the enabler."[117]

Clinton's sexual addiction has certainly been detrimental to Hillary. Yet she stays. She has stayed for more than thirty years. She makes excuses. She blames the vast right-wing conspiracy. She pays private investigators to threaten and terrorize women— her primary constituency! She enables her husband's sexual addiction and his predatory activities. In the trade, she gets her shot at power, her turn at the presidency.

Interestingly, Bernstein observes that, early in their relationship, it was not Clinton's philandering that bothered Hillary so much as her inability to control it. "The source of Hillary's frustration and anger...was her knowledge that she was powerless to change him," says Bernstein, adding that, "She knew that Bill's history of compulsive infidelity during their courtship meant the chances for a stable marriage, especially a marriage without adultery, were at best a crapshoot."[118] She was right about that.

An early example of Hillary's enabling was her handling of Bill's affair with Gennifer Flowers, which started within five years of their marriage. Hillary knew about Gennifer and fought with Bill about the affair, but Bill stayed with Gennifer and Hillary stayed with Bill.

But staying was the least of it. Bill Clinton has not kept his sex life private and Hillary has not just enabled him in the privacy of their marriage, but also in their political lives as public servants. We're not talking about an occasional fling during a campaign trip, and not even about promiscuity run amok. We're not even talking about his sexual addiction anymore. We're talking about a woman who enables a sexual abuser and a sexual predator.

As Levin says, "It is very often a mate who enables the addict by making excuses, reinforcing denial, getting the addict out of jams of one sort or another, and doing whatever else is needed to perpetuate the addiction."[119] That is Hillary. But in her case, "whatever else is needed" is scary. Time and again, she has proved willing to do whatever it takes. In fact, she has abused power, not just to win, not for her ideology, but to hurt innocent women, women her husband preyed upon.

After we got caught in Bill Clinton's trap, we were raked over the coals. All of us—Juanita, Gennifer, Paula, Monica, me—we have all been through a lot. We were regular women trying to get by when our paths crossed his. Through no fault of our own, we were smeared in the media, terrorized by thugs, audited by the IRS, followed by strangers, victimized by threats. Our homes were broken into and our pets were killed. And we know that Hillary and her minions were behind the terror.

I think Bill routinely confesses his infidelities to Hillary. Certainly, he skews the stories. I doubt he admitted that he raped Juanita, assaulted me, and abused probably dozens or hundreds of others. But I think he told Hillary that he'd done *something* with us, and it's likely he said we seduced him. I believe that, as part of their dysfunctional dynamic of addict and enabler, in their ugly, twisted cycle, he tells her some story to relieve his guilt. He screws up, he confesses, he asks forgiveness, she throws lamps, and then they make up and he gives her something—appoints a woman to the Supreme Court, lets Hillary spearhead the grand health care debacle, or campaigns for her presidency. I think it's been like that since the beginning. To Hillary, it is tightly wound up with her political aspirations. She came out ahead. We lost. Women lost. And feminism lost.

Even during the impeachment hearings, all that mattered to Hillary was the impact of the case on *her* aspirations. According to Christopher Andersen, who wrote *American Evita*, she was already planning to run for the New York Senate seat. "Said one party official, 'We all knew she wanted it so bad she could taste it. But she knew it would never happen if President Clinton was run out of office in disgrace.'"[120] Her plan all along was, "Eight years of Bill, eight years of Hill," as she told a friend after they moved into the White House in 1993. That was the plan and she has stuck to it, sacrificing her feminist ideology.

An avowed advocate for women, Hillary covered for her predatory husband and had a strong hand in intimidating many women, damaging our credibility, and demonizing us. It is bad enough that, all this time, she knew that her husband preys on women. But she also enabled him and participated in those attacks, playing a role in ruining our lives in order to keep her political ambition on track. Hillary is no feminist, no champion for women, no advocate for women. She is an advocate for *one* woman: Hillary Clinton.

The Nixonian Girl

"I'll do whatever it takes to get us elected," Hillary said during Clinton's first presidential bid.[121] When Gennifer Flowers then came forward to reveal the candidate as an adulterer, Hillary demonstrated what she meant by "whatever it takes." Hillary said, "We have to destroy her." Then Gennifer's home was ransacked, her career was ruined, she was threatened, and she was smeared in the media. This is not an isolated example. Over and over and over again, Hillary has shown how far she will go.

Even when she started law school, Hillary had political ambitions and strong determination that were novel for such a young woman. But as she told a friend, she believed that, "The only way to make a difference is to acquire power."[122] This statement implies a fundamental value structure that became Hillary's ethical mantra: "The ends justify the means."

Whether they do or not, of course, depends on the "means." Even more concerning is that, to Hillary, the justification seems absolute.

In *Rewriting History*, former Clinton strategist Dick Morris describes some of Hillary's strengths and some "disturbing echoes of Nixon" as well. "Like him, she has proven susceptible to temptation, paranoia, and scandal," Morris writes. "Like him, she has allowed her fierce political instincts to darken her perspective, and contrived a deceivingly positive public face behind which to hide."[123]

Bernie Nussbaum has said that "he and Hillary shared the view that 'you should do harm to your enemies.'"[124] This harkens back to Blumenthal's writing that politics is all about "humiliating one's prey, not merely defeating one's foes." This view seems pretty fundamental to Hillary in "power mode." Responding to Bill's sexual scandals, Hillary's modus operandi was *always* to crucify, destroy, and finish off the women, and *never* to confront her husband's abuse of them.

Dave Schippers, who spent years investigating the Clintons, says of Hillary, "Nothing is beneath her."

With a ruthless, Nixonian mind and the crazy heart of a compulsive enabler, Hillary stands in an ugly muck that she has been brewing for thirty years. She has abused and misused power, not to advance her ideological agenda but simply to further her political career while enabling her husband as a sexual predator. She took advantage of her position to condone sexual assault, to hurt innocent people, and to preserve power itself. A devious woman, Hillary will stop at nothing and destroy anybody in her way.

How can such a woman pretend to be an advocate for women's rights, for the downtrodden, for victims? That is not her intent. As journalist Melanie Morgan recently told me, "Hillary is one who will use the leaders of power to extract her own personal agenda. She is a woman to whom no slight has ever gone unrewarded or unpunished."[125]

Hillary will use dirty tactics and go to any lengths to clear the path to her legacy as the first woman president. Just as she did with every one of Bill's "women problems," her political strategy has no limits, is without rules. The means to the end, the means by which she will achieve her lifelong goal of assuming the presidency, continues to be: Do whatever it takes.

David Schippers recalls a story about a priest who came to see him after Clinton's impeachment. "I am an exorcist," the priest told Schippers, "and I want you to know that I saw in Bill Clinton's eyes the same thing that I saw in the last person I exorcised."

Okay, here we go, another nut, Schippers thought.

But the priest continued. "I came out here because I wanted to tell you, you need to stay the course," the priest told him. "There are satanic influences in the White House, and they all want you out of here."

"Yes, Bill Clinton is a bad guy," Schippers acknowledged.

"No, not him," the priest said. "*Her.*"

Schippers today says, "I don't know about satanic influences but, whenever I walked by the White House, I got the chills. There was an aura of evil around her."

Who knows what spiritual elements are at work in another person's psyche? Who knows what altruistic or evil intent lies in someone else's mind and heart and soul? We cannot judge such things. But we can assess a person's actions. We can judge her values when we see her at work.

Having investigated the whole Clinton saga, David Schippers has an inkling of what lies inside Hillary Clinton. "Good Lord!" he said, considering the possibility that Hillary might become president. "That woman is evil! That woman is evil…"

The First Woman President

When our granddaughters and great-granddaughters study American history, they will learn the momentous legacy of the first woman president of the United States. Yes, the time has come. We are ready for a woman to lead our country—and a woman will. But Hillary Clinton is the wrong woman.

As the presidential primary race led up to 2008, Joan Walsh talked with Elizabeth Edwards, wife of presidential candidate John Edwards, about Hillary's candidacy and her advocacy for women—or lack of it. "She hit Hillary Clinton particularly hard," Walsh wrote for *Salon.com*, "arguing that John Edwards is, in fact, the better candidate for women." Elizabeth Edwards added that Hillary "wants to be commander in chief. But she's just not as vocal a women's advocate as I want to see….And then she says, or maybe her supporters say, 'Support me because I'm a woman,' and I want to say to her, 'Well, then support me because I'm a woman.'"[126] Edwards went on to point out that Hillary has not articulated much ideology for her candidacy, other than shouting the obvious from the mountaintops: that she is a woman. In fact, she recalled, when Hillary announced her candidacy she said, "I'm in it to win it." Edwards challenged Hillary, "What is that? That's not a rationale."[127]

Running for her first political job as New York's senator, Hillary was up against Rudy Giuliani, who was very popular in the wake of 9/11. At the precise moment when he was diagnosed with prostate cancer, it was suddenly revealed that he'd had an affair. The one-two punch was too much and Rudy gave up his bid for the Senate seat. "Who threw the knockout punch?" pondered Dick Morris, who suspected a certain someone known to go for the jugular. "They do it secretly, clandestinely, all the while publicly acting above such revolting behavior," Morris said. By way of examples, he cited recent history. "Woman after woman has been demonized by their secret police—usually on orders from Hillary—and have had their past dragged through the mud and leaked to the press to discredit their accounts of the president's predatory practices. Did Rudy Giuliani fall victim to the same detectives who preyed on Kathleen Willey, Gennifer Flowers, Paula Jones, Juanita Broaddrick, Dolly Kyle Browning, Elizabeth Ward Gracen?"[128]

During that Senate race, feminist writer Fran Lebowitz didn't regard Hillary as much of a feminist leader. Kate Kelly, writing for the *New York Observer*, wrote that Lebowitz said, "I think she's a very poor role model for girls...I believe she's someone who decided at a young age that 'I want to be president, but I can't, because I'm a girl. So I'll marry the president.' I think that's so regressive." Kelly wrote that Lebowitz paused for breath, then added, "She's a poll-taker, she's a pulse-taker, she's not a leader. She doesn't really seem to have any ideas... And then she comes here and panders."[129]

Lebowitz wasn't the only one. "Some New York City women seem to be developing a grudge against Mrs. Clinton as a representative of their sex," Kelly wrote. "Those interviewed who said they won't support her—or who have real doubts about voting for her—said it's not so much about her politics, but rather Whitewater, Filegate, Travelgate, and health care reform." While

Kelly says the women seemed not to care about Hillary's husband's sex scandals nor Monica Lewinsky, some said they just "didn't respect her as a woman."[130] "Their resentment is an irritation with her persona, her tactics," said Kelly. She wrote that Dr. Patricia Allen, a fifty-two-year-old New York physician, described "unattractive, narcissistic tendencies" in Hillary. "I wanted to like Mrs. Clinton, because she comes from a modest, Midwestern background, as I do. She worked hard for her education and her power. But, you know, I'm ashamed of her," Allen said. She added, "The big difference is that I always went after what I wanted for me. I never lived my life through a man. I never sought to achieve power or professional aspirations through alliance with a powerful man. I always believed that I could make it happen, simply by doing what I was taught to do as a child: to get up in the morning, and do your work, and be a person whose word can be believed."[131]

But those were New Yorkers in 2000, and Hillary was running for the Senate. American women are now giddy about electing our first woman president, and it seems to matter little whether she has earned the position on her own merits or will attain it because she is married to a man who did. Nor does it seem to matter whether she is a feminist or an enabler of sexual abuse, a woman of character or a criminal, a Democrat or Republican. She is biologically female. To some voters, that is all that matters. They are just as chauvinistic as any man who would never vote for a woman just because she is a woman.

When we mark our ballots, we had better be concerned about more than gender. Has she proven to have her own strength, experience, wisdom, and integrity so she can lead our country effectively? If she has not—and we vote for her anyway—hers will be the legacy and ours will be the blame. If the first woman president of the United States is not up to the job, if her administration fails and the country suffers, it will not bode well for the women who follow—even women who will rightfully have earned the job.

Our youngest voters remember little of the Clintons' first two terms in the White House and even less of the scandal. They only remember that the former president popularized the notion that oral sex is not really sex. To voters now in their twenties, that is what his impeachment was about. They do not know about obstruction of justice, or the litany of women who were objectified, harassed, abused, and even raped. They do not know what we endured at the hands of Bill Clinton nor, more important, at Hillary's hands. They do not know what Hillary Clinton really stands for. They do not know about the smear campaigns, the hired thugs, the invasions of privacy, the threats. They do not know about the jogger or the tires full of nails or my dead cat. All they know is that Hillary Clinton is a woman, and wouldn't it be cool to elect our first woman president?

But I know who Hillary Clinton is. I know that she enabled her husband's misogyny. I know that she stepped over the bodies of countless women in her quest for power. I know what she is capable of—what she has done and what she will continue to do. A woman with her moral compass does not belong in the White House. Just as her husband's presidency was detrimental to the office and to the country, so would her presidency be. A Nixonian woman who employs any means to hurt her enemies, Hillary is a dangerous politician.

Where will it end?

It *should* end with the women of this country realizing that Hillary does not stand for them. That though she is female, Hillary is not fit to secure the legacy as *our* first woman president. If she does, it will be a sad irony.

"Somebody said to me the other day if there was ever a time for a woman president it's now, because we're going to have to do a lot of cleaning," Hillary told nearly one thousand women at a $100-a-plate breakfast. "Grab your buckets, grab your brooms," Hillary said, as if she would remember what a broom looked like. According to a CNN report on the fundraiser, the women ate it up. Hillary went on, "We're going to have to do a clean sweep because there has been a culture of cronyism, corruption, and incompetence." The woman has more than a lot of nerve to accuse her husband's successor of cronyism and corruption.[132]

According to the CNN report, the Republican National Committee responded to Hillary's housecleaning speech by arguing that female voters will not support Clinton's positions on major issues. "If Hillary Clinton thinks women will support her candidacy simply based on her gender she is mistaken," RNC spokeswoman Amber Wilkerson said. "Women, like men, will vote for a candidate because they share their views." I certainly hope so.

But activist Katherine Prudhomme-O'Brien tried to confront the Clintons at a "free and open" program at Daniel Webster College in Nashua, New Hampshire, during the primary campaign. Prudhomme-O'Brien had called Hillary's campaign headquarters a few days ahead to secure tickets and learned there would be at least half an hour for questions after Hillary's speech.

At the event, Bill Clinton spoke and then Hillary gave her speech. When she finished, music started playing, which Prudhomme-O'Brien took as an indication that the question-and-answer period she'd hoped for was not going to occur. She joined the cozy group of people pressing toward the stage to meet Hillary or Bill. People extended tickets, baseballs, and other souvenirs for Hillary's autograph and, when she had the opportunity, Prudhomme-O'Brien held out a light green postcard, which Hillary took and signed.

"Whose is this?" Hillary asked.

Prudhomme-O'Brien said it was hers and took the opportunity to ask Hillary if she believed Juanita Broaddrick.

"Who is that?" Hillary asked.

"The woman who said she was raped by Bill Clinton in 1978."

"I don't know anything about that," Hillary said, still holding the postcard.

"I sent you a videotape of the interview she gave to *Dateline NBC* and I'm sure you have received it," said Prudhomme-O'Brian. "I sent it by certified mail and that's the receipt showing your office got it that you're holding."

Hillary returned the receipt. Prudhomme-O'Brien asked her again if she believed Juanita Broaddrick.

"I don't know what you're talking about." Hillary moved away.

"That's not true!" Prudhomme-O'Brien yelled, to be heard over the music. "Why are you doing this? You've always been so good to rape survivors." According to Prudhomme-O'Brien,

Hillary started Arkansas's first rape crisis hotline and helped start its first rape crisis center.

The crowd got hostile toward Prudhomme-O'Brien and made "vehement requests to have someone get me out of there." Before long, she said, a "well groomed, handsome man in a suit with one of those clear, curly wires in his ear, a Secret Service agent perhaps, grabbed both my arms above the elbow and began pushing me backwards and telling me I had to leave."

Prudhomme-O'Brien began to leave, but stopped at the media stage to tell what had happened. She had brought with her a printed sheet for their edification. However, she said, "About four guys in suits with wires in their ears were joined by an equal number of Nashua Police officers who told me I couldn't do that," and all eight of them escorted her toward the gate. So much for a "free and open" event.

Prudhomme-O'Brien declared the event a sham. "If a candidate wants to earn the right of having said they were vetted by the tough, hard-question-asking New Hampshire citizenry, then I respond that she must earn that right," Prudhomme-O'Brien said. "Hillary is not doing that, walking away from tough questions and not being brave enough to take random ones that a whole crowd can hear."

The officers, however, couldn't care less. They sent her off the property and threatened to arrest her if she returned. They would not tell her what law she might have broken. Prudhomme-O'Brien, though, adds that she "couldn't figure out why Hillary would have ever cared about eighteen minutes of blank tape during the Watergate scandal but never wanted to know where her husband was on April 25, 1978, a date he will not account for and the date Broaddrick says the rape happened."[133]

Prudhomme-O'Brien is right. Hillary will not address the issue. But more important, she cannot address it, nor can she address the broader issue of rape, nor even the broadest issues of sexual victimization of women. Unfortunately, the question today is whether *anyone* really can advocate for women.

The "women's movement" came of age in the sixties. Led by the strong voices of feminist icons, women like me learned to be stronger people, to stand up for ourselves in the workplace, at home, and even in our doctors' offices. The great feminists of the "sexual revolution" empowered my generation to decry sexual harassment, to expect equal pay, and to demand appropriate respect. It helped us to raise our daughters, not as little girls but as women with opportunities that many in the previous generation would never have had the courage to forge.

Unfortunately, our daughters take that for granted. And we women have become complacent. Why? Where are our heroes? Don't we need our leaders any more?

The great voices who once led our empowerment were left in the wake of the Clintons' scandals and their devious campaign against women. And while the Clintons abused feminism itself, the feminists committed suicide. Thanks to the Clintons, leaders like Gloria Steinem and Patricia Ireland lost all credibility on sexual harassment, sexual abuse, assault, even domestic abuse. After condoning Bill Clinton's misogyny and Hillary's enabling, the feminists no longer have the authority to address these issues. Hillary made a mockery of feminism and now feminists can no longer advocate for women. Their great voices have been silenced, another casualty of the Clinton administration's ethics. Feminism no longer represents a fight for women's equality or strength or physical safety. Feminism now stands only for one issue: abortion. When college girls go missing, where are the feminists who once railed about predators? When domestic abuse runs amok and wives are killed in their homes, where are the feminists who once gave us the strength to leave abusive marriages? When corporate women still do not get the same compensation as men, where are the feminists, who once campaigned for our equal rights?

They are gone. And the Clintons are partly to blame.

When he assaulted me, Bill Clinton betrayed me, just as he betrayed countless women who came to him as their boss, their governor, or their president. Hillary also betrayed me—and all of the women her husband abused—when she brought her power to bear on her husband's prey. In the end, Hillary betrayed the feminism for which she has always stood. She betrayed us all.

UPDATE

ON WEDNESDAY, AUGUST 29, 2007, the *New York Daily News* published a short item about this book being written. It emphasized that the book would contain details about the threats I faced from the Clinton machine. "A rep for the publisher told us the book would also examine what it says are campaign-finance violations by Hillary."[1]

That same week, the name Norman Hsu echoed everywhere. Norman Hsu had posed as a New York apparel executive, well-connected financier, and fat-cat fund-raiser for Democratic politicians—to the tune of more than a million dollars. He hosted events and raised campaign funds, with the greatest share going to Hillary Clinton. But, suddenly, the threads of his web unraveled. The *Wall Street Journal* started looking into Hsu's fund-raising practices, providing fascinating insight into Hillary Clinton's campaign.

For one thing, Hsu seemed to have been using "straw donors" to funnel money—above federal limits—to certain politicians. For example, Hsu's friends, the Paw family, live in a tiny bungalow near a freeway in Daly City, south of San Francisco. Though they are of modest means, they managed to give Democrats, including Hillary, $200,000 in recent years. If Hsu reimbursed the Paw family, he likely broke federal campaign finance laws. Investigating Hsu a little further, the *Los Angeles Times* connected the dots and discovered that he was a fugitive.

With the media belatedly onto him, it all came crashing down. On August 31, 2007, two days after the *New York Daily News* ran the item about my book, fifty-six-year-old Hsu returned to the San Franciscio Bay area and surrendered to authorities. Then he posted $2 million bail with a cashier's check. He was released, pending a court appearance a week later when he was to surrender his passport and request a bail reduction. But with the FBI investigating possible campaign finance violations, a New York prosecutor studying whether Hsu stole a $40 million investment fund, and a Southern California investigation examining his connection to another multi-million-dollar investment fraud, Hsu skipped town. At his September 5 court date, his lawyer said he had no idea where Hsu went. It didn't take long to find him.

Hsu boarded the *California Zephyr*, a passenger train that stops in Denver en route to Chicago. As his train rolled through Colorado, Hsu fell ill and Amtrak personnel called paramedics. Hospitalized for a few days, Hsu was taken into custody and, finally, to jail. Meanwhile, a few Hsu acquaintances received explicit suicide notes, allegedly signed by Norman Hsu and mailed at about the time he got sick. A few days later, since Hsu had forfeited a measly $2 million bail just a week earlier, the Colorado prosecutor asked for $50 million bail saying, "It seems like Monopoly money at this point."[2] The judge set bail at $5 million.

In an effort to distance herself from Hsu's tangled web, Hillary pledged to return $850,000 of Hsu donations. However, a campaign spokesman said the individual contributors could make new donations. "We will accept their contributions and ask them to confirm for our records that they are from their own personal funds," Howard Wolfson wrote in an e-mail.[3]

But the Clintons' possible involvement doesn't end there. Many questions remain regarding Hillary's fundraising efforts. Did Hsu break laws to raise more than a million dollars for Hillary and other Democrats? What did Hillary or her staff know about his activities and when did they know it? How did Hsu finance the $2 million bail that he forfeited? And did he really intend to commit suicide?

These questions don't surprise me. They echo—precisely—the many lingering concerns about the Clintons' fund-raising irregularities in the 1990s, "irregularities" that may well have involved my husband and even his death.

As these echoes of my past reverberated in the press on Friday night of Labor Day weekend, I fell asleep on my couch. Groggy, I went upstairs to bed without activating my home security system. Sometime that night I heard my dogs barking, but I rolled over and went back to sleep, figuring it was a raccoon or a deer as usual. It wasn't. While I slept upstairs that night, someone climbed through a downstairs window into my home.

I woke up Saturday morning and went about my business, reading the newspaper, puttering around the house, doing my laundry and other chores. Soon, I noticed that something was wrong with my entertainment system and that my television didn't work. My laptop didn't work, either. Finally, I couldn't find my purse. It was missing—gone. That's when I realized someone had broken into my home.

I called the sheriff and two deputies came to the house, took a report, and said an investigator would contact me. After they left, I noticed that my car, a 1998 Infiniti SUV, had been vandalized, with a key scratch on the side and the antenna broken. I canceled my credit cards and tinkered with my laptop, which I eventually got to work. But, as I sat at my desk, I realized that a copy of this book manuscript was missing. I had printed two copies so I always had one at home and a second one to take with me when I was out running errands or going to appointments. But one copy was gone.

I called a friend, a seasoned investigator, and he suggested I go outside and look around in the woods beyond my yard, so I took the dogs and did so. The dogs led me to my purse, which the burglar had tossed in the woods. My credit cards were still in my wallet, a small consolation after I'd canceled all of them.

My laptop was not stolen. My jewelry was not stolen. My credit cards were not stolen. *But the book manuscript was gone.* My manuscript, with revelations about Hillary Clinton's tactics, with questions about Ed's involvement in campaign financing, and questions about Ed's suicide, had been stolen.

The break-in came only two days after the *New York Daily News* article, and on the same day that beleaguered Clinton fundraiser Norman Tsu surrendered to authorities in California. The news article had emphasized that campaign-finance violations by Hillary Clinton would be addressed in the book. It is my belief that Hillary Clinton or her cohorts, concerned about light being shed on their campaign-finance operations—especially in the wake of Tsu's arrest for such violations earlier that day—arranged to steal my manuscript. It's the only answer that makes sense.

Team Clinton did not steal the manuscript to prevent its publication. My publisher and I had many drafts on our computers. They stole the manuscript so they would know what is in it, so they could prepare their preemptive strikes, their plan of attack. Just as they devised preemptive strikes on Bill Clinton's "bimbo eruptions," just as they tried to smear me in 1998, so they will try again. Just as they damaged my tires with nails nearly ten years ago, so they vandalized my car—again. And just as they staged a "noisy investigation" and terrorized me with intruders who reminded me of my vulnerability, so they have again.

As soon as the media reported that my manuscript had been stolen, I got a call from David Schippers, who had served as the Chief Investigative Counsel for the House Judiciary Committee on Clinton's impeachment. Schippers said the same thing happened to him in 2000, when he was writing *Sellout: The Inside Story of President Clinton's Impeachment*. Schippers told Art Moore of *World Net Daily* that he wrote his manuscript in longhand and his wife, Jackie, typed it into her computer. Repeatedly, she said, she thought someone was hacking into the computer. Schippers thought she was paranoid. But, then, after he went to his office one morning, Jackie heard someone in the house. With dozens of children and grandchildren, Jackie figured it was the usual family traffic so she called out from upstairs. But no one answered. In the next couple of weeks, it happened again, a few times, until, finally, impeachment-related files were stolen. And a computer technician concluded that her computer was being accessed through a wormhole.[4]

Jayna Davis, author of *The Third Terrorist: The Middle East Connection to the Oklahoma City Bombing*, argued that she'd faced similar harassment when working on her own book. She claims that her phone was tapped and her computer hacked.[5] Gary Aldrich, author of *Unlimited Access: An FBI Agent Inside the Clinton White House*, says he sent his manuscript to the FBI for approval, as required, but the FBI immediately gave it the to the White House.[6] It is clear that I was not the only author facing such harassment while working on a less than flattering book about the Clintons.

"My suspicion was that the Clintons, or some of their toadies, were trying to find out what we were writing before we submitted the manuscript," Schippers told Moore, adding that he believes what happened to me "was deliberate and designed to scare the hell out of her" and find out what is in the book. "They will go through it page by page," Schippers said, "and they will set up their war room."[7]

Given the opportunity to respond, the Clinton camp had no comment. Not yet, anyway. But, in the midst of her campaign to return to the White House as our first woman president, Hillary will not let anything stop her. She certainly will not let me get in the way. She and her people will attack me from every angle.

Once again, I am their target. This time, I'm ready.

ACKNOWLEDGMENTS

WRITING A BOOK is a daunting task and I would like to thank the many people whose help and support brought it to fruition.

At the top of the list is Katie Vecchio without whose help, patience and enormous talent, there would never have been a book. Simple words are not enough. And thank you, Tony, Nick, Sophie and the entire Clark family for sharing her with me for the past year. You are a beautiful, courageous woman, Katie. Always remember that.

My heartfelt thanks to Dan Gecker, our guardian angel, America's best attorney, who saved us from an uncertain future after Ed's tragic death. You brought us back from the brink of total and complete ruin. Also, I would never have survived "The Troubles" without all of your help. What a journey!

I could not have contemplated this book without my dear friend, Monica Crowley, whose love, support and sage advice have kept me on track for the last eight years. You have never let me down and I value our friendship beyond words.

I am beyond grateful to Karen, for forty years of love and support and "C&D" for never leaving my side. And to "Mr. Babb" for years and years of patience, caring and unconditional love.

To the "Streakers," one and all, for twenty three years of love and laughter. Whatever would I have done without you? Thank you from the bottom of my heart to Nancy, "Shanty Irish Beth," Cindy, Sharon, Susan, Laurie, and Joan and Lea, who are no longer with us. And thank you, too, to all of you from the past whose names are too many to mention.

So very many have listened and helped me on this journey: Larry, Kristen, Lane, Ned, Keith, Sam, Teresa, Kristin, Bob, Jimmy, Alice, Jemi, Tudy, Barbara, dear Ralph, Thomas, Beverly, Marie and Michelle for putting up with my "haircut of the month" requests. I thank my two doctors, Karen, for always being available and Jo, who is talented beyond words. Thank you from the bottom of my heart.

I am forever thankful to Jared for your unfathomable loyalty and trust.

Many thanks also to Chris and Joan who listened and listened and cried with me for so many years. You both helped me so much after the loss of Ed. Thank you now to Will, Kristin, and Baxter, all of whom have continued the process! I am a walking example of your tireless and continued good talents. Thank you, too, to Dottie, for encouraging me to "come out of hiding and enjoy the world around you." You were so right.

I would also like to thank all of my friends from Douglas Freeman's Class of 1964, Bobby, Tommy, Wayne, Allen, Charlotte, Mike, Dick, Jimmy, and John and also Ken. Mere words will never be enough.

I owe a huge debt to my Tuesday Night Book Club, Kathy, Kim B, Kim P, Michael, Valerie, Noel, Janice, the "two Bills," and the "two Brendas." Also, Melinda, Seth, Heather, Noel, Terry, Lucien, Tim, Jean Marie, and all members past and present.

Special thanks, also, to my dear friends, Debbie and Judy, who keep me grounded and who are always there to listen and help. I treasure our friendship.

Thank you, Sherman. You have helped me and so very many others. You gave my life back to me! Thanks also to Lynn. I hope you are up to the challenge!

I owe a debt to Senator Susan Collins, who had the courage to listen to and validate my story and also to Congressman Jim Rogan who stood by me through thick and thin.

I also thank Louis from the bottom of my heart for stepping in after Ed's death and taking such good care of us.

Thank you to those who were so helpful throughout the process of writing this book, especially Dick Morris and Eileen McGann, Christopher Hitchens, and Carl Limbacher.

I owe a very huge debt to David Schippers, one of this country's greatest patriots, who believed in me and protected me, and

ACKNOWLEDGMENTS

who had the fortitude and courage to face the consequences of his beliefs.

I also thank so many of you whose names I cannot divulge for many reasons. You and I know who you are and I will be forever grateful.

I am also so grateful for the love and support of Joan Daylor, the greatest woman I have ever known, whose memory lives on in my heart and the hearts of so very many. We shall meet again. Your unconditional love got me through the worst of times. Your door was always open to me. Thank you, also, to your wonderful, steadfast family, dear Frank, John, Patty and Chris.

I was so blessed to have my big, beautiful Tess with me for so many years, who never left my side, who protected me throughout "The Troubles," my faithful companion to the very end and whom I miss so terribly. You did your job my sweet girl, and I will never, ever forget you. Now I am blessed with two cairn "terrorists," Roxie and Bridget, pure joy, who keep me laughing all the time and whose love is without fail. And those darn cats, too!

I am indebted to everyone at World Ahead for believing in me and giving me the opportunity to tell my story.

I owe so much to my brother, Michael, who stayed with me during those long, dark days and months of abject grief and hopelessness. We had such a special bond. I miss all of the laughter and I miss you, too.

I am forever indebted to my dad, who tried to be a good father in spite of it all. I think about you every day and I miss you from the very depths of my soul. I can only hope that I was the good daughter that you deserved and I hope I made you proud. I know that I will see you again.

If I have forgotten anyone, please forgive me. "Senior Moments" have come to be an everyday occurrence!

Finally, I send my love and hope to my children from your mother who loves you.

BIBLIOGRAPHY

Abramson, Jill. "Testing of a President: The Investigation; Two Witnesses Called by Starr Could Shed Some Light on the 'Talking Points'." *New York Times*, February 19, 1998. http://query.nytimes.com/gst/fullpage.html?res=950CE0D8 123FF93AA25751C0A96E958260 (accessed September 18, 2007).

———."The Nation: The Price of Being Lewinsky; Dream Team, Nightmare Tab." *New York Times*, June 7, 1998. http://query.nytimes.com/gst/fullpage.html?res=9E0CE6DD1F3BF934A35755C0A96E958260 (accessed September 18, 2007.)

Adams, Lorraine. "Into the Spotlight: The familiar Washington script for scandal casts the Other Woman as nothing but the instrument of a public man's potential disgrace. But the real story line is shaped not only by lust and greed, but also by questions of class and power." *Washington Post*, August 9, 1998.

Aldrich, Gary. *Unlimited Access: An FBI Agent Inside the Clinton White House*. Washington, D.C.: Regnery Publishing, 1996.

Alvater, Dennis. Interviews with author, June and July, 2007.

Andersen, Christopher. *American Evita: Hillary Clinton's Path to Power*. New York: HarperCollins, 2004.

———. *Bill & Hillary: The Marriage*. New York: William Morrow & Co., 1999.

Archibald, George. "Lindsey planned to discredit Willey year before *60 Minutes*." *Washington Times*, July 21, 1999.

Associated Press, "Anita Hill: Judge Clinton by his policies," *USA Today*, 1999. http://www.usatoday.com/news/index/clinton/ clin264.htm (accessed September 19, 2007).

Baker, Peter. "Clinton Unveils Agenda Heralding Contentious Fall." *Washington Post*, August, 7, 1997.

Balz, Dan. "Prosecutor, President Face Off: Lewinsky's Immunity Deal Sets Stage for Historic Confrontation." *Washington Post*, August 2, 1998, p. A1.

Bastin, Jerry. Interviews with author, July and August, 2007.

Bennett, Bob. Interview by Larry King. *Larry King Live*. CNN. March 16, 1998.

Bernstein, Carl. *A Woman in Charge: The Life of Hillary Rodham Clinton*. New York: Alfred A. Knopf, 2007.

Blitzer, Wolf with Janet Moore and Pierre Thomas. "White House Strikes Back Against Willey: Clinton says he is 'mystified and disappointed' by former supporter's allegations." CNN, March 16, 1998.

Blumenthal, Sidney. Response to Interregatory No. 42. Civil Action No. 96-2123/97-1288 (RCL) in the United States District Court for the District of Columbia, Responses and Objections to Plaintiff's Interrogatories to the Executive Office of the President, May 13, 1999.

———. *The Clinton Wars*. New York: Farrar, Straus and Giroux, 2003.

Bolton, Bennet. "Clinton Affair!" *National Enquirer*, August 19, 1997, p. 37.

Broaddrick, Juanita. "An Open Letter to Hillary Clinton: Do You Remember?" originally published on *Drudge Report*, October 15, 2000. http://www.freerepublic.com/forum/a39eb43637d6f.htm (accessed September 7, 2007).

Brown, L.D. Official deposition taken at the DoubleTree Hotel in Little Rock, Arkansas on November 10, 1997, and released on Friday, March 13, 1998. Excerpt published in the *Washington Post*, March 13, 1998. http://www.washingtonpost.com/wp-srv/politics/special/pjones/docs/brown031398.htm (accessed September 19, 2007).

Burros, Marian. "The New Presidency: Social Scene; A Highly Sensitive Post is Filled by the Clintons." *The New York Times*, January 12, 1993. http://query.nytimes.com/gst/fullpage.html?res=9F0CE4DB113AF931A2 5752C0A965958260 (accessed September 19, 2007).

Citizens United. Transcript from interview with author, June 27, 2007.

Clinton, Hillary. *Living History*. New York: Simon & Schuster, 2003.

CNN, "Willey Says Clinton Lied About Groping Her: White House statement reiterates president's denial," March 15, 1998.

———. "First lady to officially announce Senate bid February 6: Faces questions on her marriage." January 19, 2000.

———. "Clinton says 'clean sweep' needed at White House," June 30, 2007. http://politicalticker.blogs.cnn.com/2007/06/30/clinton-says-clean-sweep-needed-at-white-house/ (accessed September 19, 2007).

Collins, Nancy. "I'd do it All over Again: Linda Tripp, the *George* Interview." *George*, December/January, 2001.

Coman, Julian. "Shock! Canada's politics gets interesting with arrival of rich divorcee." *UK Telegraph*, March 13, 2004.

Coulter, Ann. *High Crimes & Misdemeanors: The Case Against Bill Clinton.* Washington, D.C.: Regnery Publishing, 1998.

Crowley, Monica, Ph.D., "Hillary the Anti-feminist." Interview with author, June 16, 2007.

Dealey, Sam. "A Vast Left-Wing conspiracy?" *New York Post*, January 22, 1999.

Dowd, Maureen. "Liberties, Sinners & Spinners on the Equator." *The New York Times*, March 25, 1998. http://query.nytimes.com/gst/fullpage.html?res= 9E0DE4DE1E38F936A15750C0A96E958260 (accessed September 19, 2007).

Drudge, Matt. "White House First Learned Willey Was Talking During Online Chat!" *Drudge Report*, March 15, 1998. http://www.drudgereportarchives. com/dsp/specialReports_pc_carden_detail.htm?reportID=%7BEFC06A59- 502F-4477-806C-954B06564D1A%7D (accessed September 7, 2007).

Edsall, Thomas B. "Strains in a Key Constituency: Some Women Reassess Clinton in Light of Willey Accusations." *Washington Post*, March 17, 1998, page A6.

Fitzpatrick, Kelly Ann with Chris Matthews. *Hardball with Chris Matthews.* MSNBC, March 16, 1998.

Flowers, Gennifer. *Passion and Betrayal*, Del Mar, California: Emory Dalton Books, 1995.

Gecker, Dan. Interview with author. July 5, 2007.

Gedda, George. "Official's kin in unauthorized, secret talks with Bosnian leader." *Associated Press*, November 11, 1998.

Gergen, David. *Eyewitness to Power: The Essence of Leadership, Nixon to Clinton.* New York: Simon & Schuster, 2000.

Graves, Florence and Jacqueline E. Sharkey. "Starr and Willey: The Untold Story." *The Nation*, May 17, 1999. http://www.thenation.com/docprint. mhtml?i=1999517&s=graves (accessed September 7, 2007).

Hannity & Colmes, "Presidential Legal Troubles." Fox News Channel, Feb. 25, 1999.

Harris, John. *The Survivor: Bill Clinton in the White House*. New York: Random House, 2005.

Healy, Patrick. "For Clintons, Delicate Dance of Married and Public Lives." *The New York Times*, May 23, 2006. http://www.nytimes.com/2006/05/23/nyregion/23clintons.html?_r=1&adxnnl=1&oref=slogin&adxnnlx=1190267371-xBljEOXh1gZ83Gnt95KP5Q (accessed September 19, 2007).

Helvarg, David. "All the President's P.I.s." *Mother Jones*, March 24, 1998.

Hitchens, Christopher. Interviews with author, June 26 and July 8, 2007.

Interview with former CBS News producer, conducted on the condition that this source would remain anonymous. July 10, 2007.

Interviews with former Prudential contractor, conducted on the condition that this source would remain anonymous. June 2007.

Investor's Business Daily, "Not-So-Secret Police?" May 20, 1999.

Ireland, Patricia. MSNBC, March 16, 1998.

Isikoff, Michael. "Clinton Team Works to Deflect Allegations on Nominee's Private Life." *Washington Post*, July 26, 1992, p. A18.

———. *Uncovering Clinton: A Reporter's Story*. New York: Crown Pub., 1999.

Jackson, Candice E., *Their Lives: The Women Targeted by the Clinton Machine*, Los Angeles: World Ahead Publishing, 2005.

Judd, Jackie and Chris Vlasto. "Witness Backs Willey Claims: Starr Probes Obstruction Allegations." *ABC News*, January 29, 1999.

Kelly, Kate. "Meet the Smart New York Women Who Can't Stand Hillary Clinton." *The New York Observer*, January 17, 2000. http://www.freerepublic.com/forum/a387c1dff5c1c.htm (accessed September 7, 2007).

Kessler, Ronald. *Inside the White House*. New York: Pocket, 1996.

Klein, Ed. *The Truth About Hillary What She Knew, When She Knew It, And How Far She'll Go to Become President*. New York: Sentinel, 2005.

Kuiper, Thomas, D. *I've Always Been a Yankees Fan: Hillary Clinton in Her Own Words*. Los Angeles: World Ahead Publishing, 2006.

Lauer, Matt and Ann Curry. *Today*. NBC News, March 17, 1998.

Lemire, J. "Stalk rap for Monica prober: Married & chasing mistress, says sister-in-law." *New York Daily News*, May 13, 2006. http://www.nydailynews.com/news/2006/05/13/2006-05-13_stalk_rap_for_monica_prober_married__cha_print.html.

Levin, Jerome. *The Clinton Syndrome: The President and the Self-Destructive Nature of Sexual Addiction.* Rocklin, California: Prima Publishing, 1998.

Lindsey, Bruce. Response to Interrogatory 15. Civil Action No. 96-2123/97-1288 (RCL) in the United States District Court for the District of Columbia, Responses and Objections to Plaintiff's Interrogatories to the Executive Office of the President, May 13, 1999.

Liasson, Mara. "Clinton's Christmas woes." *All Things Considered,* NPR, December 21, 1993.

Milton, Joyce. *The First Partner: Hillary Rodham Clinton.* New York: Harper Paperbacks, 2000.

Morgan, Melanie. Interview with author. San Francisco, July 13, 2007.

Morris, Dick. "Bill's Sexgate Rx Might Kill Him: Alarming 'Secret Police' Operations." *New York Post,* October 1, 1998.

Morris, Dick. "Who Knocked Out Rudy?" *New York Post,* May 22, 2000.

Morris, Dick with Eileen McGann. *Rewriting History.* New York: Regan Books/Harper Collins, 2004.

Nagourney, Adam and David Colton. "Tapes Still Entangle Clinton." *USA Today,* January 30, 1992, page 1A.

New York Times, "The Nation: The Price of Being Lewinsky; Dream Team, Nightmare Tab," June 7, 1998. http://query.nytimes.com/gst/fullpage.html?res=9E0CE6DD1F3BF934A35755C0A96E958260 (accessed September 19, 2007).

Newsmax, "Clinton Questions Dwarf Deep Throat's ID." *NewsMax.com,* June 1, 2005. http://www.newsmax.com/archives/ ic/2005/6/1/93644.shtml.

National Organization for Women. "NOW President Patricia Ireland Challenges Livingston to Rein in Conservatives and Calls upon Women to Lobby against Impeachment." NOW press release, December 11, 1998. http://www.now.org/press/12-98/12-11-98.html.

Olson, Barbara. *The Final Days: The Last Desperate Abuses of Power by the Clinton White House.* Washington, D.C.: Regnery Publishing, 2001.

———. *Hell to Pay: The Unfolding Story of Hillary Rodham Clinton.* Washington, D.C.: Regnery Publishing, 2001.

Patterson, Lt. Col. Robert "Buzz," USAF (Ret.). *Dereliction of Duty: The Eyewitness Account of How President Bill Clinton Endangered America's Long-Term National Security*. Washington, D.C.: Regnery Publishing, 2003.

Plante, Bill. *CBS Evening News*. CBS, March 16, 1998.

Prudhomme-O'Brien, Katherine. "Today I Met Hillary in Nashua, N.H. also known as 'The Gate City.'" *FreeRepublic.com*, July 13, 2007. http://www. freerepublic.com/focus/f-news/ 1865782/ posts (accessed September 7, 2007).

Ross, Andrew. Interview by Marshall Frady. "Civil rights movement: R.I.P? In a time of crisis, Jesse and other black leaders are unheard." *Salon.com*. http://www.salon.com/news/ news960624.html.

Royko, Mike. "Talking Trash; The Class Warfare Against Paula Jones is A Media Disgrace." *Pittsburgh-Post Gazette*, January 19, 1997.

Schippers, David. Interview with author, July 5, 2007.

———. Personal interview, July 5, 2007.

Serrano, Barbara A. "Steinem Fires Back—The Feminist Icon Replies to Criticism of Her Remarks Regarding the President, Monica, Paula and Others." *Seattle Times*, April 17, 1998.

Shapiro, Bruce. "A new woman? New bankruptcy documents make the murky finances of Ken Starr's key witness look even shadier." *Salon.com*, July 12, 2000. http://archive.salon.com/ news/feature/2000/07/12/willey/ (accessed September 7, 2007).

Sheehy, Gail. *Hillary's Choice*. New York: Random House, 2000.

Shiflett, Dave. "Media Selective With Its Scandals." *Rocky Mountain News* (Denver), February 21, 1994.

Sperry, Paul. "A Bully in the White House?" *Investor's Business Daily*, March 11, 1999. http://www.investors.com/editorial/editorialcontent.asp?secid= 1501&status=article&id=161263&secure=6896 (accessed Sept. 7, 2007).

Stern, Jared. Interviews with author. April to July, 2007.

Stout, David. "Federal Judge Rules President Broke Privacy Law by Releasing Letters." *The New York Times*, March 30, 2000. http://query. nytimes.com/gst/fullpage.html?res=9A04E2DA153CF933A05750C0A966 9C8B63 (accessed September 19, 2007).

Thompson, Doug. "Bill Clinton is a violent, profane man who wants to 'kill' his enemies." *CapitolHillBlue.com*, April 8, 1999.

Tripp, Linda. Interview by Larry King. *Larry King Live*. CNN, Feb. 15, 1999.

United States District Court for the District of Columbia. Motion filed in Case No. 98-1991 (WBB), June 28, 1999.

USA Today, "Starr decides not to pursue retrials for McDougal, Steele." May 26, 1999, p. 8A.

Walsh, Joan. "The *Salon* Interview with Elizabeth Edwards." *Salon.com*, July 17, 2007. http://www.salon.com/news/feature/2007/07/17/elizabeth_ edwards/index.html (accessed September 7, 2007).

Walsh, Kenneth T. "Air Force One: The inside story of how the presidential aircraft helped change the course of history." *US News and World Report*, May 11 2003. http://www.usnews.com/snews/news/articles/030519/ 19one_4.htm (accessed September 7, 2007.)

Weinraub, Bernard. "Hollywood Investigator Gets 30-Month Term in Weapons Case." *New York Times*, January 24, 2004. http://query. nytimes.com/gst/fullpage.html?res=9A06E4DF1F39F937A15752C0A9629 C8B63 (accessed September 19, 2007).

Weisman, Jonathan. "Scandal throws women a curve; Democrats' reaction raises a question of double standard." *Baltimore Sun*, March 17, 1998.

Woodward, Bob. *Shadow: Five Presidents and the Legacy of Watergate*. New York: Simon & Schuster, 1999.

WorldNetDaily, "Clinton dirty trickster faces 110-count indictment: Private investigator Pellicano allegedly wiretapped Sylvester Stallone's phone." *WorldNetDaily.com*, February 6, 2006. http://www.worldnetdaily.com/ news/article.asp?ARTICLE_ID=48693.

Young, Cathy. "Who says women never lie about rape? The 'believe the woman' zealotry promoted by Juanita Broaddrick's defenders is bad for feminism." *Salon.com*, March 3, 1999. http://www.salon.com/news/1999/ 03/cov_10news.html.

NOTES

Preface

1. "The Big Smack," *Style Weekly*, February 9, 1998.

Chapter Two: The First Campaign

1. Shapiro, "A new woman?"
2. Sheehy, *Hillary's Choice*, 226.

Chapter Three: The First Term

1. Shapiro, "A new woman?"
2. Clinton, *Living History*, 134.
3. Bernstein, *A Woman in Charge*, 315, 318-319.
4. Ibid.
5. Ibid.
6. Burros, "The New Presidency."
7. Bernstein, *A Woman in Charge*, 316.
8. Ibid., 129.
9. Ibid.
10. Collins, "I'd do It All over Again."
11. Bernstein, *A Woman in Charge*, 282.
12. Ibid.
13. Collins, "I'd do It All over Again."
14. Tripp, *Larry King Live* interview.
15. Collins, "I'd do It All over Again."
16. Ibid
17. Schippers, interview with author.

Chapter Four: Assault in the Oval Office

1. Collins, "I'd do It All over Again."
2. Ibid.
3. "The Cocaine Candidacy." http://www.whatreallyhappened.com/RAN CHO/ POLITICS/ARTICLES/CC.html.

Chapter Five: Promises, Promises

1. Tripp, *Larry King Live* interview.
2. Levin, *Clinton Syndrome*, 115.
3. Andersen, Christopher, "Hillary Clinton: They Were Terrified of Her'" ET Online interview, July 7, 2004. http://www.etonline.com/celebrities/33967/index.html.
4. Gergen, *Eyewitness to Power*, 274.
5. Aldrich, *Unlimited Access*, 192.
6. Patterson, *Dereliction of Duty*, 68.
7. Andersen, *American Evita*, 90.
8. Kuiper, *I've Always Been a Yankees Fan*, 3.
9. Milton, *First Partner*, 259.
10. Aldrich, *Unlimited Access*, 139.
11. Broaddrick, "Open Letter to Hillary Clinton."
12. Andersen, *Bill & Hillary*, 165.
13. Olson, *Hell to Pay*, 308.
14. Andersen, *American Evita*, 68.

Chapter Six: Exposed

1. Graves and Sharkey, "Starr and Willey."
2. Isikoff, *Uncovering Clinton*, 123.
3. Graves and Sharkey, "Starr and Willey."
4. Ibid.
5. Drudge, "White House First Learned Willey Was Talking During Online Chat!"
6. Isikoff, *Uncovering Clinton*, 156.
7. Ibid., 367.
8. Baker, "Clinton Unveils Agenda."
9. Bolton, "Clinton Affair!"

Chapter Seven: Terror Campaign

1. Alvater, Interviews with author.
2. Gecker, Interview with author, July 5, 2007.
3. CNN, "Willey Says Clinton Lied."
4. Gedda, "Official's kin in unauthorized, secret talks with Bosnian leader."
5. Blumenthal, *Clinton Wars*, 625, 627.
6. Collins, "I'd do It All over Again."
7. Tripp, *Larry King Live* interview.
8. Morris with McGann, *Rewriting History*, 212.

9. Ibid., 214.
10. Ibid., 206.
11. Abramson, "Testing of a President."
12. Tripp, *Larry King Live* interview.
13. Ibid.
14. Ibid.
15. Ibid.
16. Collins, "I'd do It All over Again."
17. Gecker, Interview with author, July 5, 2007.
18. Bennett, *Larry King Live* interview.
19. Abramson, "The Nation."
20. CNN, "First lady to officially announce Senate bid."
21. Gecker, Interview with author, July 5, 2007.
22. Former CBS News producer, Interview with author.   July 10, 2007.
23. Fitzpatrick with Chris Matthews, *Hardball*, March 16, 1998.
24. Patricia Ireland, MSNBC, March 16, 1998.
25. Graves and Sharkey, "Starr and Willey."
26. Bill Plante, *CBS Evening News*, March 16, 1998.
27. Patricia Ireland, MSNBC, March 16, 1998.
28. Fitzpatrick with Chris Matthews, *Hardball with Chris Matthews*, March 16, 1998.

Chapter Eight: Smear Campaign

1. Bernstein, *A Woman in Charge*, 225.
2. Ibid., 496.
3. Blumenthal, *Clinton Wars*, 365.
4. Ibid., 364.
5. Ibid., 438.
6. Blumenthal, Response to Interrogatory No.   42.
7. Archibald, "Lindsey planned to discredit Willey."
8. Blumenthal, Response to Interrogatory No.   42.
9. Lindsey, Response to Interrogatory No.   15.
10. Hitchens, Interview with author, June 26, 2007.
11. Ibid.
12. Blumenthal, *Clinton Wars*, 627.
13. Ibid, 601.
14. Blumenthal, Response to Interrogatory No.   42.
15. Hitchens, Interview with author, July 8, 2007.
16. Ibid., June 26, 2007.
17. Lindsey with Mike McCurry, Responses to Interrogatory No. 15.

18. Blitzer with Janet Moore and Pierre Thomas, "White House Strikes Back Against Willey."
19. Kurtz, Howard. "Bennett Angry at '60 Minutes'," *Washington Post*, March 23, 1998, page E1.
20. Lauer and Ann Curry, *Today*, March 17, 1998.
21. Gecker, Interview with author, July 5, 2007.
22. Graves and Sharkey, "Starr and Willey."
23. Blumenthal, *Clinton Wars*, 437.
24. Bernstein, *A Woman in Charge*, 120.
25. Ireland, Patricia. "Wait Wait Don't Tell Me," NPR, December 9, 2002. http://www.npr.org/programs/waitwait/archquiz/2003/030705.html.
26. Young, "Who says women never lie about rape?"
27. Patricia Ireland with Lisa Meyers, CNBC, March, 1998.
28. Edsall, "Strains in a Key Constituency."
29. NOW, "NOW President Patricia Ireland Challenges Livingston."
30. Levin, *Clinton Syndrome*, 5.
31. Serrano, "Steinem Fires Back."
32. Jackson, *Their Lives*, 168.
33. Dowd, "Liberties, Sinners and Spinners on the Equator."
34. Edsall, "Strains in a Key Constituency."
35. Weisman, "Scandal throws women a curve."
36. *Associated Press*, "Anita Hill: Judge Clinton by his policies."
37. Crowley, Interview with author, June 16, 2007.
38. Simon, Roger and William Neikirk. "Cover-Up Charges Embroil Clinton; Taping of Intern Key to Inquiry." *Chicago Tribune*, January 22, 1998.
39. Jackson, *Their Lives*, 256-257.
40. Crowley, Interview with author, June 16, 2007.
41. Jackson, *Their Lives*, 258.
42. Ibid., 247.

Chapter Nine: Obstruction of Justice

1. Clinton, Bill, Transcript of grand jury testimony, August 17, 1998, at: http://www.pbs.org/newshour/starr_report/clinton9-21.html.
2. Andersen, *Bill & Hillary*, 27.
3. Schippers, Personal interview, July 5, 2007.
4. Ibid.
5. Ibid.
6. Ibid.
7. Collins, "I'd do It All over Again."
8. Graves and Sharkey, "Starr and Willey."
9. Graves and Sharkey, "Starr and Willey."

10. Tripp, *Larry King Live* interview.
11. Ibid.
12. Alvater, Interview with author, July 5, 2007.
13. Isikoff, *Uncovering Clinton*, 148.
14. *USA Today*, "Starr decides not to pursue retrials for McDougal, Steele."
15. http://www.juliehiattsteele.com/.
16. Schippers, Interview with author, July 5, 2007.
17. Lemire, "Stalk rap for Monica prober."
18. David Stout, "Judge Rules Clinton Broke Privacy Law."

Chapter Ten: A Third Clinton Term?

1. Levin, *Clinton Syndrome*, 83-84.
2. *American Spectator*, August, 1996.
3. Kuiper, *I've Always Been a Yankees Fan*, 69.
4. Klein, *Truth About Hillary*, 98-99.
5. Levin, *Clinton Syndrome*, 93.
6. Ibid.
7. Andersen, *Bill & Hillary*, 220.
8. Bernstein, *A Woman in Charge*, 479.
9. Milton, *First Partner*, 216.
10. Judd and Vlasto, "Witness Backs Willey Claims."
11. Ibid.
12. Ibid.
13. Stern, Interviews with author.
14. Judd and Vlasto, "Witness Backs Willey Claims."
15. Interview with former Prudential contractor.
16. Ibid.
17. Stern, Interviews with author.
18. Ibid.
19. Interview with former Prudential contractor.
20. Stern, Interviews with author.
21. Interview with former Prudential contractor.
22. Prudential Associates website, http://www.prudentrisk.com/bios/bio-Stern.html.
23. Interview with former Prudential contractor.
24. Stern, Interviews with author.
25. Interview with former Prudential contractor.
26. Stern, Interviews with author.
27. Jackson, *Their Lives*, 230.
28. Ibid., 241.
29. Ibid., 247.

30. Motion filed in The United States District Court For the District of Columbia, Case No. 98-1991 (WBB), June 28, 1999.
31. Shiflett, "Media Selective With Its Scandals."
32. Jackson, *Their Lives*, 28-29, 35.
33. Ibid., 67.
34. Sperry, "A Bully in the White House?"
35. Jackson, *Their Lives*, 73.
36. Jackson, *Their Lives*, 79.
37. Sheehy, *Hillary's Choice*, 13.
38. Jackson, *Their Lives*, 83.
39. Ibid., 84, 91.
40. Ibid., 108.
41. Liasson, "Clinton's Christmas woes."
42. Jackson, *Their Lives*, 115.
43. Jackson, *Their Lives*, 123.
44. *Newsmax*, "Clinton Questions Dwarf Deep Throat's ID."
45. Kuiper, *I've Always Been a Yankees Fan*, 42.
46. Thompson, "Bill Clinton is a violent, profane man."
47. Morgan, Interview with author.
48. Tripp, *Larry King Live* interview.
49. Ibid.
50. Morris with McGann, *Rewriting History*, 206.
51. Ibid., 216.
52. Balz, "Prosecutor, President Face Off."
53. Milton, *First Partner*, 196.
54. *Investor's Business Daily*, "Not-So-Secret Police?"
55. Dealey, "A Vast Left-Wing conspiracy?"
56. Milton, *First Partner*, 244.
57. Ibid.
58. Dealey, "A Vast Left-Wing conspiracy?"
59. Ibid.
60. Milton, *First Partner*, 244.
61. *Investor's Business Daily*, "Not-So-Secret Police?"
62. Helvarg, "All the President's P.I.s."
63. Blumenthal, *Clinton Wars*, 419-420.
64. Ibid., 412.
65. Interview with CBS News producer, July 10, 2007
66. Adams, "Into the Spotlight."
67. Citizens United, Interview with author.
68. Isikoff, "Clinton Team Works to Deflect Allegations."
69. Helvarg, "All the President's P.I.s."

70. Ibid.
71. *Newsmax*, "Clinton Questions Dwarf Deep Throat's ID."
72. Helvarg, "All the President's P.I.s."
73. Morgan, Interview with author.
74. Nagourney and Colton, "Tapes Still Entangle Clinton."
75. Morris with McGann, *Rewriting History*, 204.
76. *WorldNetDaily*, "Clinton dirty trickster faces 110-count indictment."
77. *GQ*, January, 1992.
78. *WorldNetDaily*, "Clinton dirty trickster faces 110-count indic.tment."
79. Weinraub, "Hollywood Investigator Gets 30-Month Term."
80. *WorldNetDaily*, "Clinton dirty trickster faces 110-count indictment."
81. Weinraub, "Hollywood Investigator Gets 30-Month Term."
82. *WorldNetDaily*, "Clinton dirty trickster faces 110-count indictment."
83. Olson, *Hell to Pay*, 5.
84. Levin, *Clinton Syndrome*, p. xii.
85. Ibid., 100, 117.
86. Ibid., 80-82.
87. Ibid., 106.
88. Ibid., 143.
89. Ibid., 137, 138, 145.
90. Harris, *Survivor*, 229.
91. Patterson, *Dereliction of Duty*, 86-87.
92. Jackson, *Their Lives*, 129, 134.
93. Morgan, Interview with author.
94. ABC News, 2000, available at: http://www.pbs.org/wgbh/pages/ frontline/shows/clinton/interviews/gergen2.html.
95. Walsh, Kenneth, "Air Force One."
96. Levin, *Clinton Syndrome*, 51, 61, 73.
97. Ross, Interview with Marshall Frady.
98. Healy, "For Clintons, Delicate Dance."
99. Levin, *Clinton Syndrome*, 134.
100. Healy, "For Clintons, Delicate Dance."
101. Coman, "Shock!"
102. Levin, *Clinton Syndrome*, 96-97.
103. Ibid.
104. Flowers, *Passion and Betrayal*.
105. Jackson, *Their Lives*, 216.
106. Levin, *Clinton Syndrome*, 87.
107. Coulter, *High Crimes & Misdemeanors*, 80.
108. Andersen, *Bill & Hillary*, 238.

109. Brown, Deposition.

110. Levin, *Clinton Syndrome*, 103.

111. Andersen, *Bill & Hillary*, 220.

112. Kessler, *Inside the White House*, p.   243.

113. Levin, *Clinton Syndrome*, 80-82.

114. Bernstein, *A Woman in Charge*, 98, 103.

115. Ibid., 84.

116. Levin, *Clinton Syndrome*, 83-84.

117. Ibid., 48, 84.

118. Bernstein, *A Woman in Charge*, 88, 89.

119. Levin, *Clinton Syndrome*, 48.

120. Andersen, *American Evita*, 173.

121. Andersen, *Bill & Hillary*, 247.

122. Ibid., 100.

123. Morris with McGann, *Rewriting History*, 264.

124. Woodward, *Shadow*, 247.

125. Morgan, Interview with author.

126. Walsh, Joan, "The *Salon* Interview with Elizabeth Edwards."

127. Ibid.

128. Morris, "Who Knocked Out Rudy?"

129. Kelly, "Meet the Smart New York Women Who Can't Stand Hillary Clinton."

130. Ibid.

131. Ibid.

132. CNN, "Clinton says 'clean sweep' needed at White House."

133. Prudhomme-O'Brien, "Today I Met Hillary in Nashua, N.H."

Afterword

1. Widdicombe, Ben. "Hoping to give Hil the Willeys." *New York Daily News*, August 29, 2007.

2. Frosch, Dan. "Judge in Colorado Sets Bond of $5 Million for Democratic Fund-Raiser." *New York Times*, September 14, 2007.

3. Jordan, Lara Jakes. "Clinton to Return $850,000 Raised by Hsu." Associated Press, *My Way News*, September 10, 2007. http://apnews.myway.com/article/20070911/D8RIVR8G0.html

4. Moore, Art. "David Schippers: Clinton gang broke into my house, too." *WorldNetDaily.com*, September 9, 2007. http://www.wnd.com/news/article.asp?ARTICLE_ID=57556

5. Ibid.

6. Ibid.

7. Ibid.

INDEX